Editor
Kim Fields

Managing Editor
Mara Ellen Guckian

Illustrator
Kelly McMahon

Cover Artist
Kevin Barnes

Editor in Chief
Ina Massler Levin, M.A.

Creative Director
Karen J. Goldfluss, M.S. Ed.

Art Coordinator
Renée Christine Yates

Imaging
Rosa C. See
Craig Gunnell

Publisher
Mary D. Smith, M.S. Ed.

Author
Deanna Reynolds

The classroom teacher may reproduce the materials in this book and/or CD for use in a single classroom only. The reproduction of any part of this book and/or CD for other classrooms or for an entire school or school system is strictly prohibited. No part of this publication may be transmitted or recorded in any form without written permission from the publisher with the exception of electronic material, which may be stored on the purchaser's computer only.

Teacher Created Resources, Inc.
6421 Industry Way
Westminster, CA 92683
www.teachercreated.com

ISBN: 978-1-4206-2340-6

©*2009 Teacher Created Resources, Inc.*
Reprinted, 2013
Made in U.S.A.

Table of Contents

Introduction 4	
Assembly Instructions 5	
Parent Notes 6	

Letter Aa 8
  Aa Is for Apple 8
  Apple Lacing Activity 9
  Apple Wheel 9
  Aa Minibook 10
  Spiced Apples Cooking Project 10

Letter Bb 16
  Bb Is for Balloon 16
  Butterfly Mask Activity 17
  Balloon Wheel 17
  Bb Minibook 18
  Blue Sky Balloons Cooking Project 18

Letter Cc 24
  Cc Is for Candle 24
  Clay Cake Activity 25
  Cake Wheel 25
  Cc Minibook 26
  Carrot Mini Cakes with
    Candles Cooking Project 26

Letter Dd 31
  Dd Is for Drum 31
  Dinosaur Pop-Up Activity 32
  Dinosaur Wheel 32
  Dd Minibook 33
  Dinosaur Delights Cooking Project 33

Letter Ee 39
  Ee Is for Elephant 39
  Elephant Stick Puppets Activity 40
  Egg Wheel 40
  Ee Minibook 41
  Elephant Munch Cooking Project 41

Letter Ff 47
  Ff Is for Flower 47
  Five Fish in a Bottle Activity 48
  Fish Wheel 48
  Ff Minibook 49
  Fish Aquarium Cooking Project 49

Letter Gg 54

  Gg Is for Goat 54
  Gate Picture Activity 55
  Gate Wheel 55
  Gg Minibook 56
  Gates Cooking Project 56

Letter Hh 62
  Hh Is for Hammer 62
  House Building Activity 63
  House Wheel 63
  Hh Minibook 64
  Houses Cooking Project 64

Letter Ii 70
  Ii Is for Igloo 70
  Iguana Magnet Activity 71
  Ice Cream Wheel 71
  Ii Minibook 72
  Ice Cream Cooking Project 72

Letter Jj 78
  Jj Is for Jewels 78
  Jewel Friendship Bracelet Activity 79
  Jack-in-the-Box Wheel 79
  Jj Minibook 80
  Jewels to Eat Cooking Project 80

Letter Kk 85
  Kk Is for Key 85
  Kite Sun Catcher Activity 86
  Kite Wheel 86
  Kk Minibook 87
  Kangaroo Pouch Cooking Project 87

Letter Ll 94
  Ll Is for Ladder 94
  Ladybug Rock Activity 95
  Ladybug Wheel 95
  Ll Minibook 96
  Ladybug Cookies Cooking Project 96

Letter Mm 102
  Mm Is for Monkey 102
  Mouse and Cheese Activity 103
  Mitten Wheel 103
  Mm Minibook 104
  Monkey Faces Cooking Project 104

Table of Contents (cont.)

Letter Nn	110
Nn Is for Nest	110
Nest with Eggs Activity	111
Noodles Wheel	111
Nn Minibook	112
Noodles Cooking Project	112
Letter Oo	117
Oo Is for Octopus	117
Owl Wind Sock Activity	118
Owl Wheel	118
Oo Minibook	119
Octopus Cooking Project	119
Letter Pp	125
Pp Is for Pencil	125
Pencil Topper Activity	126
Penguin Wheel	126
Pp Minibook	127
Pretzels Cooking Project	127
Letter Qq	132
Qq Is for Quilt	132
Queen Puppet Activity	133
Quarter Wheel	133
Qq Minibook	134
Quilts Cooking Project	134
Letter Rr	140
Rr Is for Ring	140
Rabbit Hide-and-Seek Activity	141
Rabbit Wheel	141
Rr Minibook	142
Rabbit Salad Cooking Project	142
Letter Ss	148
Ss Is for Snake	148
Star Magnet Activity	149
Star Wheel	149
Ss Minibook	150
Star Sandwiches Cooking Project	150
Letter Tt	156
Tt Is for Tree	156
Tree of Many Colors Activity	157
Turtle Wheel	157
Tt Minibook	158
Turkey Toast Cooking Project	158
Letter Uu	164
Uu Is for Umbrella	164
Unicorn Horn Activity	165
Unicycle Wheel	165
Uu Minibook	166
Umbrellas Cooking Project	166
Letter Vv	171
Vv Is for Vase of Violets	171
Violet Vase Activity	172
Van Wheel	172
Vv Minibook	173
Valentine Veggies with Heart-Smart Dip Cooking Project	173
Letter Ww	179
Ww Is for Watch	179
Whale Activity	180
Whale Wheel	180
Ww Minibook	181
Watch Pizza Cooking Project	181
Letter Xx	186
Xx Is for Fox	186
Fox Mask Activity	187
X-ray Wheel	187
Xx Minibook	188
X-ray Sandwiches Cooking Project	188
Letter Yy	194
Yy Is for Yo-Yo	194
Yucca Plant Activity	195
Yarn Wheel	195
Yy Minibook	196
Yummy Yogurt Cooking Project	196
Letter Zz	201
Zz Is for Zebra	201
Zany Zero Lacing Activity	202
Zipper Wheel	202
Zz Minibook	203
Zebra Stripes Cooking Project	203

©Teacher Created Resources, Inc.   #2340 Alphabet Treasury

Introduction

Alphabet Treasury was designed with preschoolers in mind. The activities in this book will prepare children to learn and develop phonemic and phonological awareness skills through gross motor, fine motor, and tactile activities while having fun at the same time!

This book is set up to fill the entire week with letter activities. An easy-to-follow, 5-day lesson plan format is included for each letter. Maximum exposure to letters is a must at this stage. Young children need frequent repetition. They have to see a letter often and learn the sound or sounds associated with the letter. The activities in *Alphabet Treasury* enable children to see, hear, and touch while learning about the alphabet. These visual, auditory, and hands-on experiences reinforce literacy development.

Alphabet Treasury provides busy preschool teachers, childcare providers, and parents with finger plays, art activities, cooking projects, writing experiences, games, and more—all designed to reinforce each letter of the alphabet. Each unit includes the following components:

- Actions/finger plays to introduce the letter
- Reproducible activity to practice writing the letter and tracing a picture
- Art activity (with any necessary patterns) featuring the letter
- Picture wheel activity for the letter
- Minibook for the letter tracing
- Cooking project

#2340 Alphabet Treasury   4   ©Teacher Created Resources, Inc.

Assembly Instructions

Making a Picture Wheel

1. Color the pattern page and pictures on the picture wheel page.

2. Cut out the pattern wheel and the picture wheel.

3. Cut out the gray picture window on the pattern. Adult assistance may be necessary to cut out the window. (Note: In most cases, the wheel will work just as well if the bottom of the picture box is cut away. See sample on top right. The ladybug pattern on page 99 would be the exception.)

4. Write your name on the back of the picture wheel. (Note: Some teachers may prefer students' names to be on the front of the pattern.)

5. Place the picture wheel behind the pattern. Make certain that one of the pictures is visible in the window on the pattern before going on to the next step.

6. Attach the pattern to the front of the wheel with a brad. Use the black dot as a guide.

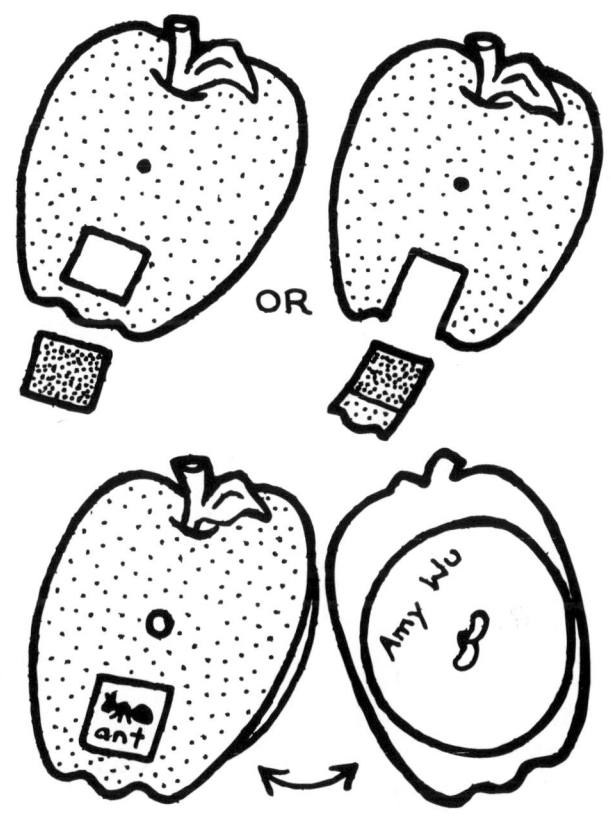

Making a Minibook

1. Cut along the outer edge of the minibook on the dashed line.

2. Fold the paper in half horizontally along the line so the pictures are visible.

3. Fold the in half again vertically along the line so the cover is on the front.

4. Write your name on the cover.

5. Trace and color each picture. Trace the letters on the lines.

©Teacher Created Resources, Inc.   #2340 Alphabet Treasury

Parent Notes

Food Allergies Alert

Dear Parents,

Our class will be cooking a variety of recipes. I realize that your child may have food allergies or dietary restrictions. Please complete this form and return it by _____. Thank you!

Sincerely,

_____
   (Teacher)

Student Name: _____

☐ Has NO food allergies or dietary restrictions.

☐ Has the food allergies or dietary restrictions checked below.

Parent Signature _____

___ apple juice
___ apples
___ banana chips
___ bananas
___ bell peppers
___ black licorice
___ black olives
___ butter
___ candy sprinkles
___ carrots
___ celery
___ cheese
___ chicken lunch meat
___ chocolate chips
___ cinnamon
___ cocoa
___ coconut (shredded)
___ crackers
___ cream cheese
___ crispy rice cereal
___ cucumbers
___ dried apple slices

___ dried pineapple slices
___ eggs or egg products
___ English muffins
___ food coloring
     (color: _____)
___ frosting (flavor: _____)
___ fruit-flavored,
     o-shaped cereal
___ gelatin (flavor: _____)
___ gluten
___ graham crackers
___ grapes
___ gummy candies
___ ham lunch meat
___ honey
___ ice cream (flavor: _____)
___ icing/gel (color/
     flavor: _____)
___ jam/jelly(flavor: _____)
___ lettuce
___ mayonnaise
___ milk or milk products
___ mustard

___ peanut butter
___ pepperoni
___ pineapple
___ pizza sauce
___ pretzels
___ pudding
___ raisins
___ ranch dressing
___ refrigerated biscuit dough
___ rice cakes
___ soy products
___ spaghetti noodles
___ spaghetti sauce
___ strawberries
___ sugar cookies
___ tomatoes
___ turkey lunch meat
___ wheat
___ whipped cream
___ white bread
___ whole-wheat bread
___ yogurt (flavor: _____)

#2340 Alphabet Treasury   ©Teacher Created Resources, Inc.

Parent Notes

Supply Request Notes

Dear Parents,

We will soon be studying the letter _____. On _____, we will be making _____.

We would appreciate your help gathering supplies. If you can donate any of the items listed below by _____, please let me know.

-
-
-

-
-
-

Thank you! _____
                    Teacher

Dear Parents,

We will soon be studying the letter _____. On _____, we will be making _____.

We would appreciate your help gathering supplies. If you can donate any of the items listed below by _____, please let me know.

-
-
-

-
-
-

Thank you! _____
                    Teacher

Dear Parents,

We will soon be studying the letter _____. On _____, we will be making _____.

We would appreciate your help gathering supplies. If you can donate any of the items listed below by _____, please let me know.

-
-
-

-
-
-

Thank you! _____
                    Teacher

Letter Aa

Aa

Introduce the letter Aa. Draw and discuss the shape of the letters using chart paper, a white board or a chalkboard. Note any students whose names begin or end with the letter Aa. This will provide opportunities to discuss how and when uppercase and lowercase letters are used.

Introduce the following sentences and accompanying actions. Repeat them often during the week.

Aa is for an **apple** that is good to eat.
(Pretend to eat an apple. Rub your stomach and say, "mmmmmm.")

Aa is for an **ant**, crawling up my arm.
(Pretend an ant is crawling up your arm.)

Aa is for an **airplane**, flying up high.
(Pretend to be an airplane flying.)

Day 1: Aa Is for Apple

Materials

- Aa Is for Apple worksheet (page 11) for each child
- pencils
- crayons

Procedure for Child

1. Write your name on the line provided at the top of the page.
2. Trace the apple and the letters provided.
3. Practice writing the letter Aa on the lines provided.
4. Finish by coloring the apple using crayons.

#2340 Alphabet Treasury   8   ©Teacher Created Resources, Inc.

Letter Aa

Aa

Day 2: Apple Lacing Activity

Materials

- red, green, and yellow poster board
- Apple Lacing Pattern (page 12)
- hole punches
- yarn in different colors, cut to 42" lengths
- crayons
- safety scissors
- tape
- cardboard

Teacher Preparation

1. Trace the Apple Lacing Pattern (page 12) onto heavy cardboard and cut it out to create a template. Precut an apple shape for each student using the red, green, and yellow poster board.
2. Punch holes around the outer border of the apples using a hole punch. Note: Slide the apple into the hole punch as far as it will go before punching. Doing so should ensure that the holes are placed away from the edge of the poster board.

Procedure for Child

1. Choose a piece of yarn. Tape the yarn to the back of the apple so that it will stay in place. (Note: For additional help, wrap a small piece of tape on the other end to form a "needle." The tape will prevent the yarn from fraying.)
2. Lace the yarn in and out of the holes around the apple. When finished, tie the ends of the yarn together and cut off the remaining yarn.

Day 3: Apple Wheel

Materials

- Apple Pattern (page 13) for each child
- Aa Picture Wheel (page 14) for each child
- brad for each child
- pencils
- markers or crayons
- safety scissors

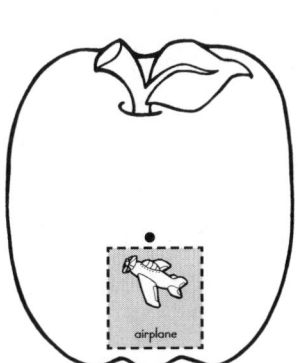

Procedure for Child

1. Color the Apple Pattern and Aa pictures on the picture wheel page.
2. Cut out the apple and the picture wheel. (See page 5 for directions.)
3. Write your name on the back of the wheel.
4. Cut out the picture window on the apple. (Note: Adult assistance may be necessary to cut out the picture window.)
5. Place the Aa Picture Wheel behind the Apple Pattern. Make certain that one of the pictures is visible in the picture window on the apple before going on to the next step.
6. Attach the apple to the front of the wheel with a brad.

©Teacher Created Resources, Inc.   9   #2340 Alphabet Treasury

Letter Aa

Aa

Day 4: Aa Minibook

Materials

- Aa Minibook (page 15) for each child
- pencils, colored pencils, crayons or markers
- safety scissors

Procedure for Child

1. Trim and fold the page to create the Aa Minibook. (See page 5 for directions.)
2. Write your name in pencil on the line on the minibook cover.
3. Complete each page of the minibook. Trace each picture and then trace the letter Aa on the lines.
4. Color the pictures using the colored pencils, crayons or markers.
5. Read the book as a group. Later it can be shared at home.

Day 5: Spiced Apples Cooking Project

(serves 10 children)

Kitchen Implements

- skillet
- apple corer
- knife (adult use only)
- large spoon
- plastic forks
- serving spoons
- small paper plate for each child
- small plastic serving bowls
- measuring cup and spoons

Ingredients

- 5 Red Delicious apples
- 1/2 cup butter
- 2 teaspoons cinnamon
- 1/4 cup sugar

Preparation

1. Peel, core, and slice apples.
2. Melt butter in the skillet and add the peeled, sliced apples. If appropriate, let children take turns stirring the apples.
3. Sauté the apples until tender. Explain to students that to *sauté* is to fry quickly in a little bit of fat.
4. Combine the sugar and cinnamon in a bowl and mix well. Add the mixture to the apples.

Presentation

1. Let the apples cool. Then serve them on paper plates.
2. Practice good table manners when you eat your treat!

#2340 Alphabet Treasury ©Teacher Created Resources, Inc.

Letter Aa

Aa Is for Apple

Name _____

1. Trace the apple.
2. Trace the Aa's.
3. Write more Aa's.
4. Color the picture.

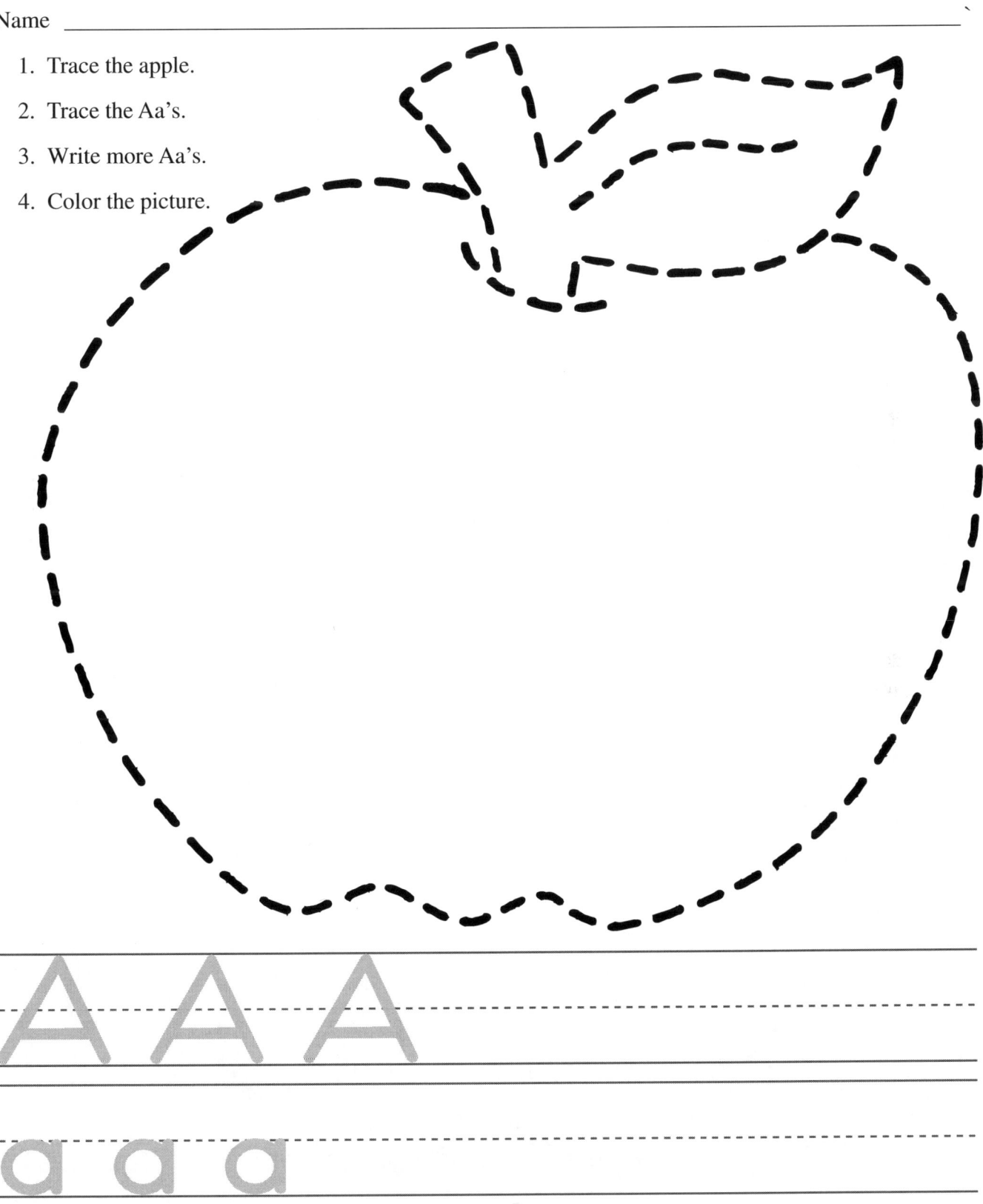

©Teacher Created Resources, Inc.   11   #2340 Alphabet Treasury

Letter Aa

Apple Lacing Pattern

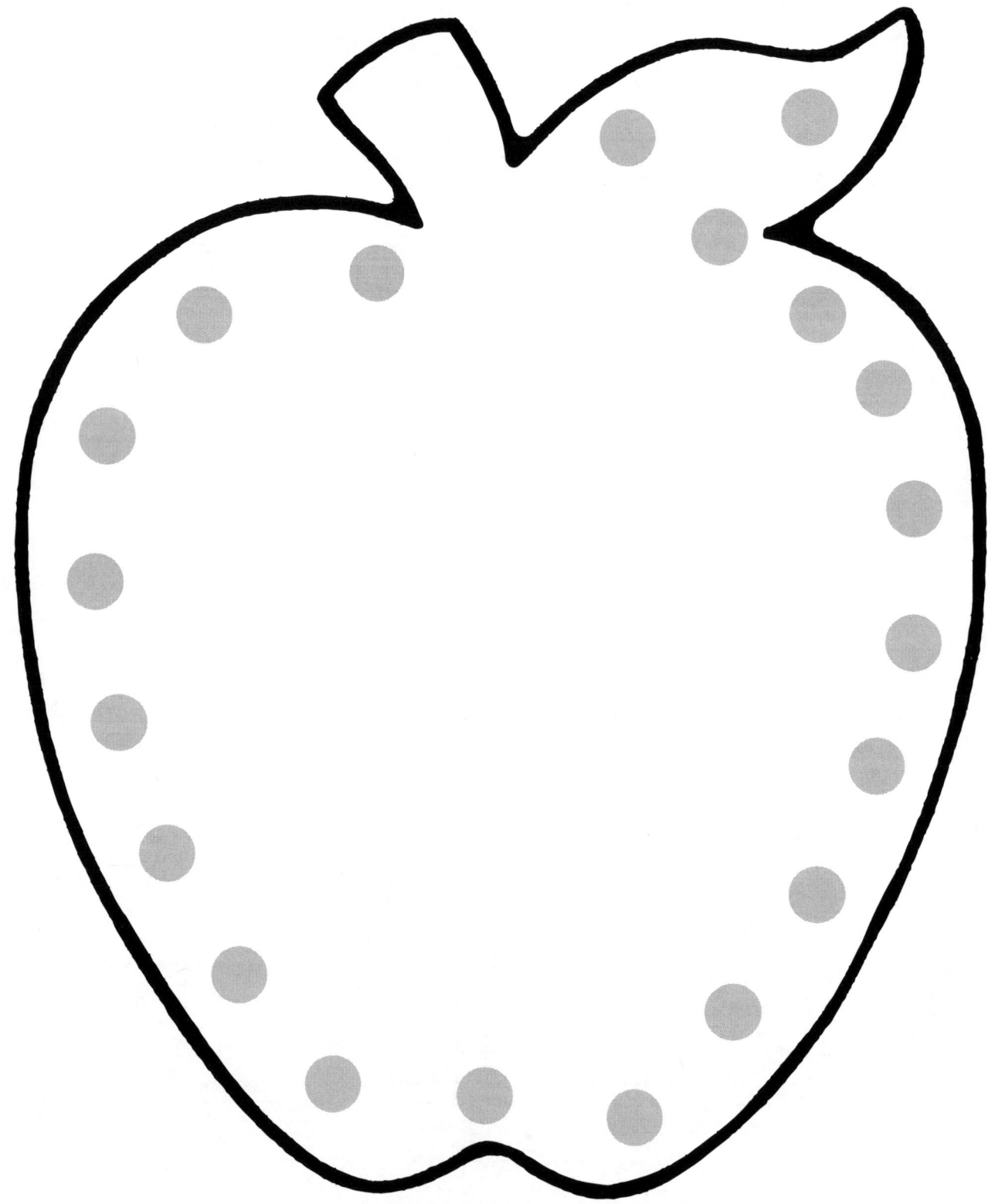

#2340 Alphabet Treasury 12 ©Teacher Created Resources, Inc.

Letter Aa

Apple Pattern

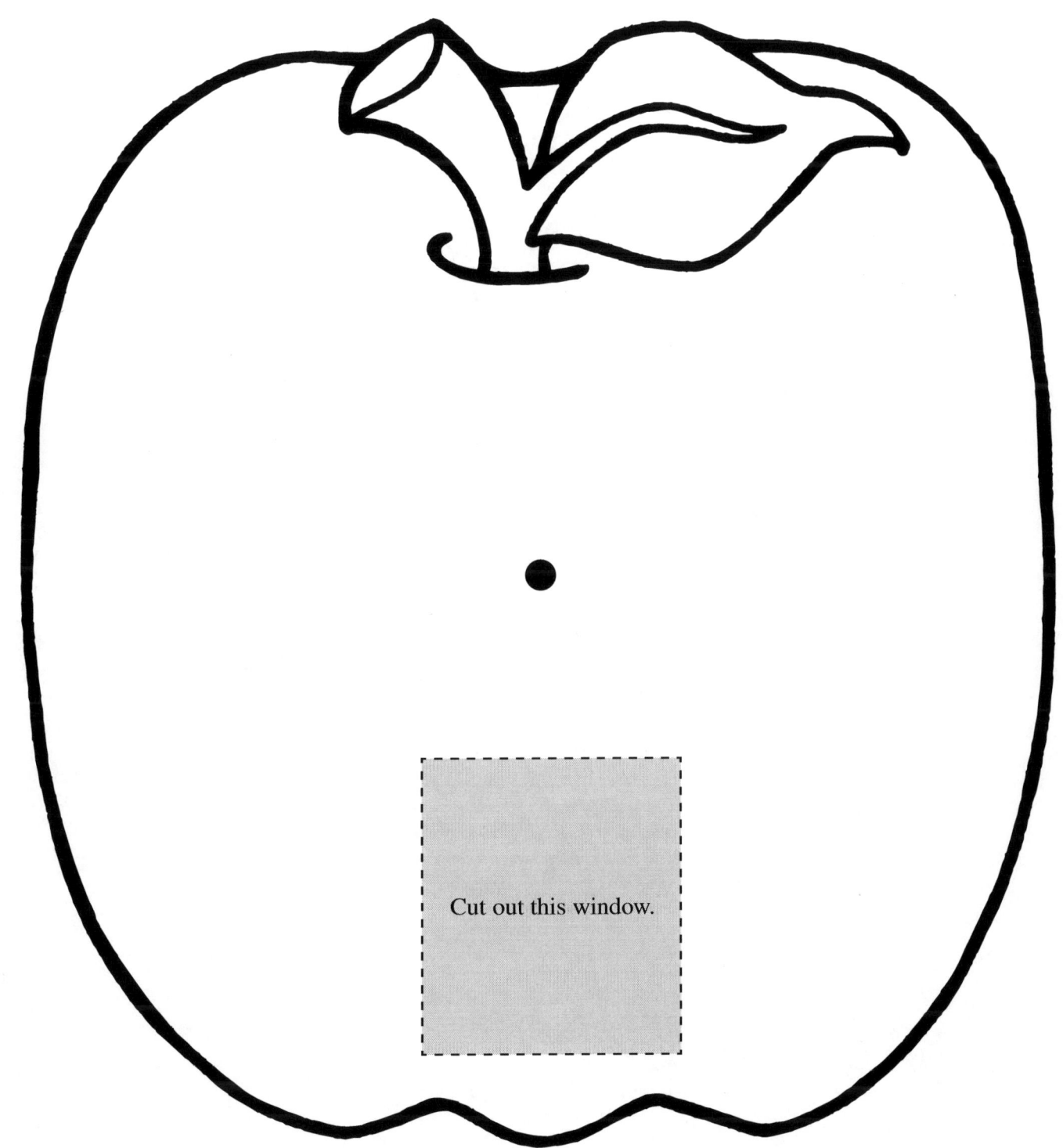

Cut out this window.

©Teacher Created Resources, Inc. #2340 Alphabet Treasury

Letter Aa

Aa Picture Wheel

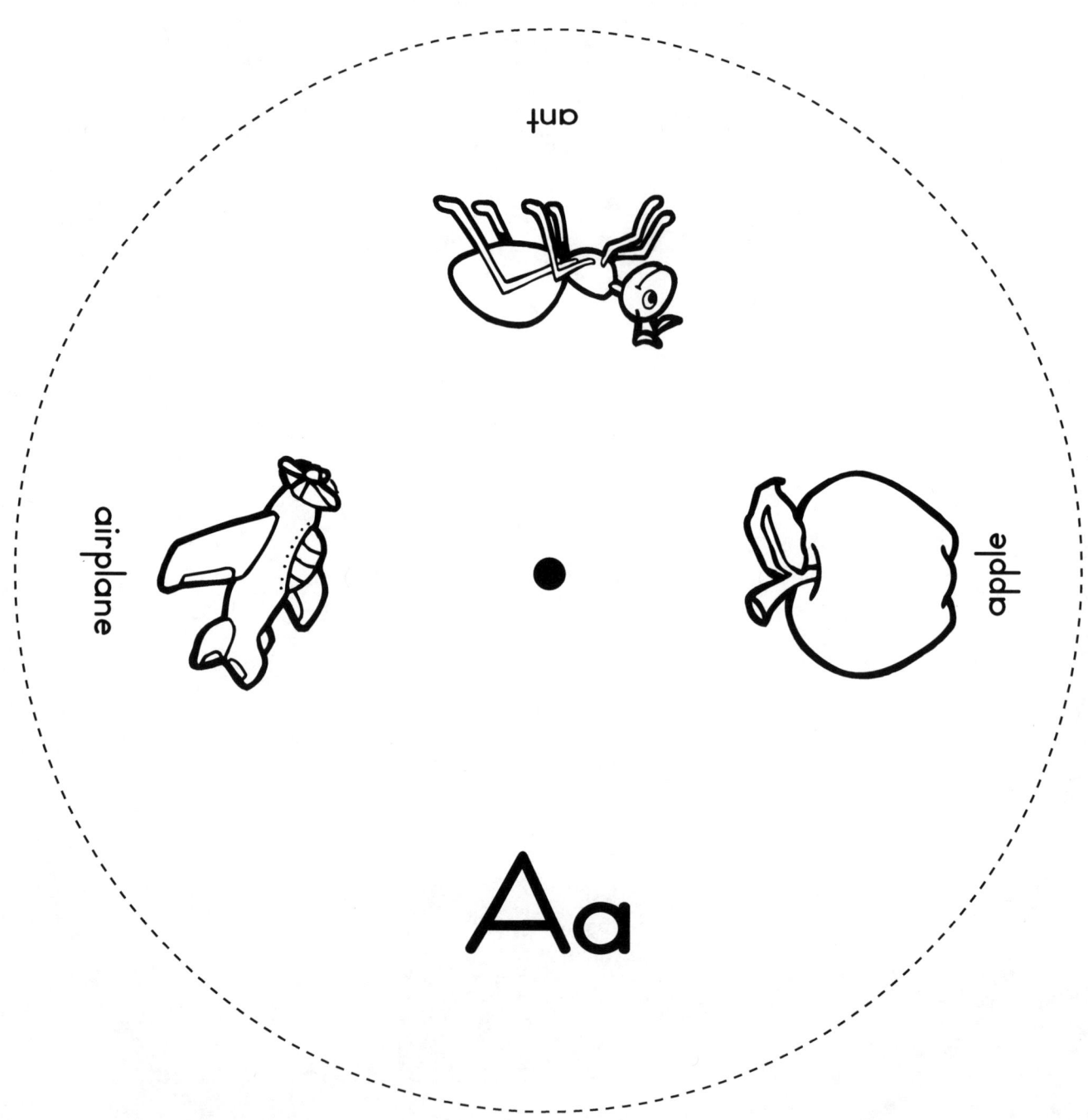

#2340 Alphabet Treasury · 14 · ©Teacher Created Resources, Inc.

Letter Aa

Aa is for an **ant**, crawling up my arm.

Aa is for an **apple** that is good to eat.

Aa is for an **airplane**, flying up high.

_____'s

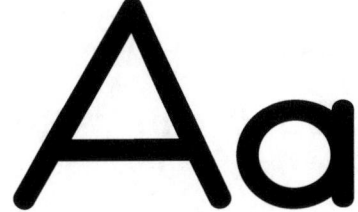

Minibook

©Teacher Created Resources, Inc.   15   #2340 Alphabet Treasury

Letter Bb

Bb

Introduce the letter Bb. Draw and discuss the shape of the letters using chart paper, a white board or a chalkboard. Note any students whose names begin or end with the letter Bb. This will provide opportunities to discuss how and when uppercase and lowercase letters are used.

Introduce the following sentences and accompanying actions. Repeat them often during the week.

Bb is for a **butterfly**, fluttering its wings.
(Pretend to be a butterfly by flapping your arms forward and back.)

Bb is for a **baby** crying, "waaa waaa."
(Pretend to be a baby crying.)

Bb is for a **balloon**, floating away.
(Pretend to be a balloon floating up and away.)

Day 1: Bb Is for Balloon

Materials

- Bb Is for Balloon worksheet (page 19) for each child
- pencils and crayons

Procedure for Child

1. Write your name on the line provided at the top of the page.
2. Trace the balloon and the letters provided.
3. Practice writing the letter Bb on the lines provided.
4. Finish by coloring the balloon using crayons.

#2340 Alphabet Treasury   16   ©Teacher Created Resources, Inc.

Letter Bb

Bb

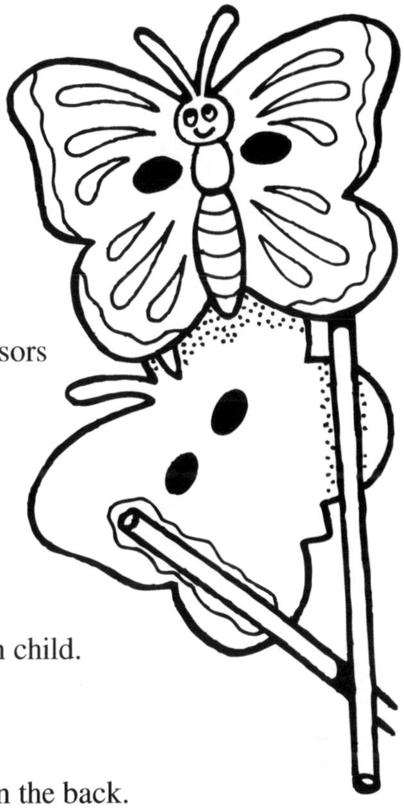

Day 2: Butterfly Mask Activity

Materials

- Butterfly Mask Pattern (page 20) for each child
- 12" dowel (1/4" wide) for each child
- assortment of feathers (different colors/sizes)
- sheet of cardstock for each child
- glue gun (adult use only)
- safety scissors
- markers
- glitter
- glue

Teacher Preparation

Copy the Butterfly Mask Pattern (page 20) onto cardstock for each child. Cut out the eye holes.

Procedure for Child

1. Color the mask using markers; then cut it out. Write your name on the back.
2. Decorate the mask by attaching glitter and feathers using glue.
3. After the mask is dry, glue or tape a dowel to the back of the mask using a glue gun. (Note: An adult needs to complete this step.)
4. Show off your new creation by participating in a Butterfly Parade!

Day 3: Balloon Wheel

Materials

- Balloon Pattern (page 21) for each child
- Bb Picture Wheel (page 22) for each child
- brad for each child
- markers or crayons
- safety scissors
- pencils

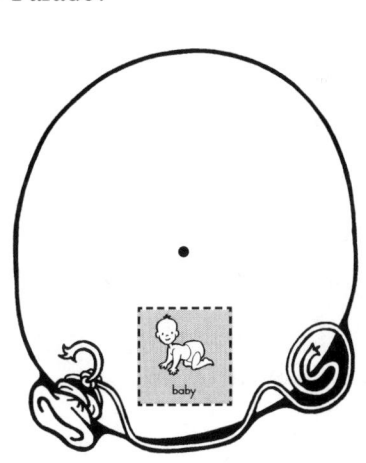

Procedure for Child

1. Color the Balloon Pattern and Bb pictures on the picture wheel page.
2. Cut out the balloon and the picture wheel. (See page 5 for directions.)
3. Write your name on the back of the wheel.
4. Cut out the picture window on the balloon. (Note: Adult assistance may be necessary to cut out the picture window.)
5. Place the Bb Picture Wheel behind the Balloon Pattern. Make certain that one of the pictures is visible in the picture window on the balloon before going on to the next step.
6. Attach the balloon to the front of the wheel with a brad. Use the black dot as a guide.

©Teacher Created Resources, Inc. #2340 Alphabet Treasury

Letter Bb

Bb

Day 4: Bb Minibook

Materials

- Bb Minibook (page 23) for each child
- pencils, colored pencils, crayons or markers
- safety scissors

Procedure for Child

1. Trim and fold the page to create the Bb Minibook. (See page 5 for directions.)
2. Write your name in pencil on the line on the minibook cover.
3. Complete each page of the minibook. Trace each picture and then trace the letter Bb on the lines.
4. Color the pictures using the colored pencils, crayons or markers.
5. Read the book as a group. Later, it can be shared at home or with friends.

Day 5: Blue Sky Balloons Cooking Project

(serves 10 children)

Kitchen Implements

- plastic spoon and small paper plate for each child
- serving spoon
- measuring cups

Ingredients

- 5 cups vanilla yogurt
- blue food coloring
- 30 grapes (variety of red, green, or white)
- cooked spaghetti noodles

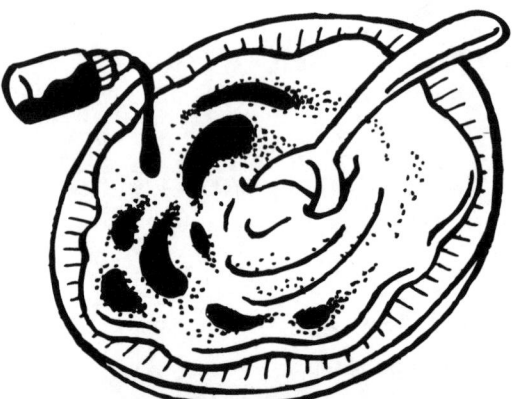

Preparation

1. Place 1/2 cup yogurt on a plate. Spread the yogurt to fill the plate.
2. Add a few drops of blue food coloring on top of the yogurt. Mix it until the yogurt is completely blue.
3. Choose 3 grapes (balloons) and place them on the blue yogurt (sky).
4. Place a spaghetti noodle under each grape (balloon) to make a string for it.
5. Practice good table manners while eating your treat!

#2340 Alphabet Treasury ©Teacher Created Resources, Inc.

Letter Bb

Bb Is for Balloon

Name _____

1. Trace the balloon.
2. Trace the Bb's.
3. Write more Bb's.
4. Color the picture.

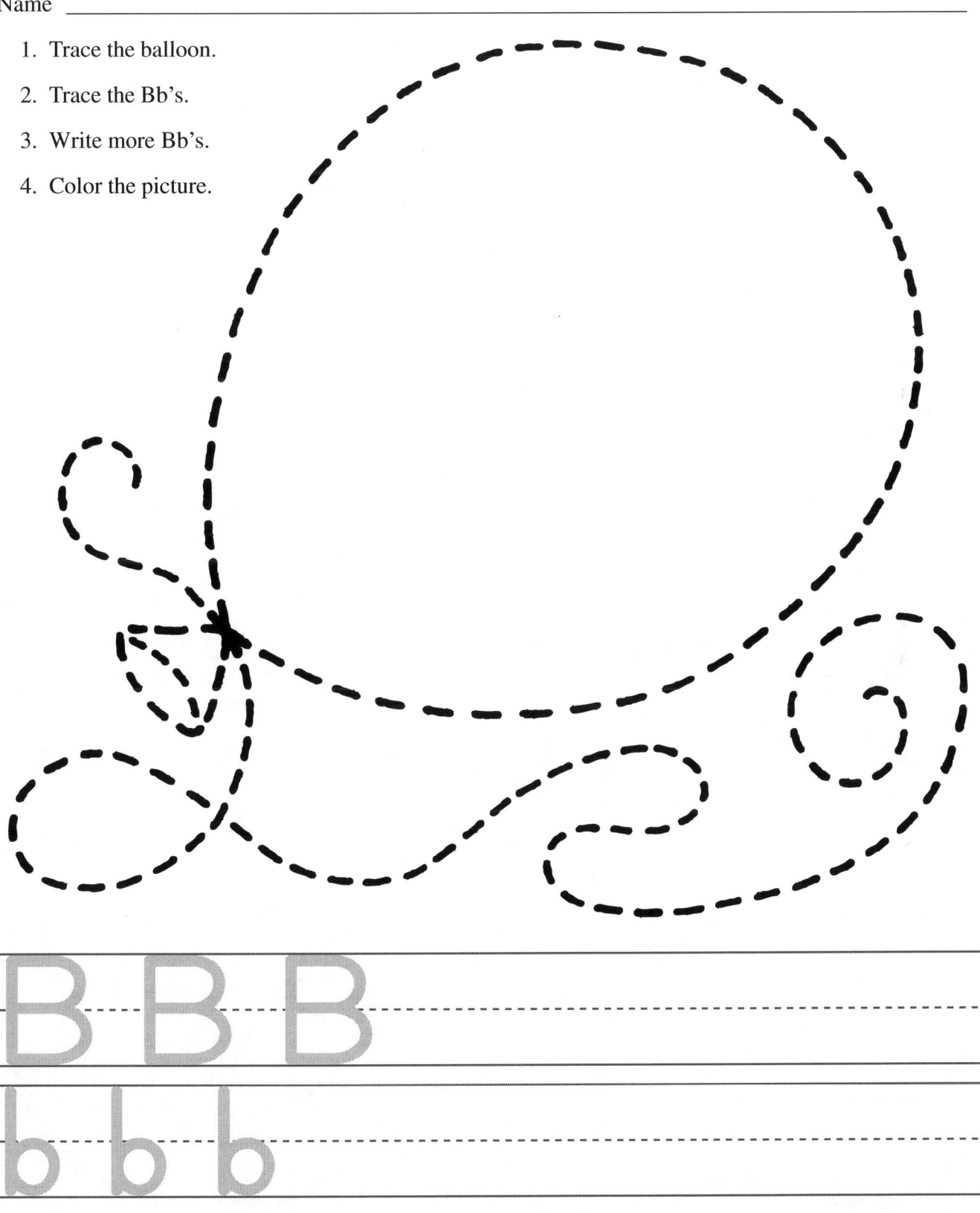

©Teacher Created Resources, Inc.   19   #2340 Alphabet Treasury

Letter Bb

Butterfly Mask Pattern

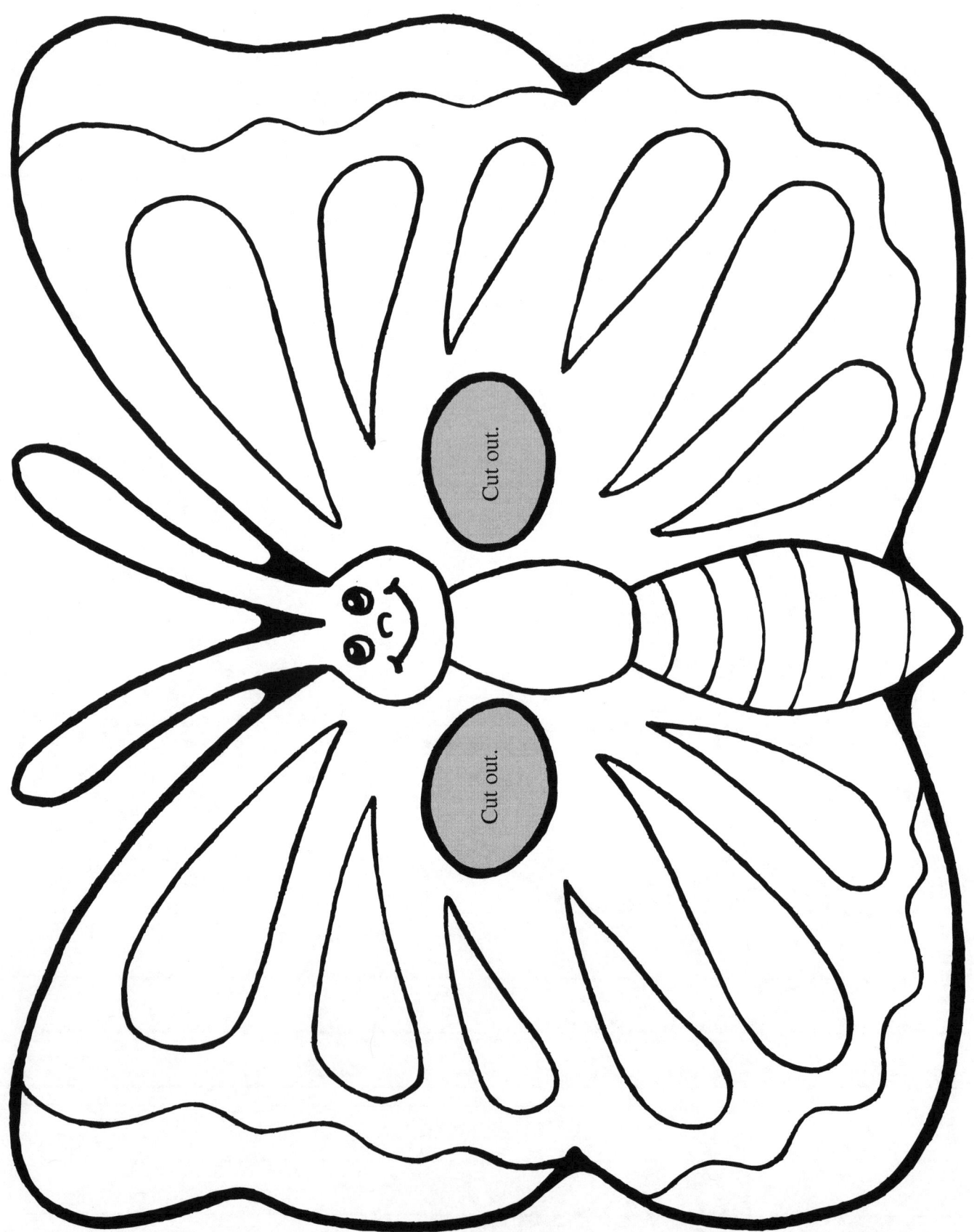

Letter Bb

Balloon Pattern

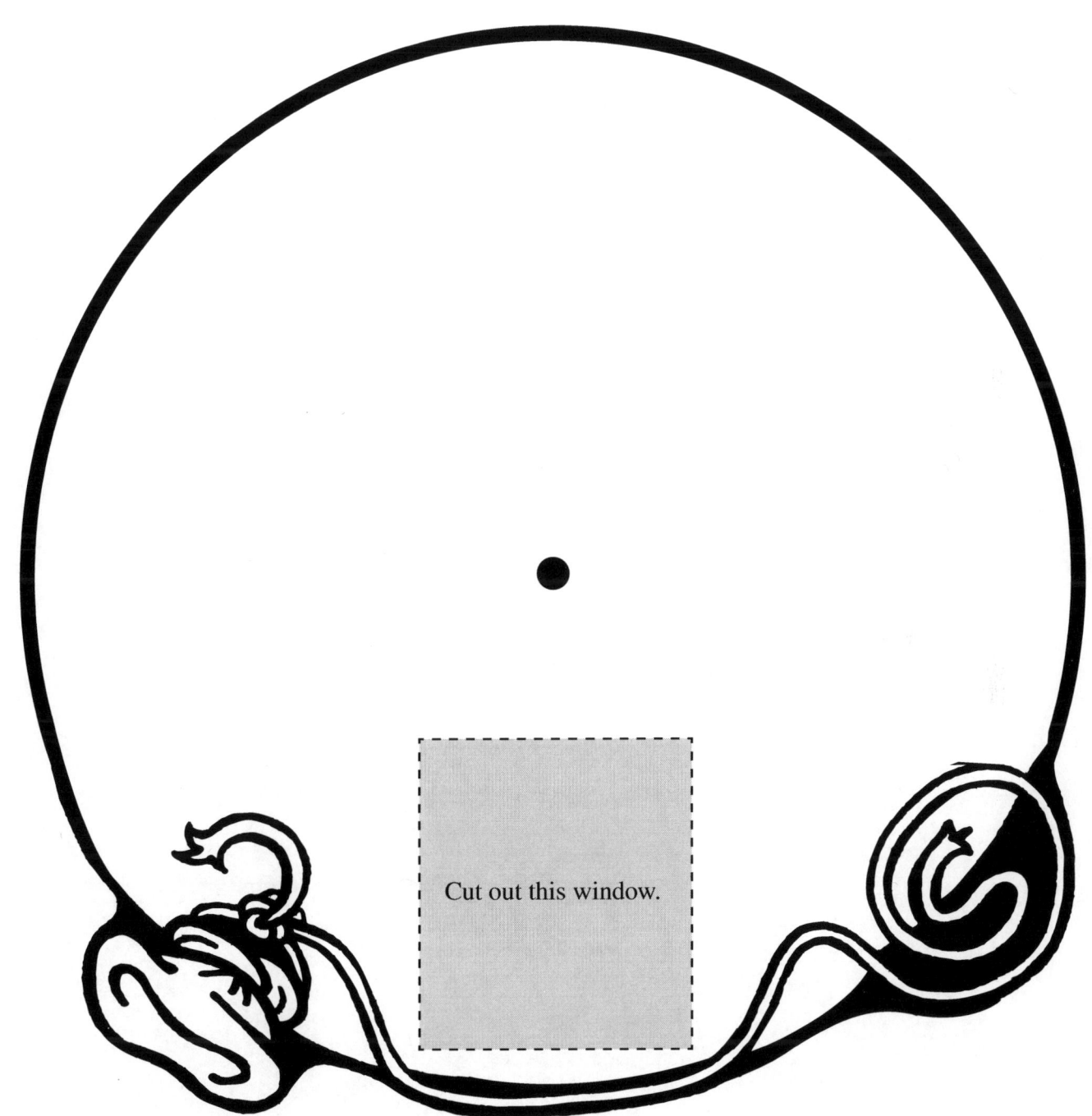

Cut out this window.

Letter Bb

Bb Picture Wheel

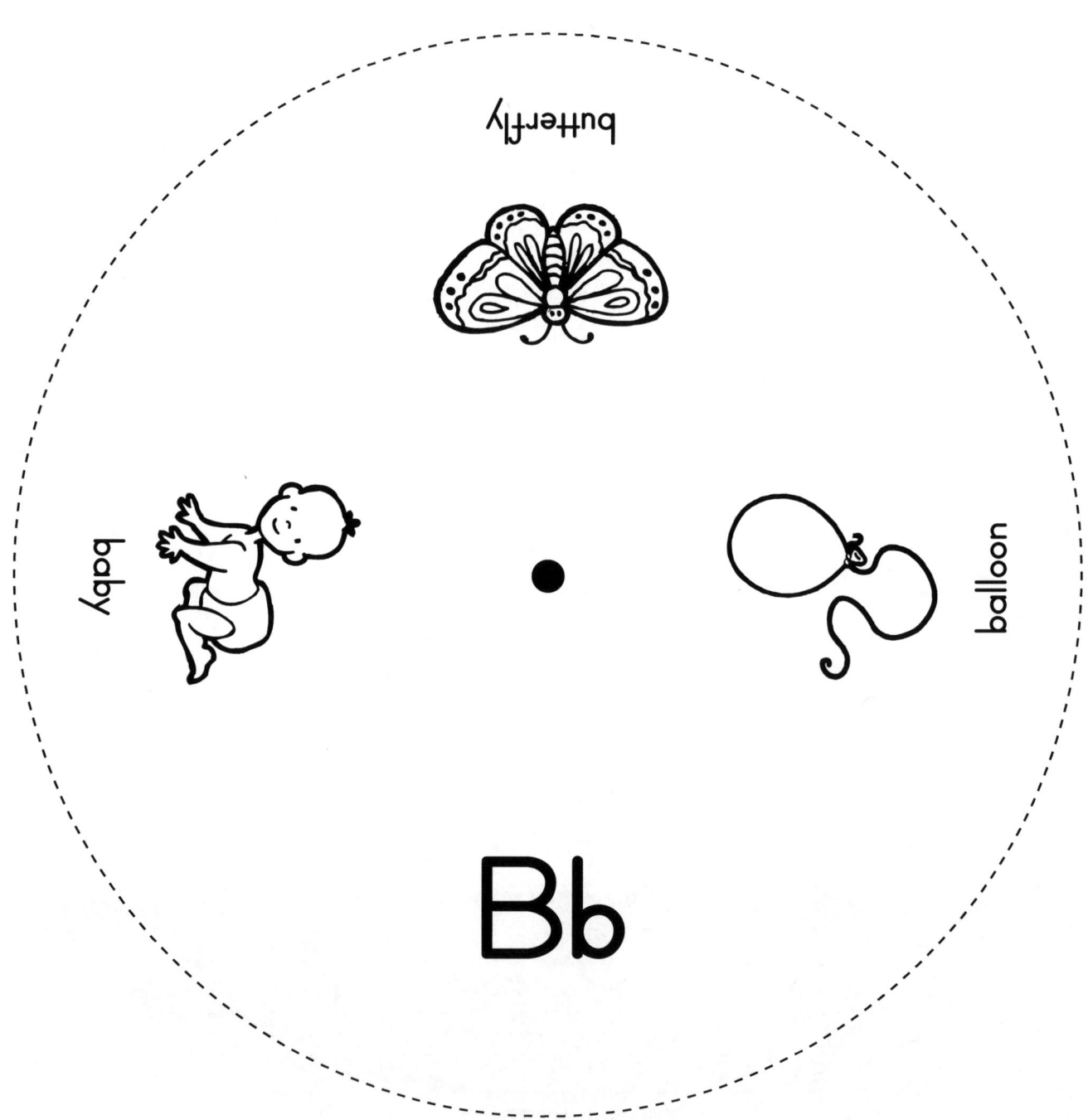

#2340 Alphabet Treasury   22   ©Teacher Created Resources, Inc.

Letter Bb

Bb is for a butterfly,
fluttering its wings.

Bb is for a baby crying,
"waa waa."

Bb is for a balloon,
floating away.

_____'s

Bb

Minibook

©Teacher Created Resources, Inc.   #2340 Alphabet Treasury

Letter Cc

Cc

Introduce the letter Cc. Draw and discuss the shape of the letters using chart paper, a white board or a chalkboard. Note any students whose names begin or end with the letter Cc. This will provide opportunities to discuss how and when uppercase and lowercase letters are used.

Introduce the following sentences and accompanying actions. Repeat them often during the week.

Cc is for a **cat**—meow, meow!
(Pretend to be a cat and meow.)

Cc is for a **candle** to blow out.
(Pretend to blow out a candle.)

Cc is for **cake** to eat, "mmmm."
(Pretend to eat cake while rubbing your tummy and saying, "mmmm.")

Day 1: Cc Is for Candle

Materials

- Cc Is for Candle worksheet (page 27) for each child
- pencils and crayons

Procedure for Child

1. Write your name on the line provided at the top of the page.
2. Trace the candle and the letters provided.
3. Practice writing the letter Cc on the lines provided.
4. Finish by coloring the candle using crayons.

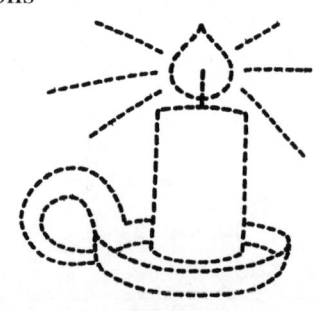

#2340 Alphabet Treasury   24   ©Teacher Created Resources, Inc.

Letter Cc

Cc

Day 2: Clay Cake Activity

Materials

- 2" lengths of plastic straws (in a variety of colors)
- heavy-duty, small paper plate for each child
- air-dry clay in assorted colors
- glitter (optional)

Procedure for Child

1. Choose a color of clay to work with.
2. Shape the clay to form a cake (about the size of a cupcake) and place it on a paper plate.
3. Place the 2" straws (candles) on the cake according to your age (example: age 4 uses 4 candles). If desired, decorate the cake using glitter.
4. Let the cakes air-dry overnight or use the speed method according to the clay package instructions.

Day 3: Cake Wheel

Materials

- Cake Pattern (page 28) for each child
- Cc Picture Wheel (page 29) for each child
- brad for each child
- markers or crayons
- safety scissors
- pencils

Procedure for Child

1. Color the Cake Pattern and Cc pictures on the picture wheel page.
2. Cut out the cake and the picture wheel. (See page 5 for directions.)
3. Write your name on the back of the wheel.
4. Cut out the picture window on the cake. (Note: Adult assistance may be necessary to cut out the picture window.)
5. Place the Cc Picture Wheel behind the Cake Pattern. Make certain that one of the pictures is visible in the picture window on the cake before going on to the next step.
6. Attach the cake to the front of the wheel with a brad. Use the black dot as a guide.

Letter Cc

Cc

Day 4: Cc Minibook

Materials

- Cc Minibook (page 30) for each child
- pencils, colored pencils, crayons or markers
- safety scissors

Procedure for Child

1. Trim and fold the page to create the Cc Minibook. (See page 5 for directions.)
2. Write your name in pencil on the line on the minibook cover.
3. Complete each page of the minibook. Trace each picture and then trace the letter Cc on the lines.
4. Color the pictures using the colored pencils, crayons or markers.
5. Read the book as a group. Later, it can be shared at home or with friends.

Day 5: Carrot Mini Cakes with Candles Cooking Project

(serves 20 children)

Kitchen Implements

- small paper plate for each child
- small plastic knife for each child
- grater
- muffin paper liners
- large mixing bowl
- measuring cups
- mixing spoon
- muffin pan
- measuring spoons

Ingredients

- 2 1/4 cups flour
- 1 1/2 teaspoons baking powder
- 1/2 teaspoon baking soda
- 1 teaspoon cinnamon
- 1 cup brown sugar
- 2 eggs
- 1/2 cup vegetable oil
- 1/2 cup sour cream
- 1 1/2 cups grated carrots
- 8 oz. can crushed pineapple, undrained
- cream cheese frosting
- baby carrots

Preparation

1. In a large mixing bowl, combine the flour, baking powder, baking soda, cinnamon, and brown sugar with a mixing spoon.
2. Add eggs, vegetable oil, sour cream, grated carrots, and pineapple to the mixture and stir until the cake batter is mixed well.
3. Add cake batter to each muffin paper liner until it is three-fourths full.
4. Bake the cakes for 20–25 minutes at 375°F until golden brown and let cool.
5. Use a plastic knife to spread cream cheese frosting on the mini carrot cake. Insert the number of baby carrots in the cake to represent your age.
6. Practice good table manners when you eat your treat!

Letter Cc

Cc Is for Candle

Name _____

1. Trace the candle.
2. Trace the Cc's.
3. Write more Cc's.
4. Color the picture.

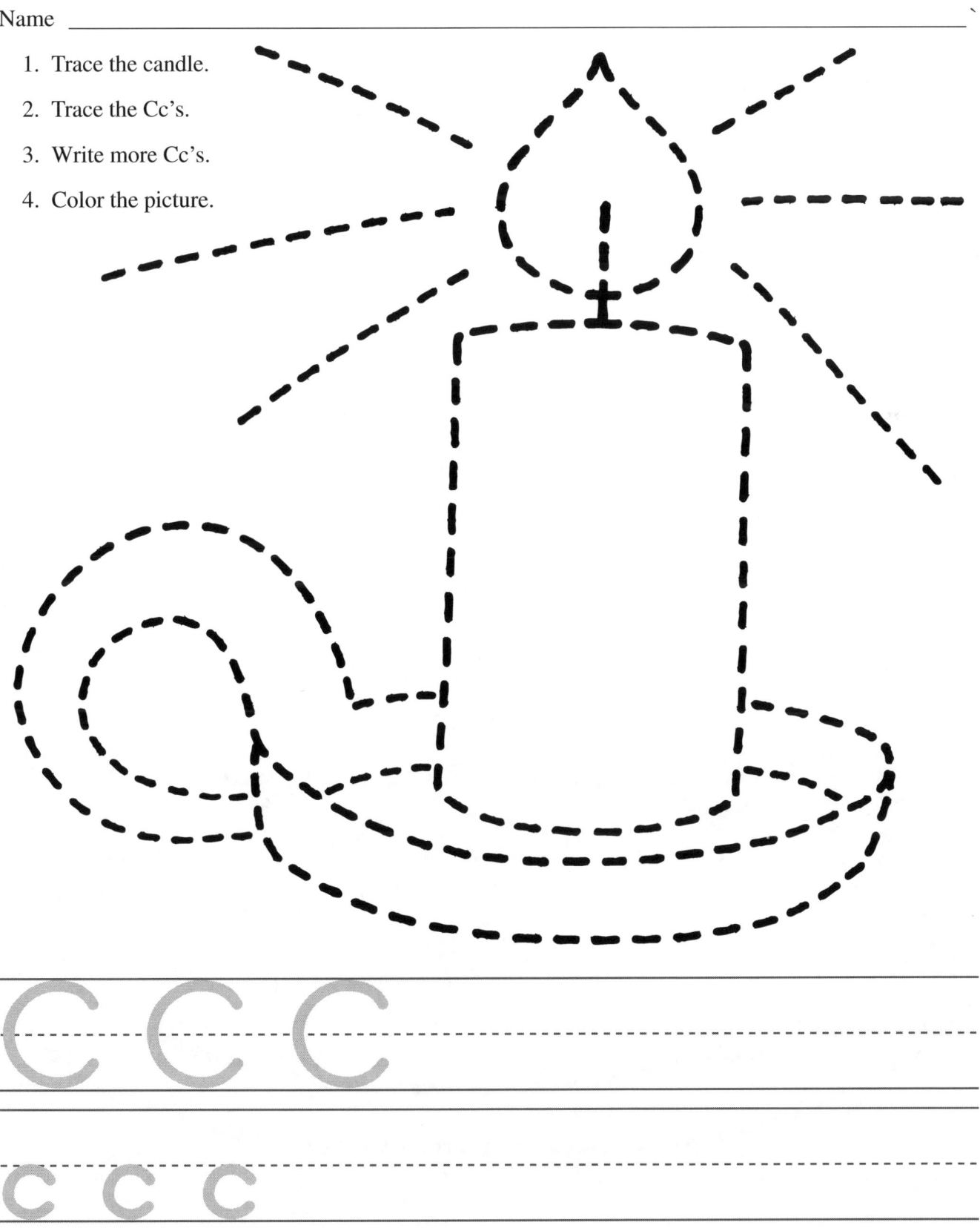

©Teacher Created Resources, Inc.   27   #2340 Alphabet Treasury

Letter Cc

Cake Pattern

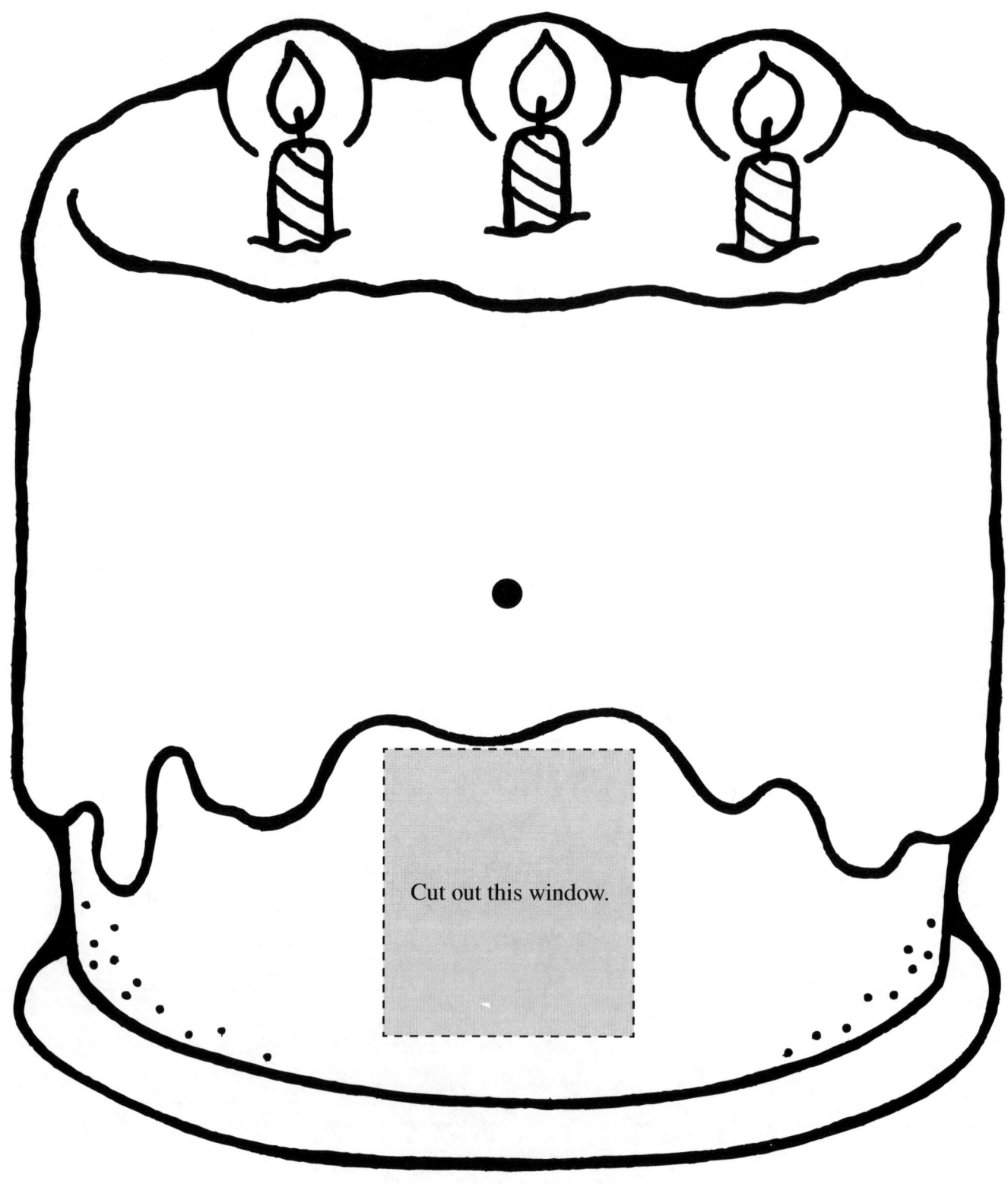

Letter Cc

Cc Picture Wheel

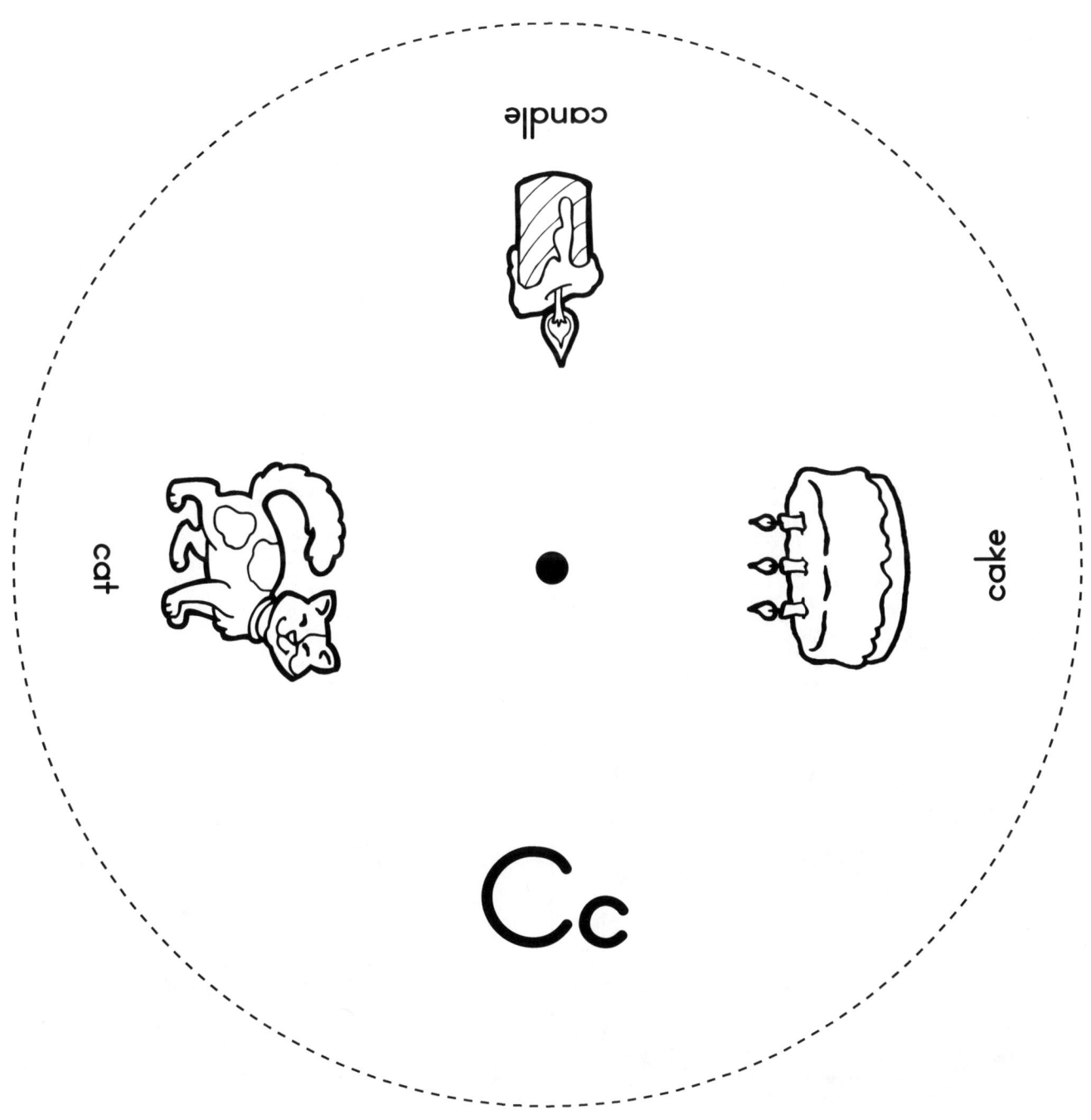

Letter Cc

Cc is for candle to blow out!

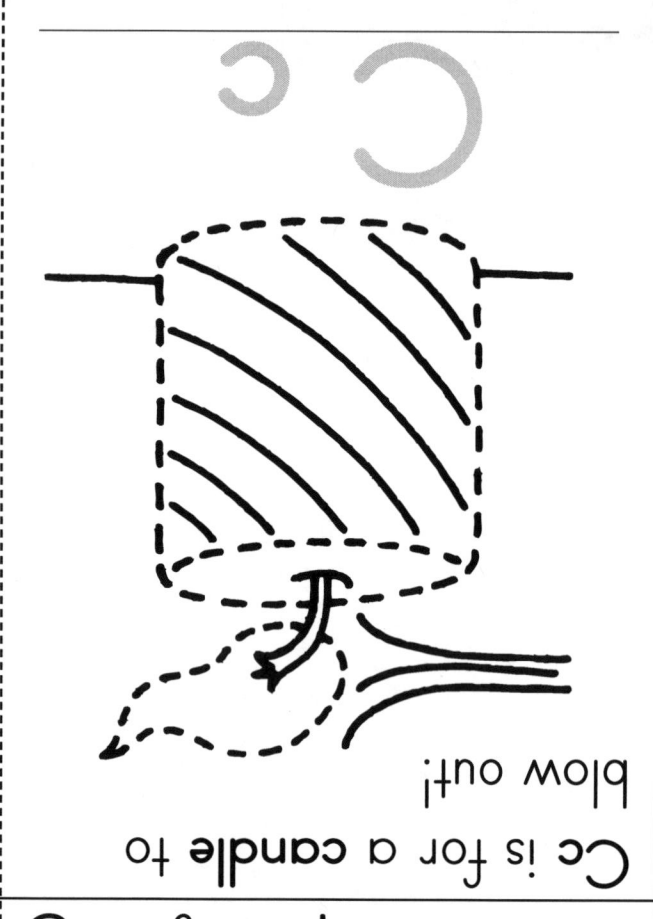

Cc is for cat—meow, meow!

Cc is for **cake** to eat, "mmmm."

_____'s

Cc

Minibook

Letter Dd

Dd

Introduce the letter Dd. Draw and discuss the shape of the letters using chart paper, a white board or a chalkboard. Note any students whose names begin or end with the letter Dd. This will provide opportunities to discuss how and when uppercase and lowercase letters are used.

Introduce the following sentences and accompanying actions. Repeat them often during the week.

Dd is for a **drum**, beating rata-tat-tat.
(Pretend to beat a drum while saying, "rata-tat-tat.")

Dd is for a **duck** saying, "quack, quack."
(Form a bill with your hands while saying, "quack, quack.")

Dd is for a **dinosaur**, roaring very loudly!
(Pretend to be a dinosaur roaring loudly.)

Day 1: Dd Is for Drum

Materials

- Dd Is for Drum worksheet (page 34) for each child
- pencils and crayons

Procedure for Child

1. Write your name on the line provided at the top of the page.
2. Trace the drum and the letters provided.
3. Practice writing the letter Dd on the lines provided.
4. Finish by coloring the drum using crayons.

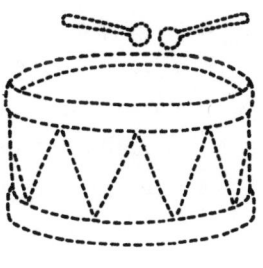

©Teacher Created Resources, Inc. 31 #2340 Alphabet Treasury

Letter Dd

Dd

Day 2: Dinosaur Pop-Up

Materials

- Dinosaur Pop-Up Patterns (page 35) copied onto cardstock for each child
- craft stick for each child
- watercolor paints
- paintbrushes
- safety scissors
- glue

Procedure for Child

1. Write your name on the back of the egg.
2. Use watercolors to paint the dinosaur egg and the dinosaur baby, and let them dry.
3. Cut out the dinosaur egg and baby. Cut the slit on the dinosaur egg.
4. Glue the craft stick to the back of the dinosaur baby.
5. Place the craft stick partly through the slit so the baby dinosaur can move up and down.

Day 3: Dinosaur Wheel

Materials

- Dinosaur Pattern (page 36) for each child
- Dd Picture Wheel (page 37) for each child
- brad for each child
- markers or crayons
- safety scissors
- pencils

Procedure for Child

1. Color the Dinosaur Pattern and Dd pictures on the picture wheel page.
2. Cut out the dinosaur and the picture wheel. (See page 5 for directions.)
3. Write your name on the back of the wheel.
4. Cut out the picture window on the dinosaur. (Note: Adult assistance may be necessary to cut out the picture window.)
5. Place the Dd Picture Wheel behind the Dinosaur Pattern. Make certain that one of the pictures is visible in the picture window on the dinosaur before going on to the next step.
6. Attach the dinosaur to the front of the wheel with a brad. Use the black dot as a guide.

#2340 Alphabet Treasury 32 ©Teacher Created Resources, Inc.

Letter Dd

Dd

Day 4: Dd Minibook

Materials

- Dd Minibook (page 38) for each child
- pencils, colored pencils, crayons or markers
- safety scissors

Procedure for Child

1. Trim and fold the page to create the Dd Minibook. (See page 5 for directions.)
2. Write your name in pencil on the line on the minibook cover.
3. Complete each page of the minibook. Trace each picture and then trace the letter Dd on the lines.
4. Color the pictures using the colored pencils, crayons or markers.
5. Read the book as a group. Later, it can be shared at home or with friends.

Day 5: Dinosaur Delights Cooking Project

(serves 10 children)

Kitchen Implements

- dinosaur cookie cutters
- paper plate for each child

Ingredients

- 20 slices of bread
- 10 slices of cheese

Preparation

1. Place a slice of cheese on top of a slice of bread.
2. Add another slice of bread on top of the cheese to create a sandwich. Place the sandwich on a plate.

Presentation

1. Using a dinosaur cookie cutter, cut out a dinosaur shape from the sandwich. (Optional: If no dinosaur cookie cutter is available, help children cut out an egg shape from the bread and cheese to create a dinosaur egg.)
2. Snack on the leftover bread while admiring the dinosaur creation!
3. Practice good table manners while eating the Dinosaur Delights!

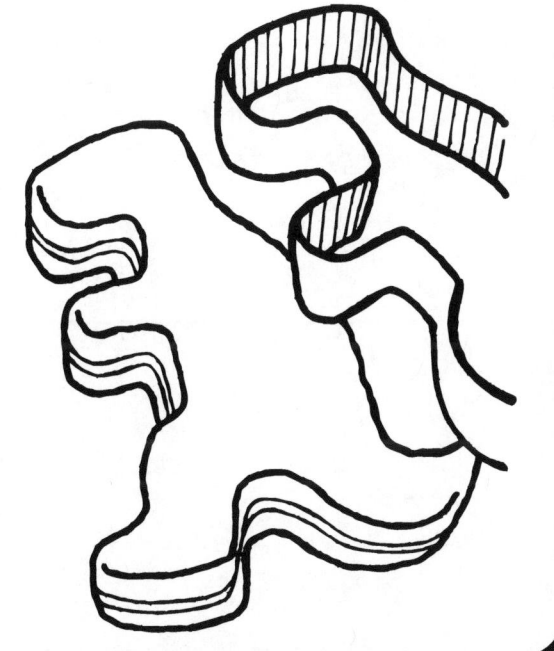

Letter Dd

Dd Is for Drum

Name _____

1. Trace the drum.
2. Trace the Dd's.
3. Write more Dd's.
4. Color the picture.

#2340 Alphabet Treasury   34   ©Teacher Created Resources, Inc.

Letter Dd

Dinosaur Pop-Up

Patterns

Slit the egg on the gray line.

Letter Dd

Dinosaur Pattern

#2340 Alphabet Treasury　　36　　©Teacher Created Resources, Inc.

Letter Dd

Dd Picture Wheel

drum

duck

dinosaur

Dd

©Teacher Created Resources, Inc. 37 #2340 Alphabet Treasury

Letter Dd

Dd is for a duck saying,
"quack, quack."

Dd is for a drum, beating
rata ta ta.

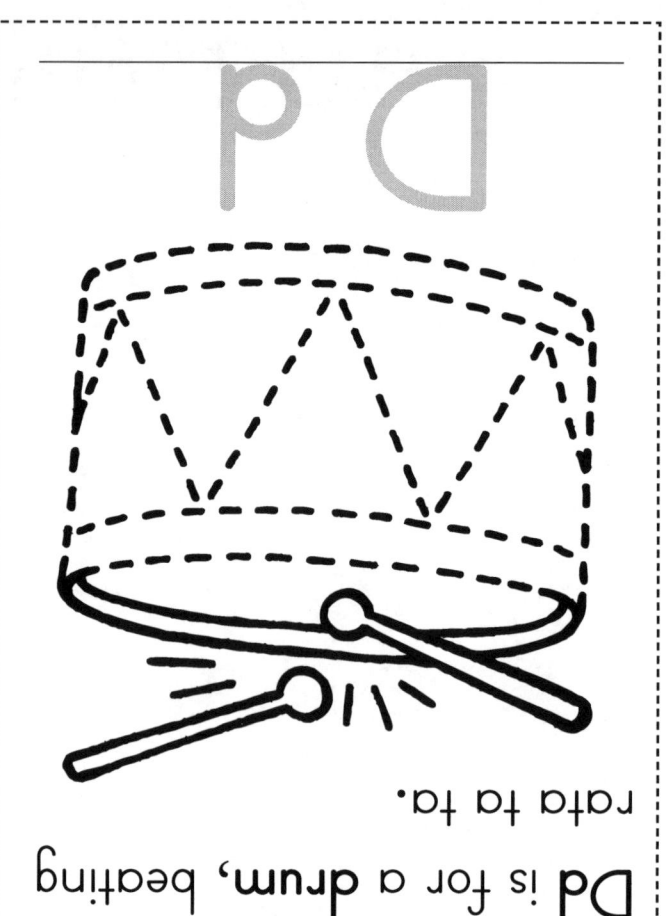

Dd is for a dinosaur,
roaring very loudly!

_____'s

Dd

Minibook

#2340 Alphabet Treasury　　38　　©Teacher Created Resources, Inc.

Letter Ee

Ee

Introduce the letter Ee. Draw and discuss the shape of the letters using chart paper, a white board or a chalkboard. Note any students whose names begin or end with the letter Ee. This will provide opportunities to discuss how and when uppercase and lowercase letters are used.

Introduce the following sentences and accompanying actions. Repeat them often during the week.

Ee is for **ears** with which to hear.
(Pretend to listen while pulling on your ear lobes.)

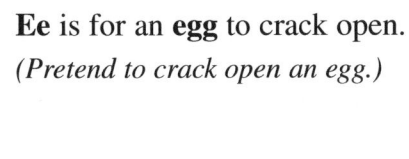

Ee is for an **egg** to crack open.
(Pretend to crack open an egg.)

Ee is for an **elephant**, stomping hard.
(Stomp your feet hard as an elephant might.)

Day 1: Ee Is for Elephant

Materials

- Ee Is for Elephant worksheet (page 42) for each child
- pencils and crayons

Procedure for Child

1. Write your name on the line provided at the top of the page.
2. Trace the elephant and the letters provided.
3. Practice writing the letter Ee on the lines provided.
4. Finish by coloring the elephant using crayons.

©Teacher Created Resources, Inc.   39   #2340 Alphabet Treasury

Letter Ee

Ee

Day 2: Elephant Stick Puppets Activity

Materials

- Elephant Stick Puppet Patterns (page 43) copied onto cardstock for each child
- 8 oz. Styrofoam cup for each child
- 3 craft sticks for each child
- markers or crayons
- safety scissors
- glue or tape

Procedure for Child

1. Color the elephant patterns and cut them out.
2. Write your name on the back of the elephants.
3. Get adult assistance making a hole in the bottom of each Styrofoam cup using scissors.
4. Glue or tape a craft stick to the back of each elephant.
5. If desired, decorate the cup using markers.
6. Slide the stick of an elephant puppet into the cup (stage). Move the elephant up and down using the craft stick.

Day 3: Egg Wheel

Materials

- Egg Pattern (page 44) for each child
- Ee Picture Wheel (page 45) for each child
- brad for each child
- markers or crayons
- safety scissors
- pencils

Procedure for Child

1. Color the Egg Pattern and Ee pictures on the picture wheel page.
2. Cut out the egg and the picture wheel. (see page 5 for directions.)
3. Write your name on the back of the wheel.
4. Cut out the picture window on the egg. (Note: Adult assistance may be necessary to cut out the picture window.)
5. Place the Ee Picture Wheel behind the Egg Pattern. Make certain that one of the pictures is visible in the picture window on the egg before going on to the next step.
6. Attach the egg to the front of the wheel with a brad.

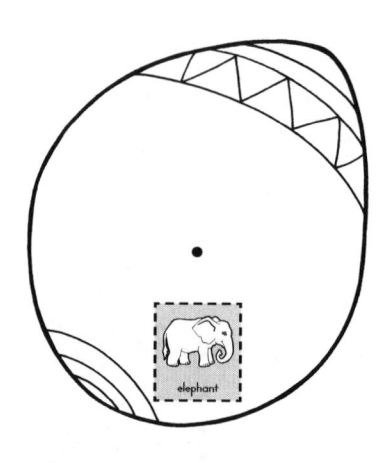

#2340 Alphabet Treasury　　　　　　　　©Teacher Created Resources, Inc.

Letter Ee

Ee

Day 4: Ee Minibook

Materials

- Ee Minibook (page 46) for each child
- pencils, colored pencils, crayons or markers
- safety scissors

Procedure for Child

1. Trim and fold the page to create the Ee Minibook. (See page 5 for directions.)
2. Write your name in pencil on the line on the minibook cover.
3. Complete each page of the minibook. Trace each picture and then trace the letter Ee on the lines.
4. Color the pictures using the colored pencils, crayons or markers.
5. Read the book as a group. Later, it can be shared at home or with friends.

Day 5: Elephant Munch Cooking Project

(serves 10 children)

Kitchen Implements

- measuring cups
- large mixing spoon
- large mixing bowl
- small plate for each child
- small, resealable plastic bag for each child

Ingredients

- 1 cup shredded coconut
- 1 cup dried apple slices
- 1 cup dried banana chips
- 1 cup raisins
- 1 cup dried pineapple slices

Preparation

1. Pour shredded coconut, raisins, and the dried fruit in the large mixing bowl.
2. Take turns mixing the ingredients using the mixing spoon.

Presentation

1. Place a 1/2-cup serving of Elephant Munch on each paper plate.
2. Practice good table manners while munching your treat!

©Teacher Created Resources, Inc.   #2340 Alphabet Treasury

Letter Ee

Ee Is for Elephant

Name _____

1. Trace the elephant.
2. Trace the Ee's.
3. Write more Ee's.
4. Color the picture.

#2340 Alphabet Treasury · ©Teacher Created Resources, Inc.

Letter Ee

Elephant Stick Puppets

Patterns

©*Teacher Created Resources, Inc.* #2340 *Alphabet Treasury*

Letter Ee

Egg Pattern

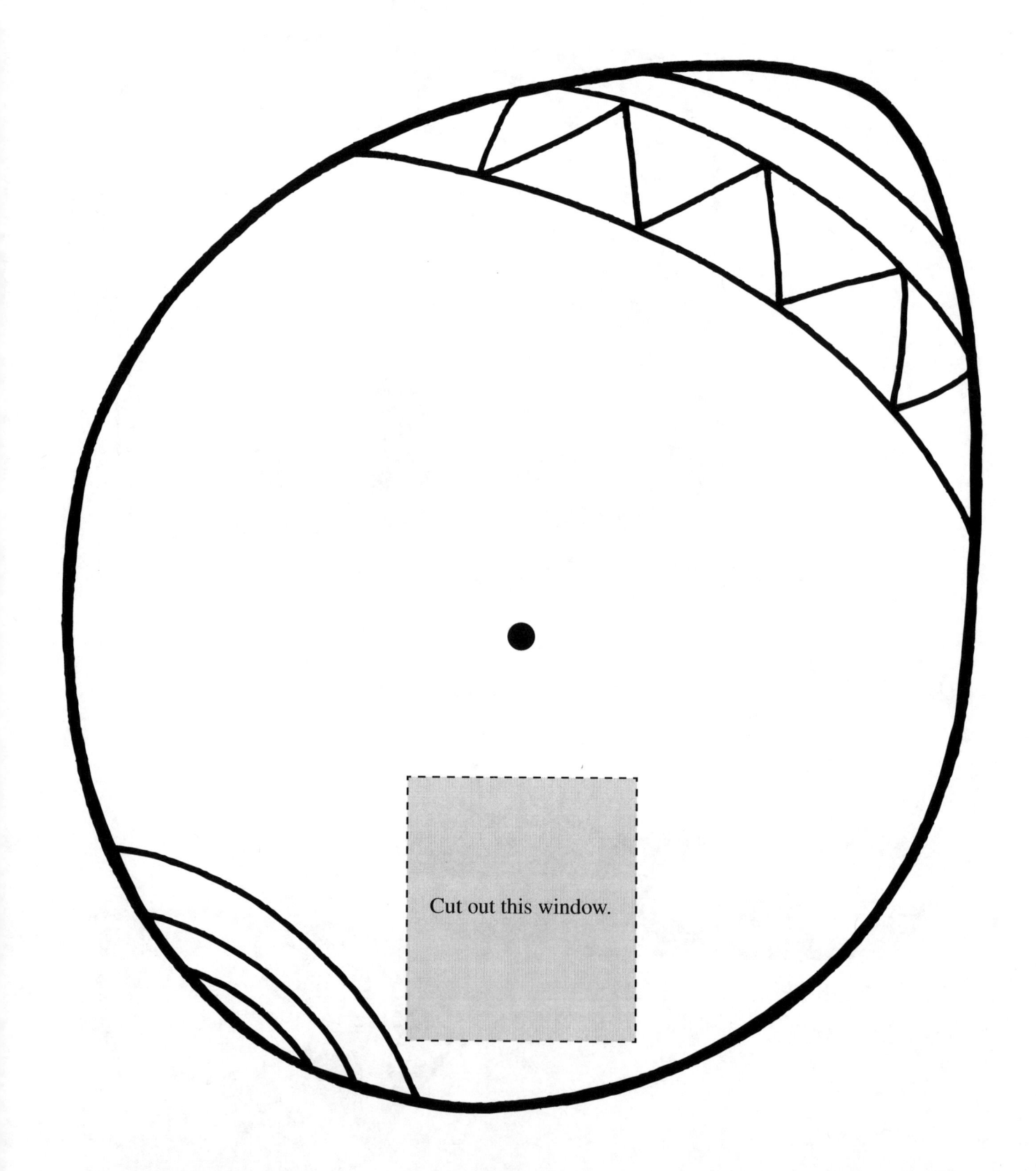

Cut out this window.

#2340 Alphabet Treasury 44 ©Teacher Created Resources, Inc.

Letter Ee

Ee Picture Wheel

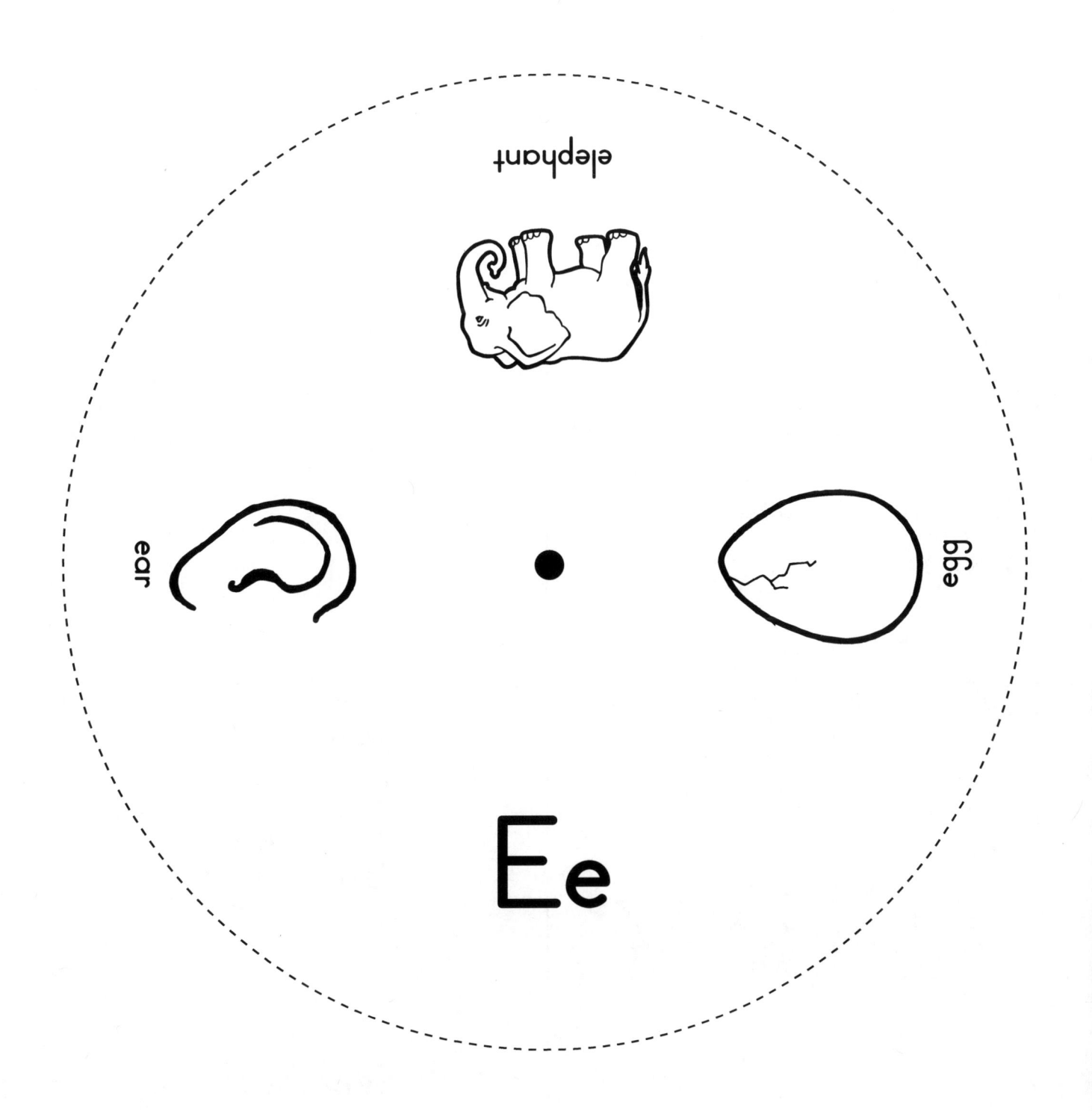

elephant

ear

egg

Ee

©Teacher Created Resources, Inc. #2340 Alphabet Treasury

Letter Ee

Ee is for an **egg** to crack.

Ee is for an **ear** to hear.

Ee is for an **elephant**, stomping hard.

_____'s

Ee

Minibook

#2340 Alphabet Treasury — 46 — ©Teacher Created Resources, Inc.

Letter Ff

Ff

Introduce the letter Ff. Draw and discuss the shape of the letters using chart paper, a white board or a chalkboard. Note any students whose names begin or end with the letter Ff. This will provide opportunities to discuss how and when uppercase and lowercase letters are used.

Introduce the following sentences and accompanying actions. Repeat them often during the week.

Ff is for a **flower** to smell.
(Pretend to smell a flower.)

Ff is for a **fish**, blowing bubbles.
(Pretend to blow bubbles.)

Ff is for a **frog**, leaping up and down.
(Pretend to be a frog leaping.)

Day 1: Ff Is for Flower

Materials

- Ff Is for Flower worksheet (page 50) for each child
- pencils and crayons

Procedure for Child

1. Write your name on the line provided at the top of the page.
2. Trace the flower and the letters provided.
3. Practice writing the letter Ff on the lines provided.
4. Finish by coloring the flower using crayons.

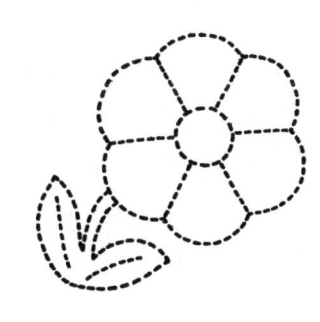

©Teacher Created Resources, Inc. #2340 Alphabet Treasury

Letter Ff

Ff

Day 2: Five Fish in a Bottle Activity

Materials

- empty 16 oz. plastic bottle for each child
- 1/4 c. baby oil for each child
- glue gun (adult use only)
- 5 plastic fish for each child
- small beads
- glitter
- water

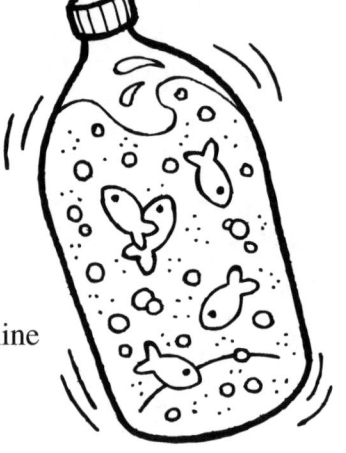

Note: Plastic fish can be found at most hobby shops, craft shops and online at *www.orientaltrading.com*.

Procedure for Child

1. Place 5 plastic fish, beads, and glitter in an empty bottle.
2. Pour 1/4 c. baby oil into the bottle. Then fill the bottle with water.
3. Use the glue gun to attach the bottle cap securely to the bottle. (Adult must complete this step.)

Day 3: Fish Wheel

Materials

- Fish Pattern (page 51) for each child
- Ff Picture Wheel (page 52) for each child
- brad for each child
- markers or crayons
- safety scissors
- pencils

Procedure for Child

1. Color the Fish Pattern and Ff pictures on the picture wheel page.
2. Cut out the fish and the picture wheel. (See page 5 for directions.)
3. Write your name on the back of the wheel.
4. Cut out the picture window on the fish. (Note: Adult assistance may be necessary to cut out the picture window.)
5. Place the Ff Picture Wheel behind the Fish Pattern. Make certain that one of the pictures is visible in the picture window on the fish before going on to the next step.
6. Attach the fish to the front of the wheel with a brad.

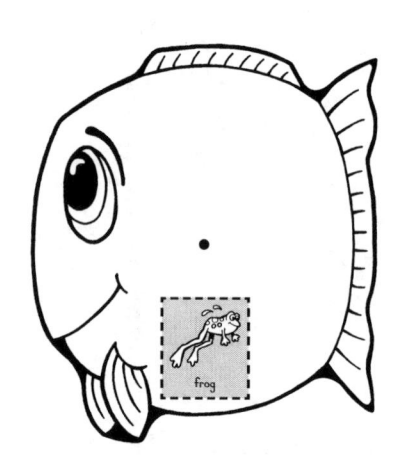

#2340 Alphabet Treasury ©Teacher Created Resources, Inc.

Letter Ff

Ff

Day 4: Ff Minibook

Materials

- Ff Minibook (page 53) for each child
- pencils, colored pencils, crayons or markers
- safety glasses

Procedure for Child

1. Trim and fold the page to create the Ff Minibook. (See page 5 for directions.)
2. Write your name in pencil on the line on the minibook cover.
3. Complete each page of the minibook. Trace each picture and then trace the letter Ff on the lines.
4. Color the pictures using the colored pencils, crayons or markers.
5. Read the book as a group. Later it can be shared at home or with friends.

Day 5: Fish Aquarium Cooking Project

(serves 10 children)

Kitchen Implements

- pot
- large bowl
- measuring cup
- clear plastic dessert cup for each child
- plastic spoon for each child

Ingredients

- three 3 oz. boxes of blue gelatin
- gummy fish
- water

Preparation

1. Make the gelatin. Follow the instructions on the gelatin package and pour it into the dessert cups.
2. Refrigerate the gelatin.

Presentation

1. When the gelatin begins to set, add gummy fish to the dessert cup (aquarium) so it looks like they are swimming. Refrigerate the gelatin until fully set.
2. Serve each child his or her fish in an aquarium.
3. Practice good table manners.

©Teacher Created Resources, Inc. #2340 Alphabet Treasury

Letter Ff

Ff Is for Flower

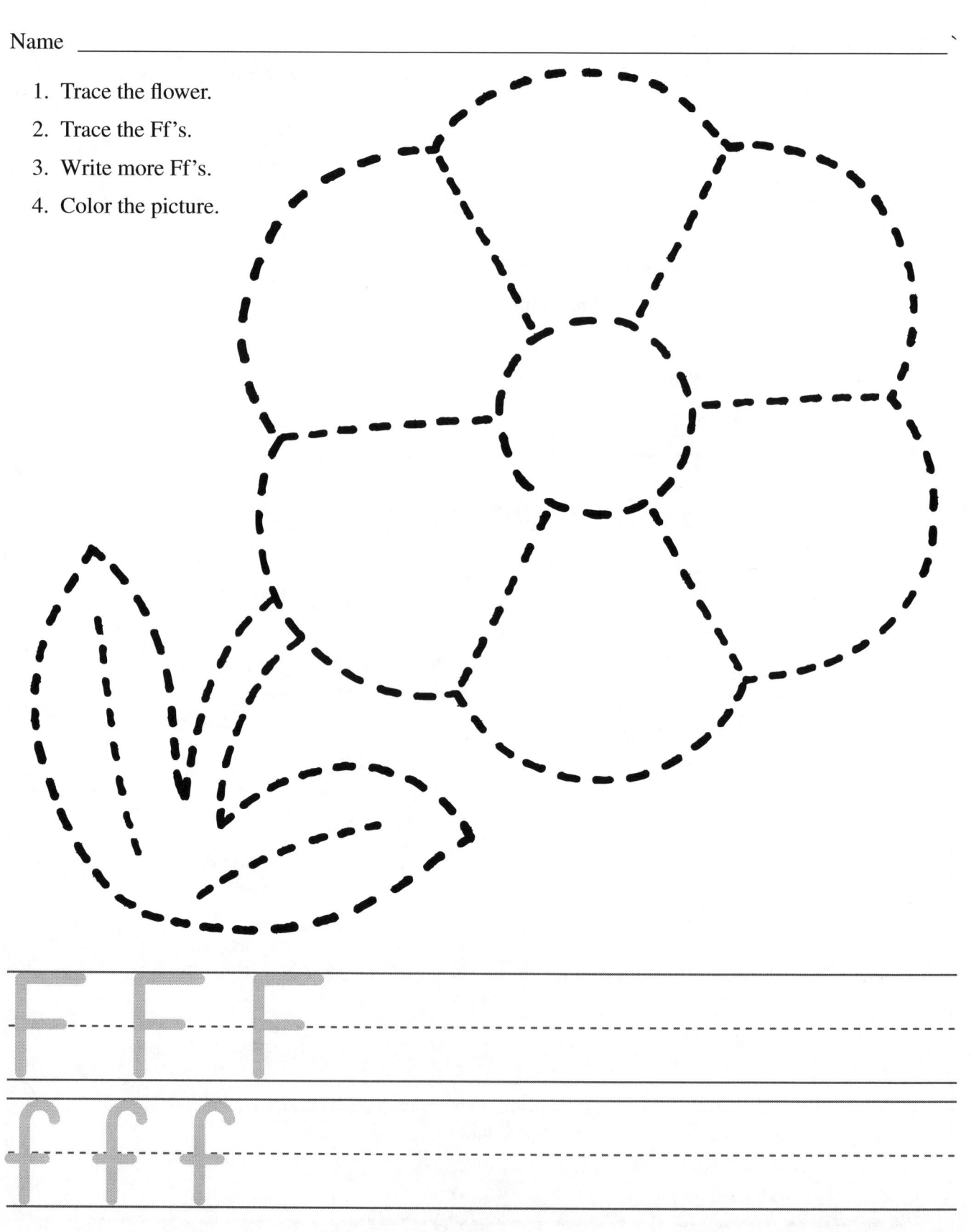

Name _____

1. Trace the flower.
2. Trace the Ff's.
3. Write more Ff's.
4. Color the picture.

#2340 Alphabet Treasury 50 ©Teacher Created Resources, Inc.

Letter Ff

Fish Pattern

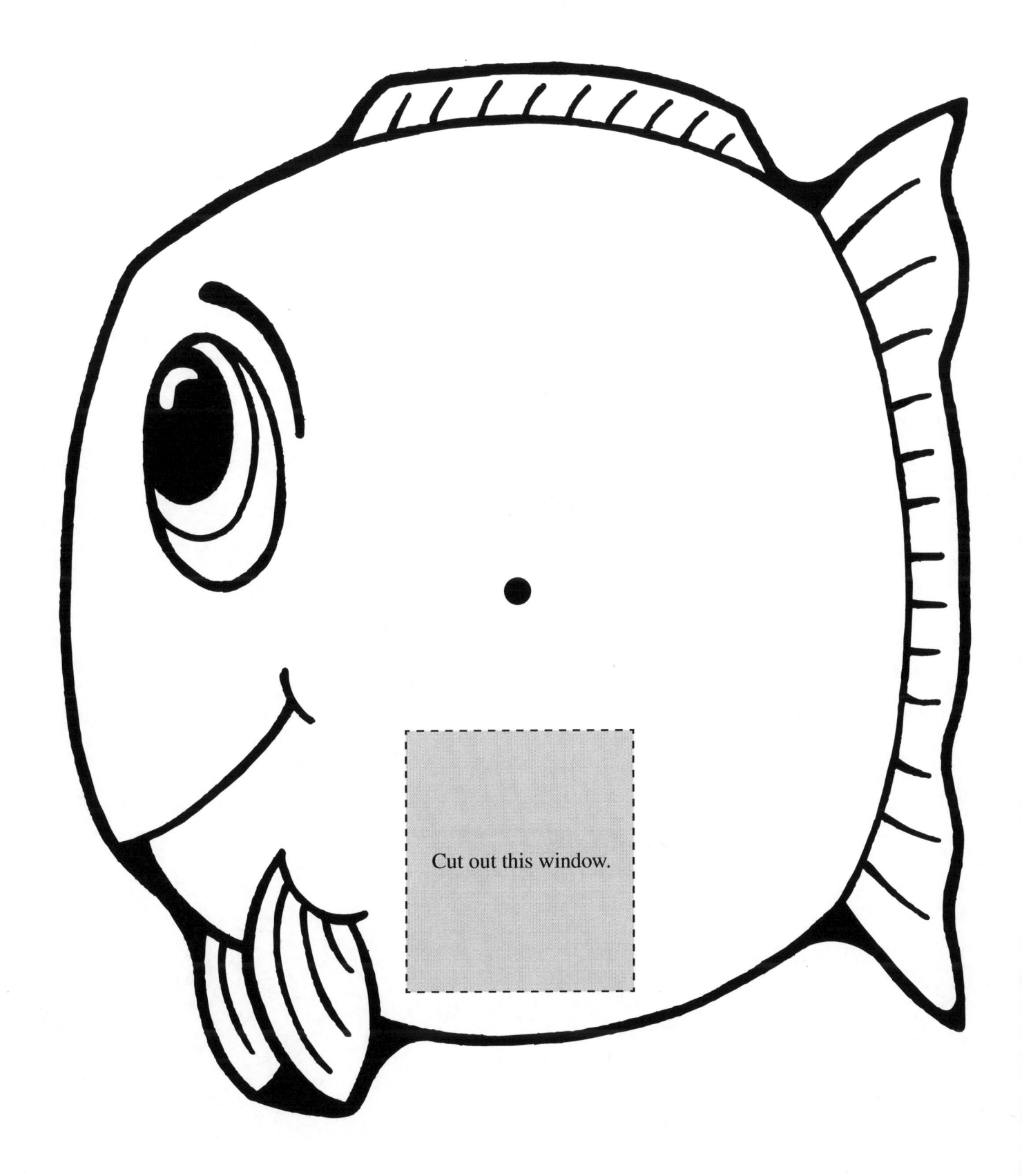

Cut out this window.

©*Teacher Created Resources, Inc.* #2340 *Alphabet Treasury*

Letter Ff

Ff Picture Wheel

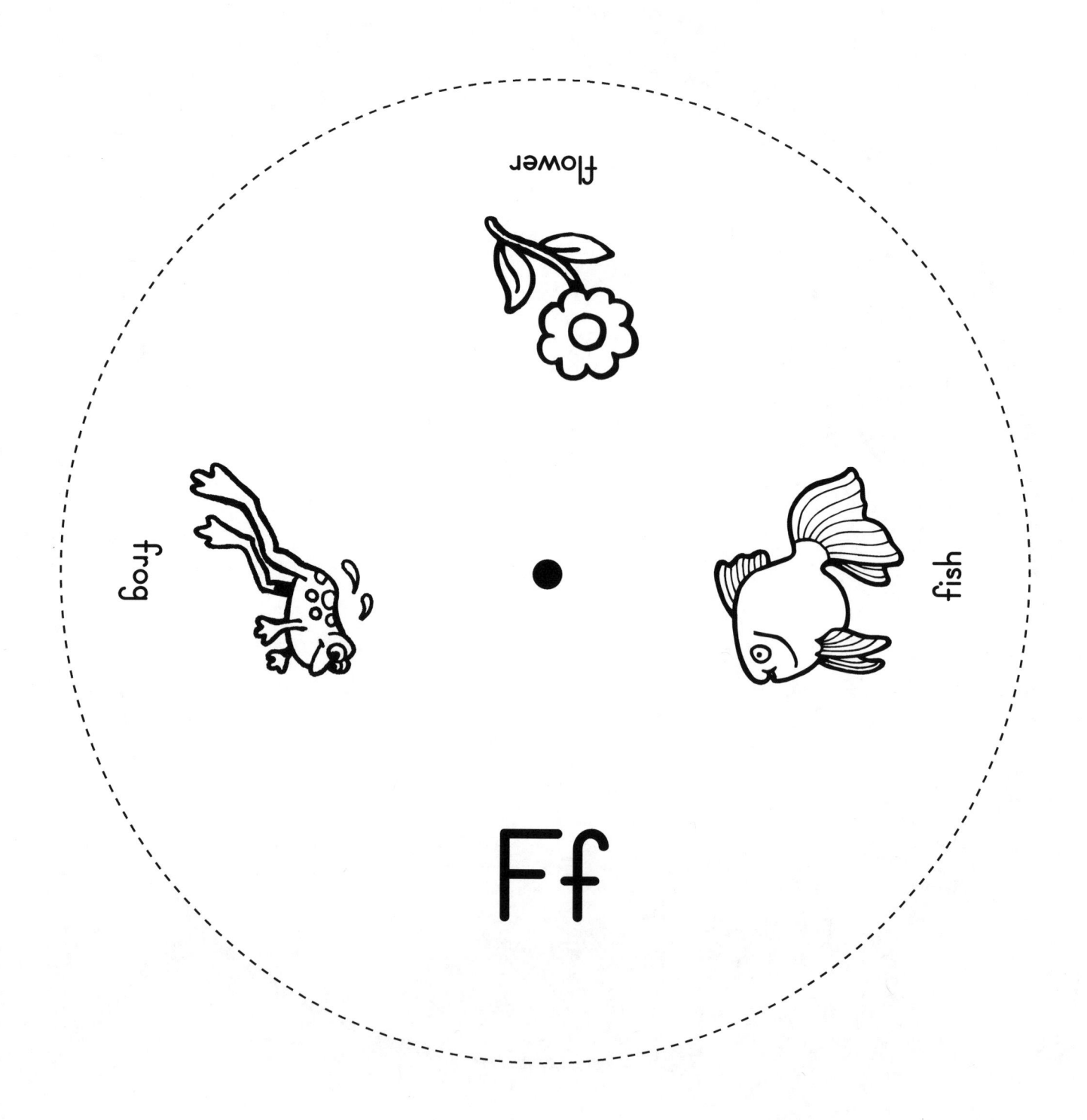

flower

frog

fish

Ff

#2340 Alphabet Treasury ©Teacher Created Resources, Inc.

Letter *Ff*

Ff is for a **flower** to smell.

Ff is for a **fish**, blowing bubbles.

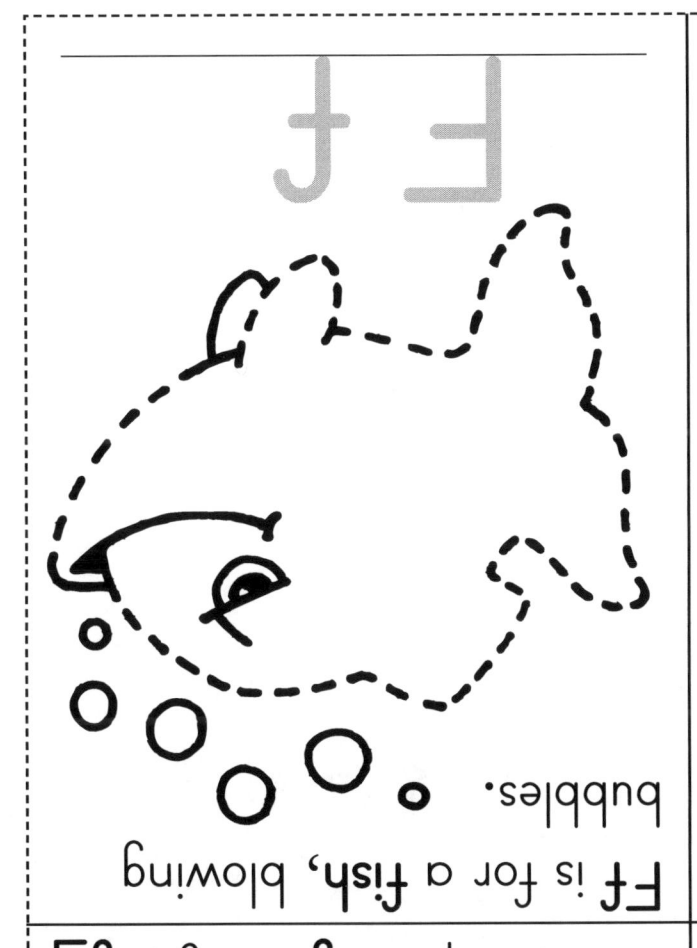

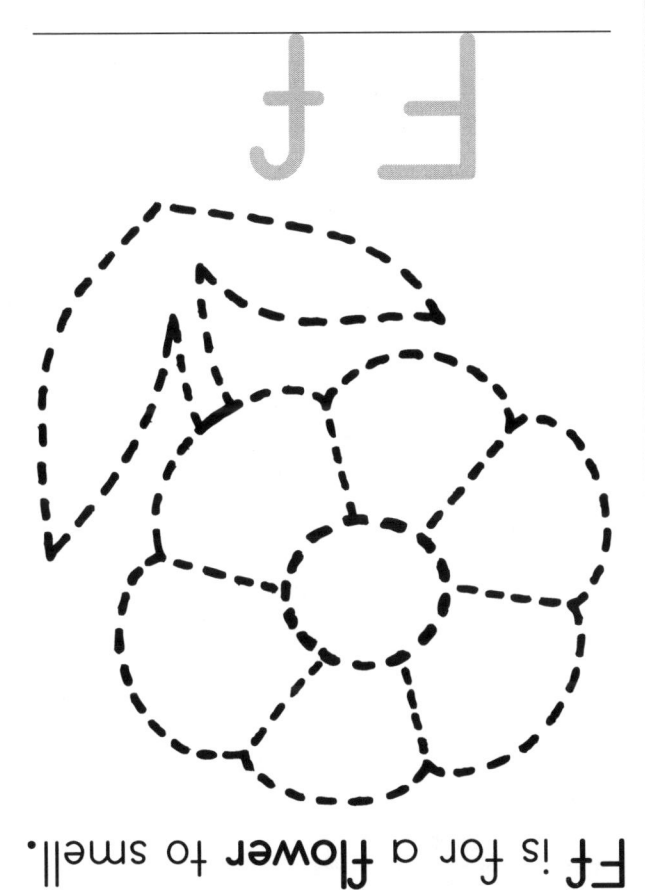

Ff is for a **frog**, leaping up and down.

_____'s

Ff

Minibook

letter Ff

©*Teacher Created Resources, Inc.* 53 #2340 *Alphabet Treasury*

Letter Gg

Gg

Introduce the letter Gg. Draw and discuss the shape of the letters using chart paper, a white board or a chalkboard. Note any students whose names begin or end with the letter Gg. This will provide opportunities to discuss how and when uppercase and lowercase letters are used.

Introduce the following sentences and accompanying actions. Repeat them often during the week.

Gg is for a **girl**, running quickly.
(Run in place.)

Gg is for a **gate**, swinging open.
(Pretend to open and close a gate.)

Gg is for a **goat**, climbing up a hill.
(Pretend to climb up a tall hill.)

Day 1: Gg Is for Goat

Materials

- Gg Is for Goat worksheet (page 57) for each child
- pencils and crayons

Procedure for Child

1. Write your name on the line provided at the top of the page.
2. Trace the goat and the letters provided.
3. Practice writing the letter Gg on the lines provided.
4. Finish by coloring the goat.

#2340 Alphabet Treasury · ©Teacher Created Resources, Inc.

Letter Gg

Gg

Day 2: Gate Picture Activity

Materials

- Gate Picture Pattern (page 58) copied onto copied onto card for each child
- 3" x 4" photo of each child
- crayons or markers
- safety scissors • glitter • glue
- self-adhesive magnet for each child (optional)

Procedure for Child

1. Cut out the gate and fold it as indicated.
2. Write your name on the back of the pattern.
3. On the inside of the gate, glue the child's photo as shown.
4. Color the front of the gate, add glitter using glue, and let dry.
5. If desired, attach a self-adhesive magnet to the back of the glittery gate to display it on a metallic surface.

Day 3: Gate Wheel

Materials

- Gate Pattern (page 59) for each child
- Gg Picture Wheel (page 60) for each child
- brad for each child
- markers or crayons
- safety scissors
- pencils

Procedure for Child

1. Color the Gate Pattern and Gg pictures on the picture wheel page.
2. Cut out the gate and the picture wheel. (See page 5 for directions.)
3. Write your name on the back of the wheel.
4. Cut out the picture window on the gate. (Note: Adult assistance may be necessary to cut out the picture window.)
5. Place the Gg Picture Wheel behind the Gate Pattern. Make certain that one of the pictures is visible in the picture window on the gate before going on to the next step.
6. Attach the gate to the front of the wheel with a brad.

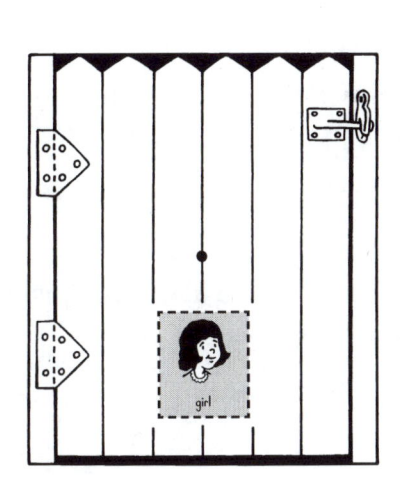

©Teacher Created Resources, Inc. #2340 Alphabet Treasury

Letter Gg

Gg

Day 4: Gg Minibook

Materials

- Gg Minibook (page 61) for each child
- pencils, colored pencils, crayons or markers
- safety sissors

Procedure for Child

1. Trim and fold the page to create the Gg Minibook. (See page 5 for directions.)
2. Write your name in pencil on the line on the minibook cover.
3. Complete each page of the minibook. Trace each picture and then trace the letter Gg on the lines.
4. Color the pictures using the colored pencils, crayons or markers.
5. Read the book as a group. Later, it can be shared at home or with friends.

Day 5: Gates Cooking Project *(serves 10 children)*

Kitchen Implements

- small paper plate for each child
- plastic knife for each child
- small serving spoon

Ingredients

- 1 cup cream cheese (or peanut butter)
- graham crackers
- pretzel sticks

Preparation

1. Gather 6 pretzel sticks, a graham cracker, a plastic knife, and a spoonful of cream cheese on a plate.
2. Spread the cream cheese evenly on the graham cracker using a plastic knife.
3. Arrange the pretzels on the cream cheese to resemble a gate.
4. Practice good table manners as you enjoy your treat!

Letter Gg

Gg Is for Goat

Name _____

1. Trace the goat.
2. Trace the Gg's.
3. Write more Gg's.
4. Color the picture.

G G G

g g g

©Teacher Created Resources, Inc.   #2340 Alphabet Treasury

Letter Gg

Gate Picture Pattern

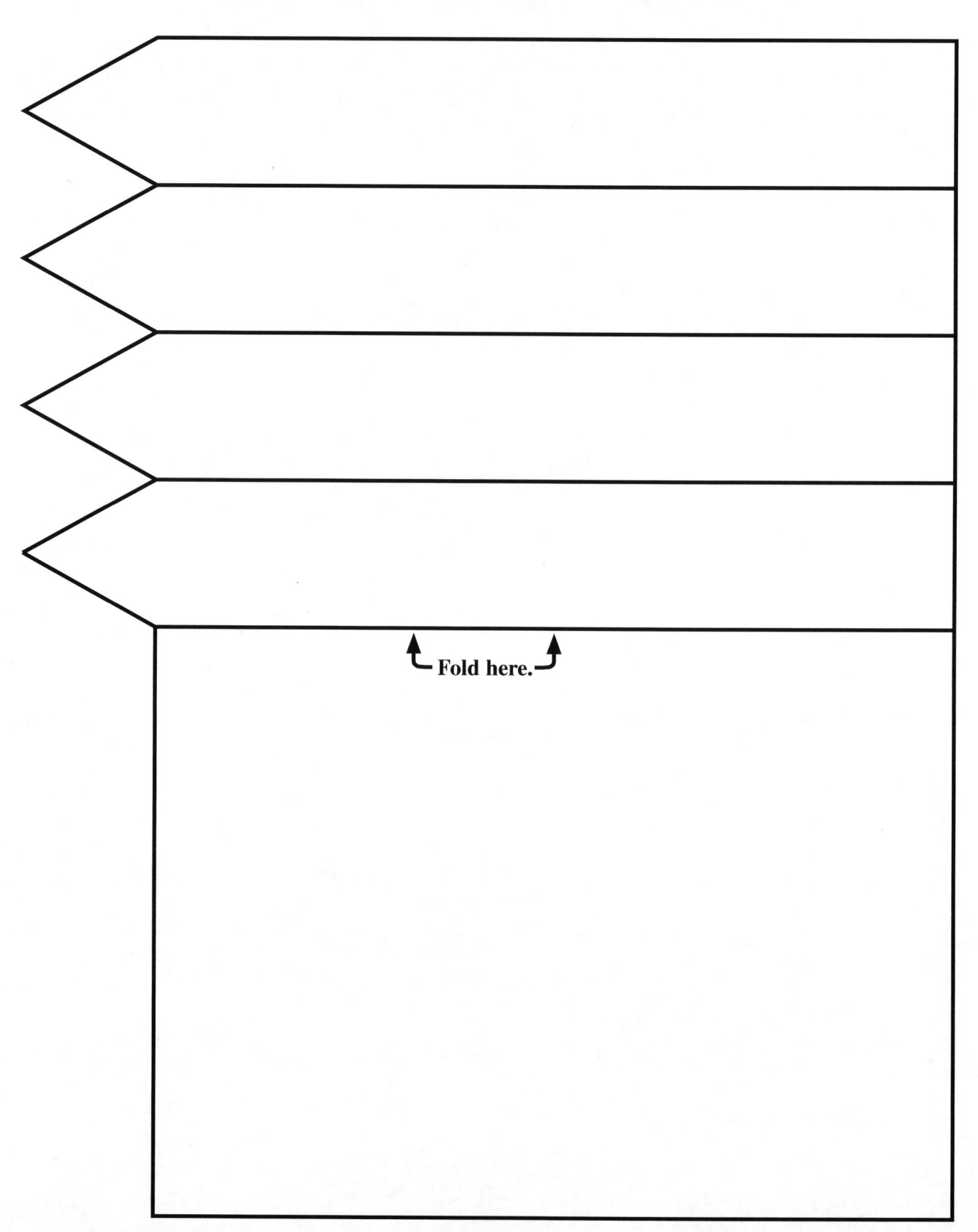

Fold here.

Letter Gg

Gate Pattern

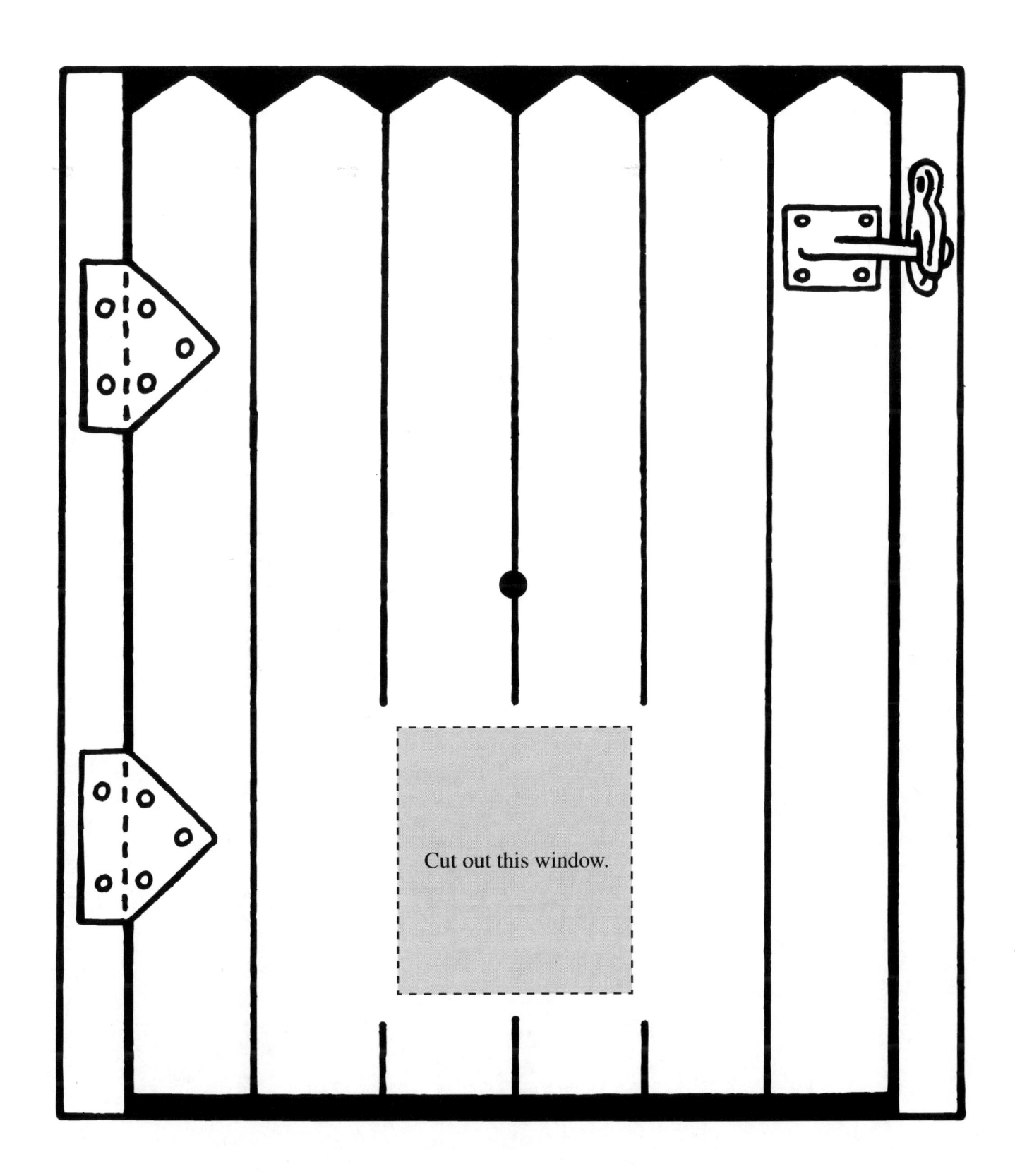

Cut out this window.

©Teacher Created Resources, Inc. 59 #2340 Alphabet Treasury

Letter Gg

Gg Picture Wheel

girl

goat

gate

Gg

#2340 Alphabet Treasury ©Teacher Created Resources, Inc.

Letter Gg

Gg is for a gate, swinging open.

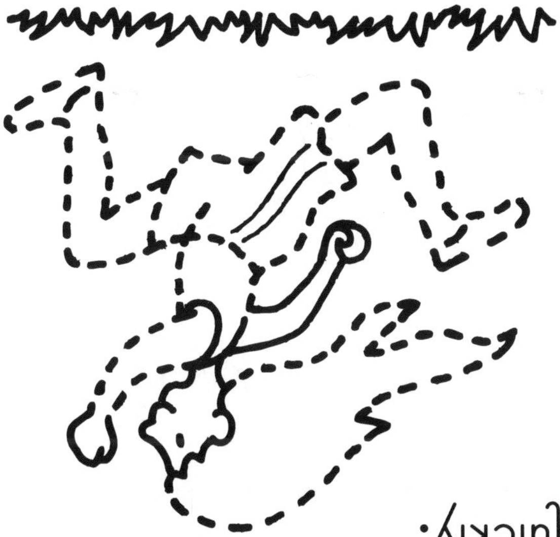

Gg is for a girl, running quickly.

Gg is for a goat, climbing up a hill.

_____'s

Gg

Minibook

©Teacher Created Resources, Inc. 61 #2340 Alphabet Treasury

Letter Hh

Hh

Introduce the letter Hh. Draw and discuss the shape of the letters using chart paper, a white board or a chalkboard. Note any students whose names begin or end with the letter Hh. This will provide opportunities to discuss how and when uppercase and lowercase letters are used.

Introduce the following sentences and accompanying actions. Repeat them often during the week.

Hh is for **hands** to clap.
(Clap your hands.)

Hh is for a **hammer** to bang.
(Pretend to bang a hammer by pounding one fist into one palm.)

Hh is for the **house** we live in.
(Pretend to put a roof over your head to form a house.)

Day 1: Hh Is for Hammer

Materials

- Hh Is for Hammer worksheet (page 65) for each child
- pencils and crayons

Procedure for Child

1. Write your name on the line provided at the top of the page.
2. Trace the hammer and the letters provided.
3. Practice writing the letter Hh on the lines provided.
4. Finish by coloring the hammer.

Letter Hh

Hh

Day 2: House-Building Activity

Materials

- House-Building Patterns (page 66) for each child
- small paper bag for each child (different colors, if possible)
- assortment of stickers
- old newspapers
- crayons or markers
- safety scissors
- stapler
- markers
- glue

Procedure for Child

1. Color and cut out the House-Building Patterns.
2. Attach the window and door patterns to the paper bag using glue and let dry.
3. Decorate the bag with crayons or markers and stickers.
4. Crumple the old newspapers into small balls and stuff the bag with newspaper balls until it is full.
5. Fold down the top of the bag. Then attach the folded roof pattern over the top. Staple across the top of the bag to create a house.

Day 3: House Wheel

Materials

- House Pattern (page 67) for each child
- Hh Picture Wheel (page 68) for each child
- brad for each child
- safety scissors
- markers or crayons
- pencils

Procedure for Child

1. Color the House Pattern and Hh pictures on the picture wheel page.
2. Cut out the house and the picture wheel. (See page 5 for directions.)
3. Write your name on the back of the wheel.
4. Cut out the picture window on the house. (Note: Adult assistance may be necessary to cut out the picture window.)
5. Place the Hh Picture Wheel behind the House Pattern. Make certain that one of the pictures is visible in the picture window on the house before going on to the next step.
6. Attach the house to the front of the wheel with a brad.

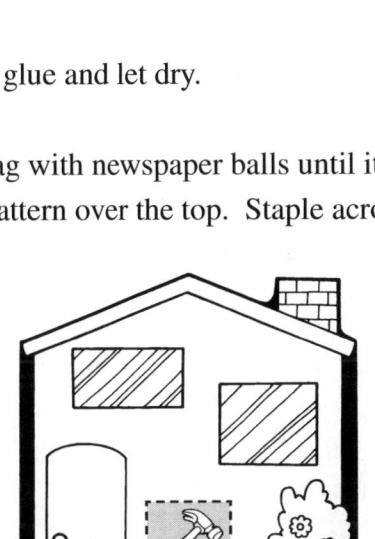

©Teacher Created Resources, Inc.   #2340 Alphabet Treasury

Letter Hh

Hh

Day 4: Hh Minibook

Materials

- Hh Minibook (page 69) for each child
- pencils, colored pencils, crayons or markers
- safety scissors

Procedure for Child

1. Trim and fold the page to create the Hh Minibook. (See page 5 for directions.)
2. Write your name in pencil on the line on the minibook cover.
3. Complete each page of the minibook. Trace each picture and then trace the letter Hh on the lines.
4. Color the pictures using the colored pencils, crayons or markers.
5. Read the book as a group. Later, it can be shared at home or with friends.

Day 5: Houses Cooking Project *(serves 10 children)*

Kitchen Implements

- sheet of wax paper for each child
- measuring cups
- large mixing bowl
- large mixing spoon

Ingredients

- 10 cups peanut butter (or cream cheese)
- 10 cups crispy rice cereal
- 5 cups dry powdered milk
- raisins

Preparation

1. Measure 10 cups of peanut butter and place it in a large mixing bowl. Add the cereal and powdered milk to the bowl.
2. Take turns mixing the mixture with a large spoon until smooth.
3. Place a small amount of the mixture on each child's sheet of wax paper.
4. Form most of the mixture into the shape of a square for the house. Form the remainder of the mixture into a triangle for the roof of the house.
5. Add raisins to the house to create a door, windows, and shingles for the roof.
6. Practice good table manners.

Letter Hh

Hh Is for Hammer

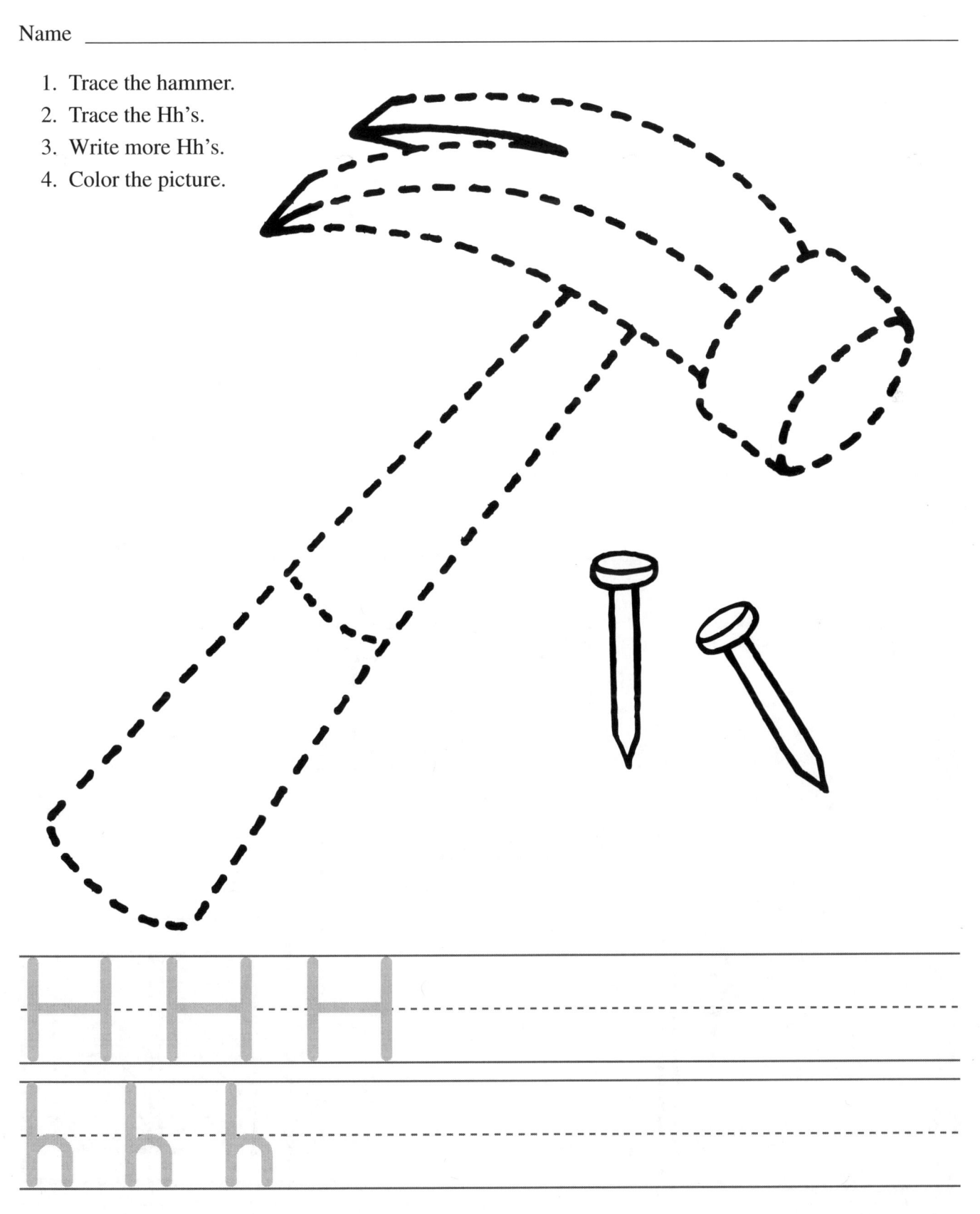

Name _____

1. Trace the hammer.
2. Trace the Hh's.
3. Write more Hh's.
4. Color the picture.

©Teacher Created Resources, Inc.   65   #2340 Alphabet Treasury

Letter Hh

House Building Patterns

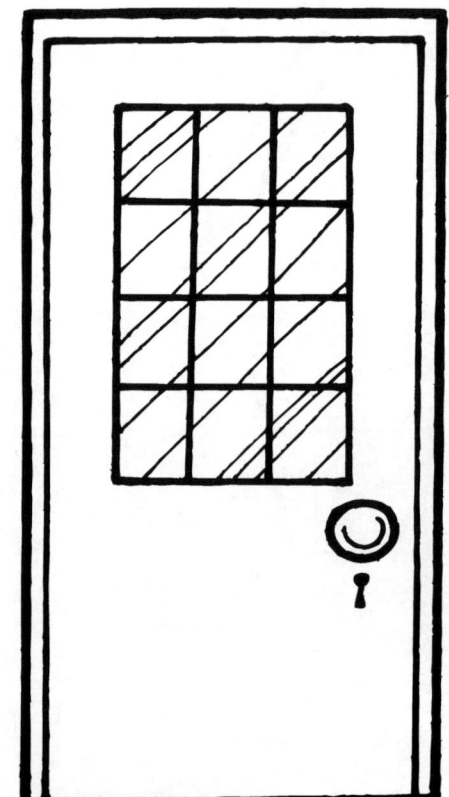

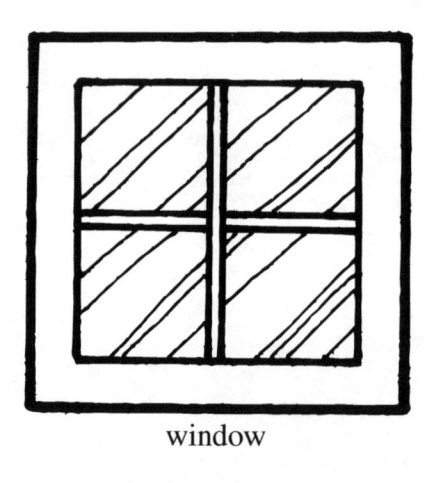

Fold here.

roof

window

window

door

#2340 Alphabet Treasury

Letter Hh

House Pattern

Cut out this window.

Letter Hh

Hh Picture Wheel

hammer

hand

house

Hh

#2340 Alphabet Treasury ©Teacher Created Resources, Inc.

Letter Hh

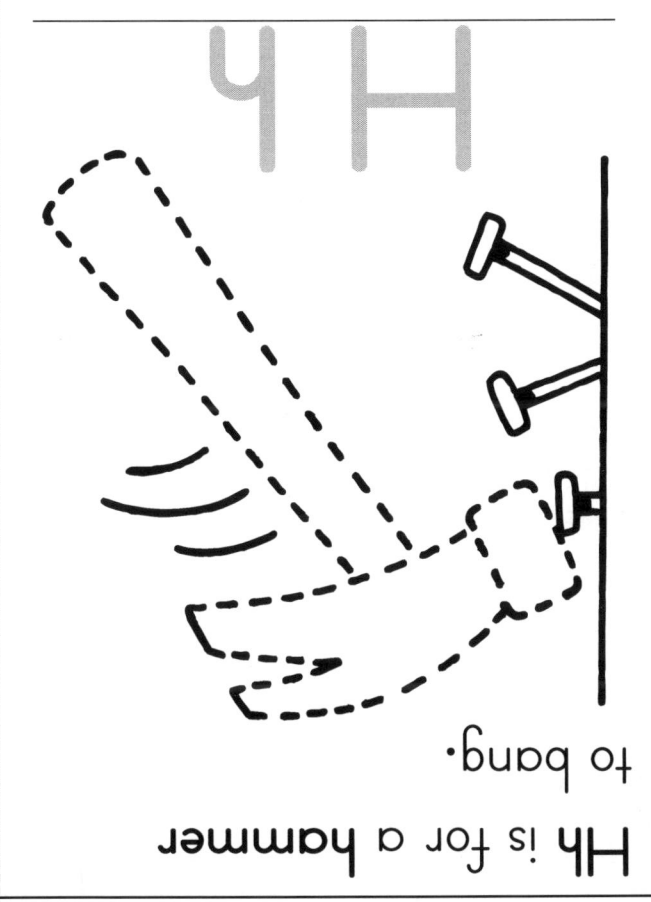

Hh is for hands to clap.

Hh is for a hammer to bang.

Hh is for the house we live in.

Hh

_____'s

Hh

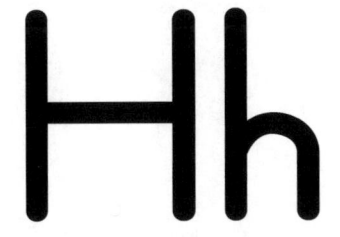

Minibook

Letter Ii

Ii

Introduce the letter Ii. Draw and discuss the shape of the letters using chart paper, a white board or a chalkboard. Note any students whose names begin or end with the letter Ii. This will provide opportunities to discuss how and when uppercase and lowercase letters are used.

Introduce the following sentences and accompanying actions. Repeat them often during the week.

Ii is for an **iguana**, scurrying across the ground.
(Pretend to be an iguana, scurrying across the ground.)

Ii is for an **igloo** to build when it snows.
(Pretend to build an igloo.)

Ii is for an **ice cream** to eat, "mmmm."
(Pretend to eat ice cream and say, "mmmm.")

Day 1: Ii Is for Igloo

Materials

- Ii Is for Igloo worksheet (page 73) for each child
- pencils and crayons

Procedure for Child

1. Write your name on the line provided at the top of the page.
2. Trace the igloo and the letters provided.
3. Practice writing the letter Ii on the lines provided.
4. Finish by coloring the igloo using crayons.

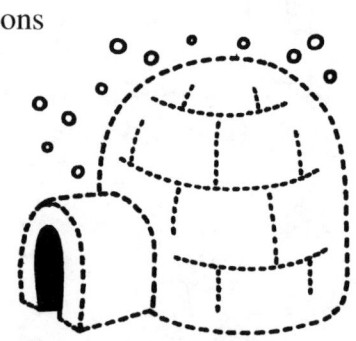

#2340 Alphabet Treasury ©Teacher Created Resources, Inc.

Letter Ii

Ii

Day 2: Iguana Magnet Activity

Materials

- Iguana Pattern (page 74) copied onto cardstock for each child
- safety scissors
- paintbrushes
- spring-type clothespin for each child
- green tempera paint
- self-adhesive magnet for each child
- glue
- 4 mm wiggle eye for each child

Procedure for Child

1. Write your name on the back of the pattern.
2. Paint the iguana and spring-type clothespin green and let dry.
3. Cut out the iguana.
4. Attach the wiggle eye to the iguana using glue.
5. Glue the iguana onto the clothespin as shown. Attach the self-adhesive magnet to the back of the clothespin.
6. Use the completed iguana magnet clip to display your favorite artwork!

Day 3: Ice-Cream Cone Wheel

Materials

- Ice-Cream Cone Pattern (page 75) for each child
- Ii Picture Wheel (page 76) for each child
- brad for each child
- safety scissors
- markers or crayons
- pencils

Procedure for Child

1. Color the Ice-Cream Cone Pattern and Ii pictures on the picture wheel page.
2. Cut out the ice-cream cone and the picture wheel. (See page 5 for directions.)
3. Write your name on the back of the wheel.
4. Cut out the picture window on the ice-cream cone. (Note: Adult assistance may be necessary to cut out the picture window.)
5. Place the Ii Picture Wheel behind the Ice-Cream Cone Pattern. Make certain that one of the pictures is visible in the picture window on the ice-cream cone before going on to the next step.
6. Attach the ice-cream cone to the front of the wheel with a brad.

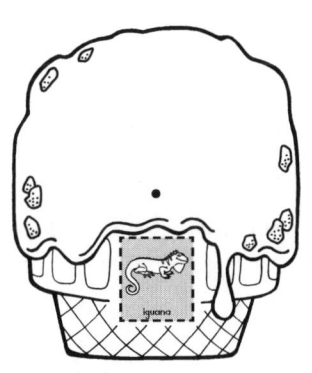

©Teacher Created Resources, Inc.   71   #2340 Alphabet Treasury

Letter Ii

Ii

Day 4: Ii Minibook

Materials

- Ii Minibook (page 77) for each child
- pencils, colored pencils, crayons or markers

Procedure for Child

1. Fold the page to create the Ii Minibook.
2. Have students write their names in pencil on the line on the minibook cover.
3. Complete each page of the minibook. Trace each picture and then trace and write the letter Ii on the lines.
4. Color the pictures using the colored pencils, crayons or markers.
5. Read the book as a group. Later it can be shared at home or with friends.

Day 5: Ice Cream Cooking Project *(serves 10 children)*

Kitchen Implement

- ice-cream scoop

Ingredients

- ice cream (variety of flavors)
- 10 ice-cream cones
- candy sprinkles
- whipped cream (optional)

Preparation

1. Choose the flavor of ice cream you want. Use the ice-cream scoop to scoop the ice cream onto a cone.
2. Sprinkle the assorted candy sprinkles onto the ice cream.

Presentation

1. Add whipped cream atop the ice cream if desired.
2. Practice good table manners.

#2340 Alphabet Treasury ©Teacher Created Resources, Inc.

Letter Ii

Ii Is for Igloo

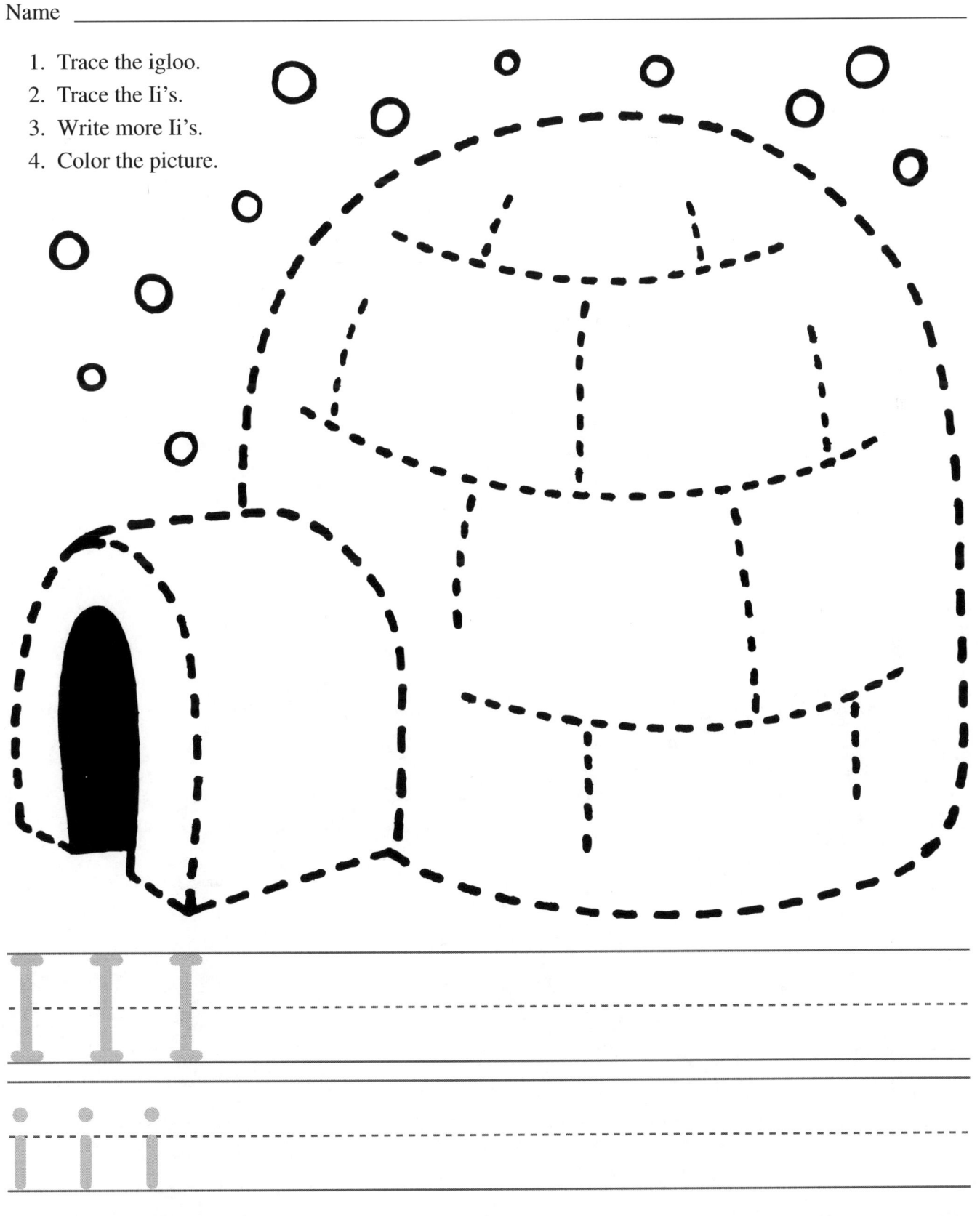

Name _____

1. Trace the igloo.
2. Trace the Ii's.
3. Write more Ii's.
4. Color the picture.

©Teacher Created Resources, Inc.   73   #2340 Alphabet Treasury

Letter Ii

Iguana Pattern

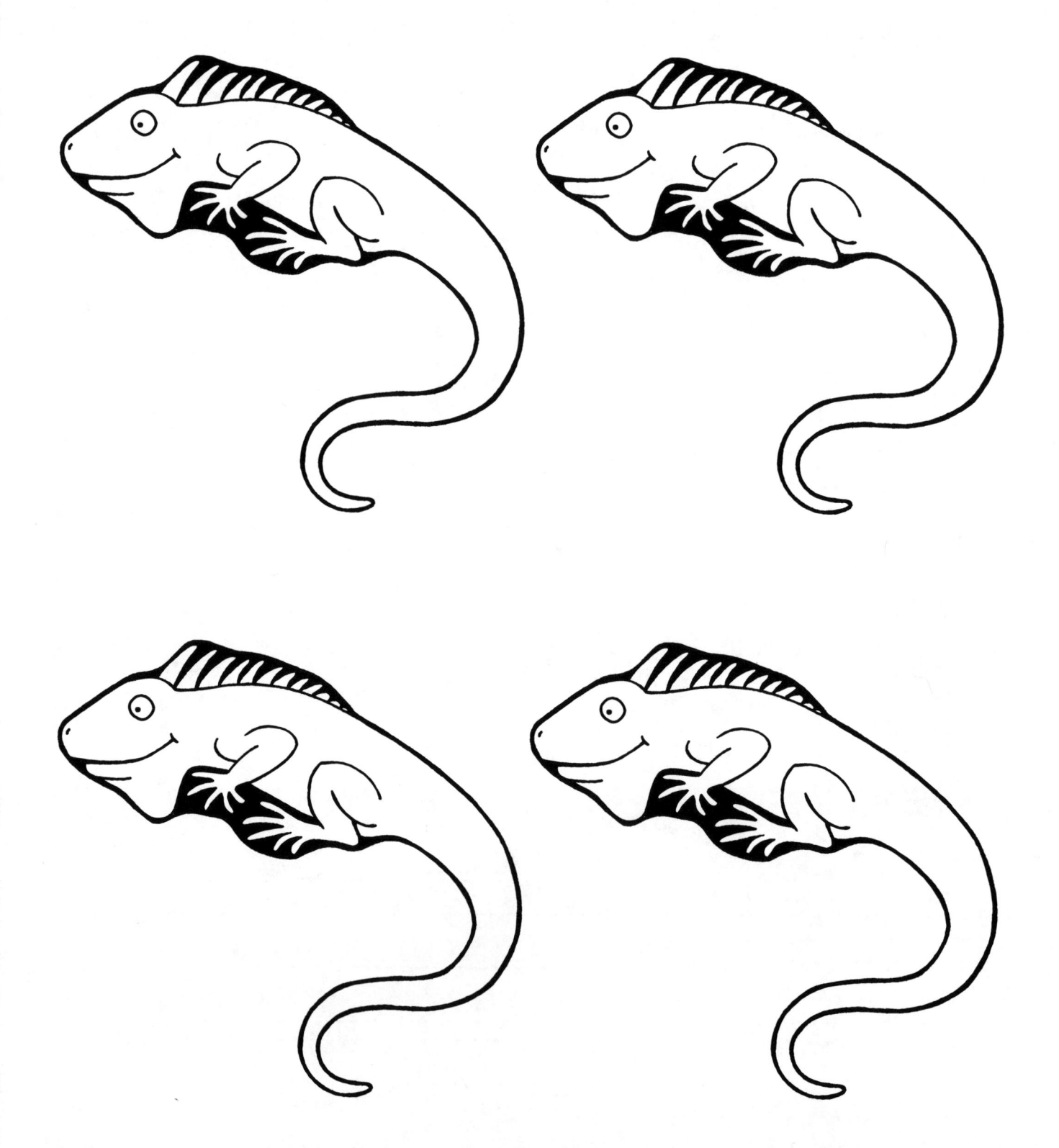

#2340 Alphabet Treasury 74 ©Teacher Created Resources, Inc.

Letter Ii

Ice-Cream Cone Pattern

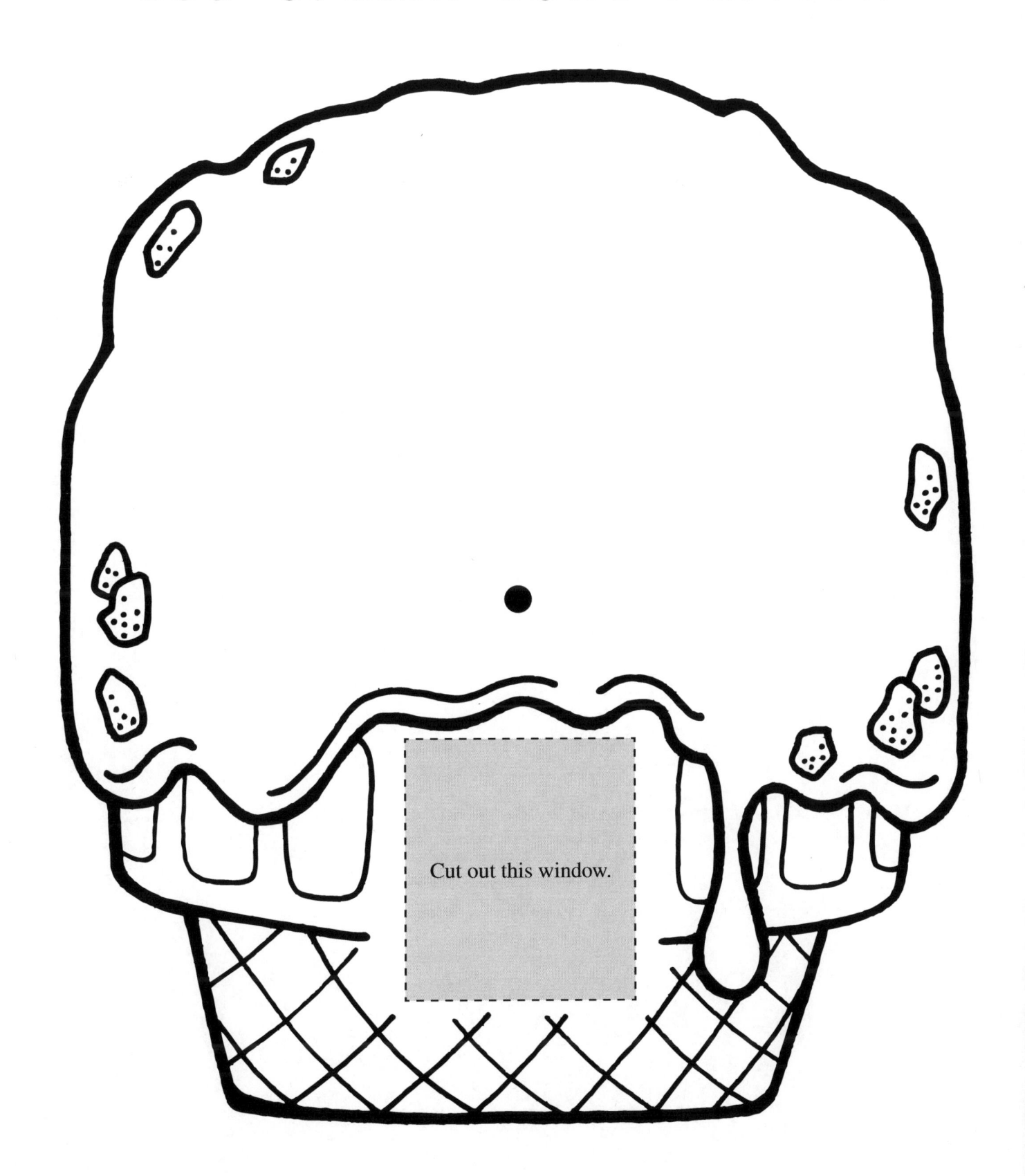

Cut out this window.

©Teacher Created Resources, Inc. 75 #2340 Alphabet Treasury

Letter Ii

Ii Picture Wheel

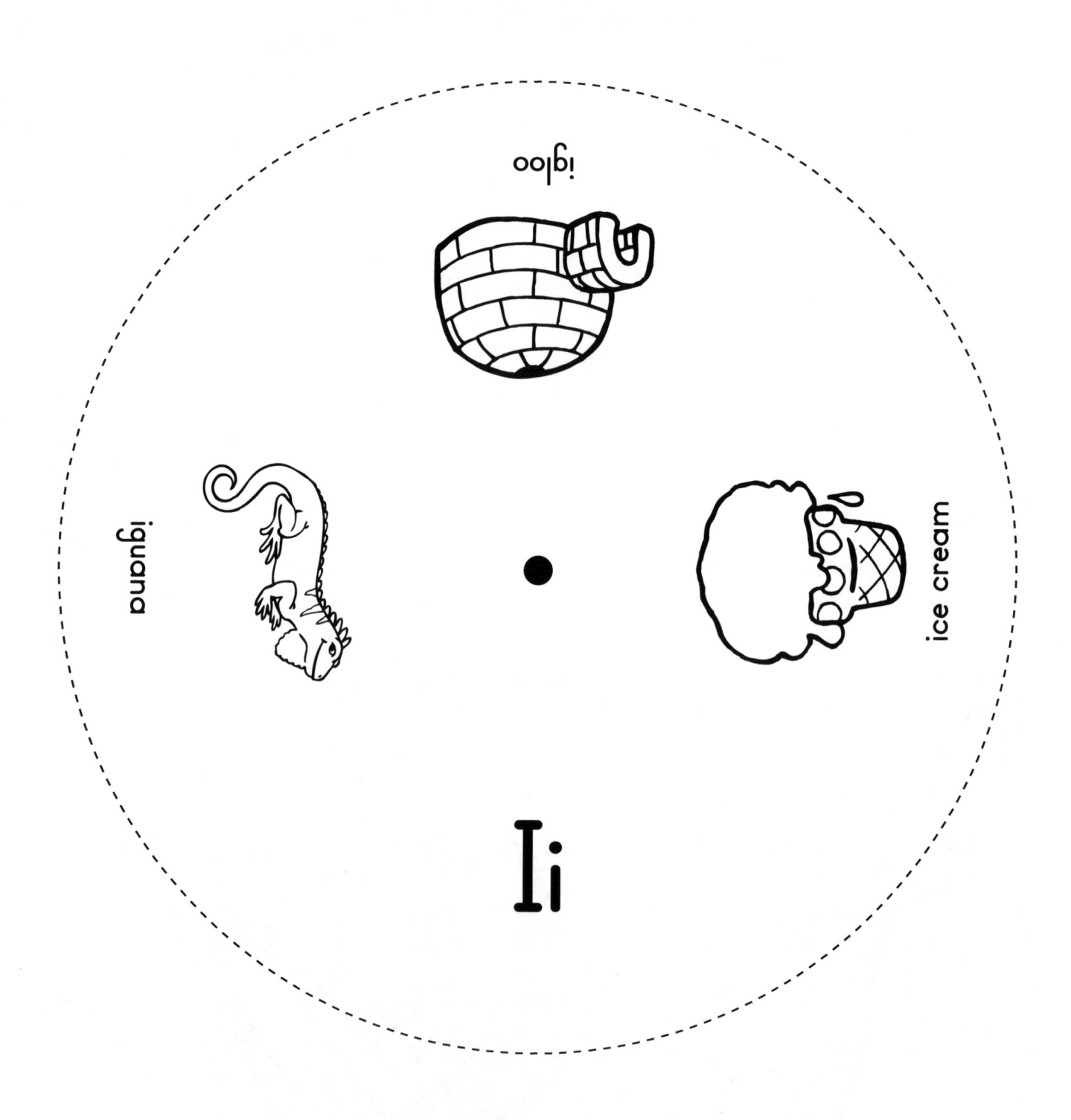

igloo

iguana

ice cream

Ii

#2340 Alphabet Treasury 76 ©Teacher Created Resources, Inc.

Letter Ii

Ii is for an iguana,
scurrying across the ground.

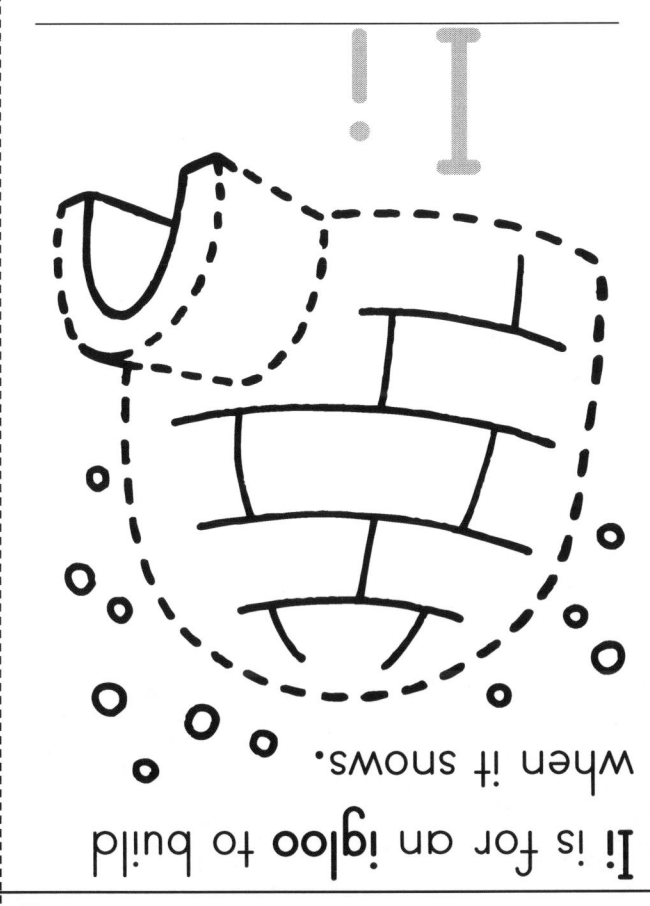

Ii is for an igloo to build
when it snows.

Ii is for **ice cream** to eat,
"mmmm."

Ii

_____'s

Ii

Minibook

©Teacher Created Resources, Inc.   77   #2340 Alphabet Treasury

Letter Jj

Jj

Introduce the letter Jj. Draw and discuss the shape of the letters using chart paper, a white board or a chalkboard. Note any students whose names begin or end with the letter Jj. This will provide opportunities to discuss how and when uppercase and lowercase letters are used.

Introduce the following sentences and accompanying actions. Repeat them often during the week.

Jj is for **jewels** that sparkle.
(Flick fingers to five to create the illusion of sparkling.)

Jj is for a **Jack-in-the-box** jumping.
(Starting from a squatting position, jump up and down.)

Jj is for a **jump rope** to jump with.
(Pretend to jump rope.)

Day 1: Jj Is for Jewels

Materials

- Jj Is for Jewels worksheet (page 81) for each child
- pencils and crayons

Procedure for Child

1. Write your name on the line provided at the top of the page.
2. Trace the jewels and the letters provided.
3. Practice writing the letter Jj on the lines provided.
4. Finish by coloring the jewels using crayons.

Letter Jj

Jj

Day 2: Jewel Friendship Bracelet Activity

Materials

- 8" length of yarn for each child
- assortment of beads (different colors/shapes)
- safety scissors
- clear tape (optional)

Procedure for Child

1. Tie the first bead to one end of the yarn. Then string the beads (jewels) onto the yarn. (Note: For additional help, wrap a small piece of tape on the other end of the yarn to form a "needle." The tape will prevent the yarn from fraying.)
2. When finished, tie the two ends together. Make sure you can slide the bracelet on and off after the ends are tied together.
3. Cut off the excess yarn and the bead on the end.
4. Children may trade bracelets with friends, if desired.

Day 3: Jack-in-the-Box Wheel

Materials

- Jack-in-the-Box Pattern (page 82) for each child
- Jj Picture Wheel (page 83) for each child
- brad for each child
- markers or crayons
- safety scissors
- pencils

Procedure for Child

1. Color the Jack-in-the-Box Pattern and Jj pictures on the picture wheel page.
2. Cut out the Jack-in-the-box and the picture wheel. (See page 5 for directions.)
3. Write your name on the back of the wheel.
4. Cut out the picture window on the Jack-in-the-box. (Note: Adult assistance may be necessary to cut out the picture window.)
5. Place the Jj Picture Wheel behind the Jack-in-the-Box Pattern. Make certain that one of the pictures is visible in the picture window on the Jack-in-the-box before going on to the next step.
6. Attach the Jack-in-the-box to the front of the wheel with a brad.

©Teacher Created Resources, Inc. 79 #2340 Alphabet Treasury

Letter Jj

Jj

Day 4: Jj Minibook

Materials

- Jj Minibook (page 84) for each child
- pencils, colored pencils, crayons or markers
- safety scissors

Procedure for Child

1. Trim and fold the page to create the Jj Minibook. (See page 5 for directions.)
2. Write your name in pencil on the line on the minibook cover.
3. Complete each page of the minibook. Trace each picture and then trace the letter Jj on the lines.
4. Color the pictures using the colored pencils, crayons or markers.
5. Read the book as a group. Later, it can be shared at home or with friends.

Day 5: Jewels to Eat Cooking Project *(serves 10 children)*

Kitchen Implements

- 3 pots
- measuring cups
- 3 mixing spoons
- three 9" x 13" baking pans
- cookie cutters (variety of simple shapes)
- small paper plate for each child

Ingredients

- three 3 oz. boxes of gelatin (3 different colors)
- 7 1/2 cups apple juice or water

Preparation

1. Measure 2 1/2 cups of juice or water and pour it into a pot.
2. Follow the instructions on the gelatin package.
3. Pour each color of gelatin into a 9" x 13" baking pan and refrigerate it for at least 3 hours. It should bounce back when touched.
4. Repeat Steps 1 and 2 for the other boxes of gelatin.

Presentation

1. Use the cookie cutters to cut out a variety of shapes (jewels) from the set gelatin.
2. Place some jewels on each paper plate.
3. Practice good table manners.

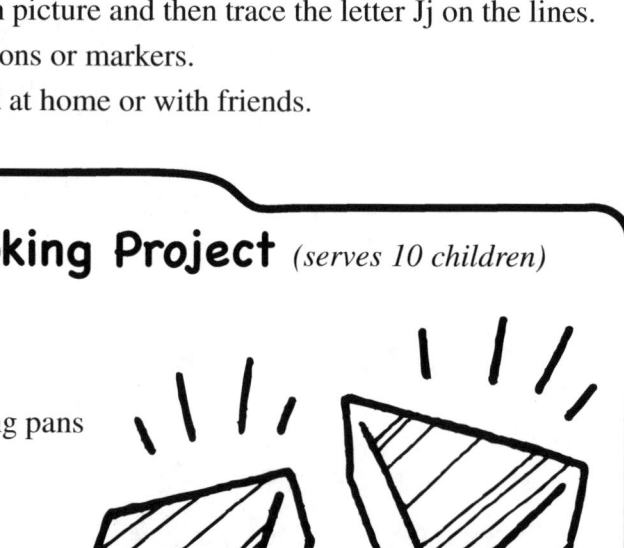

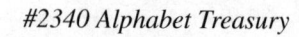

#2340 Alphabet Treasury

Letter Jj

Jj Is for Jewels

Name _____

1. Trace the jewels.
2. Trace the Jj's.
3. Write more Jj's.
4. Color the picture.

Letter Jj

Jack-in-the-Box Pattern

Cut out this window.

#2340 Alphabet Treasury　　82　　©Teacher Created Resources, Inc.

Letter Jj

Jj Picture Wheel

jewel

jump rope

Jack-in-the-box

Jj

Letter Jj

Jj is for a Jack-in-the-box jumping.

Jj is for jewels that sparkle.

Jj is for a **jump rope** to jump with.

_____'s

Jj

Minibook

#2340 Alphabet Treasury ©Teacher Created Resources, Inc.

Letter Kk

Kk

Introduce the letter Kk. Draw and discuss the shape of the letters using chart paper, a white board or a chalkboard. Note any students whose names begin or end with the letter Kk. This will provide opportunities to discuss how and when uppercase and lowercase letters are used.

Introduce the following sentences and accompanying actions. Repeat them often during the week.

Kk is for a **kangaroo** hopping.
(Hop up and down holding your arms up in front like a kangaroo.)

Kk is for a **key** to unlock a lock.
(Pretend to hold a key, then turn it in a lock.)

Kk is for a **kite**, flying high.
(Pretend to fly a kite.)

Day 1: Kk Is for Key

Materials

- Kk Is for Key worksheet (page 88) for each child
- pencil and crayons

Procedure for Child

1. Write your name on the line provided at the top of the page.
2. Trace the key and the letters provided.
3. Practice tracing and writing the letter Kk on the lines provided.
4. Finish by coloring the key using crayons.

©Teacher Created Resources, Inc. 85 #2340 Alphabet Treasury

Letter Kk

Kk

Day 2: Kite Sun Catcher Activity

Materials
- Kite Sun Catcher Patterns (page 89) for each child
- Kite Template (page 90)
- 2 sheets of 8" x 10" clear contact paper for each child
- 2 sheets of colored construction paper for each child
- assortment of confetti and glitter
- different colors of yarn
- hole punch
- cardboard
- glue
- markers

Teacher Preparation
1. Copy the Sun Catcher Patterns on different colors of construction paper. Make two sheets for each child.
2. Cut out 2 sets of Sun Catcher Patterns for each child.
3. Trace the Kite Template onto cardboard and use it to make two clear contact paper kite shapes for each child.

Procedure for Child
1. Peel off the contact paper backing on one of the pieces of contact paper.
2. Sprinkle the sticky side of the contact paper with glitter and confetti. Set aside.
3. Peel off the contact paper backing on the second sheet. With the help of an adult, match up the second sheet of contact paper to the decorated one and press the sticky sides together.
4. Glue a frame atop the contact-paper kite. Then glue another frame on the other side of the contact-paper kite.
5. Punch a hole in the bottom of the kite, thread a 24" length of yarn through the hole, and tie it in place. Glue the bows on the yarn.
6. Punch a hole at the top of the kite. Thread a short length through the hole and tie a knot. Use the hanger to display the completed kite sun catcher in a window.

Day 3: Kite Wheel

Materials
- Kite Pattern (page 91) for each child
- Kk Picture Wheel (page 92) for each child
- brad for each child
- markers or crayons
- safety scissors
- pencils

Procedure for Child
1. Color the Kite Pattern and Kk pictures on the picture wheel page.
2. Cut out the kite and the picture wheel. (See page 5 for directions.)
3. Write your name on the back of the picture wheel.
4. Cut out the picture window on the kite. (Note: Adult assistance may be necessary to cut out the picture window.)
5. Place the Kk Picture Wheel behind the Kite Pattern. Make certain that one of the pictures is visible in the picture window on the kite before going on to the next step.
6. Attach the kite to the front of the wheel with a brad.

#2340 Alphabet Treasury ©Teacher Created Resources, Inc.

Letter Kk

Kk

Day 4: Kk Minibook

Materials

- Kk Minibook (page 93) for each child
- pencils, colored pencils, crayons or markers

Procedure for Child

1. Trim and fold the page to create the Kk Minibook. (See page 5 for directions.)
2. Write your name in pencil on the line on the minibook cover.
3. Complete each page of the minibook. Trace each picture and then trace the letter Kk on the lines.
4. Color the pictures using the colored pencils, crayons or markers.
5. Read the book as a group. Later, it can be shared at home or with friends.

Day 5: Kangaroo Pouch Cooking Project *(serves 10 children)*

Kitchen Implements

- small serving bowls and serving spoons
- small paper plate for each child
- measuring cups
- sharp knife

Ingredients

- 1/2 pita pocket for each child
- 8 oz. shredded cheese
- 10 oz. shredded lettuce
- 10 oz. shredded carrots
- 10 oz. shredded turkey
- 1 cup thinly sliced cucumbers
- squeeze-bottle of ranch dressing

Preparation

1. Place the cheese, lettuce, carrots, turkey, and cucumbers in separate serving bowls with serving spoons.
2. Fill a pita pocket (kangaroo pouch) with desired ingredients.
3. Squeeze a small amount of the ranch dressing (if desired) on a plate. Dip the kangaroo pouch in the dressing.
4. Practice good table manners when eating the treat!

Letter Kk

Kk Is for Key

Name _____

1. Trace the key.
2. Trace the Kk's.
3. Write more Kk's.
4. Color the picture.

#2340 Alphabet Treasury ©Teacher Created Resources, Inc.

Letter Kk

Kite Sun Catcher Patterns

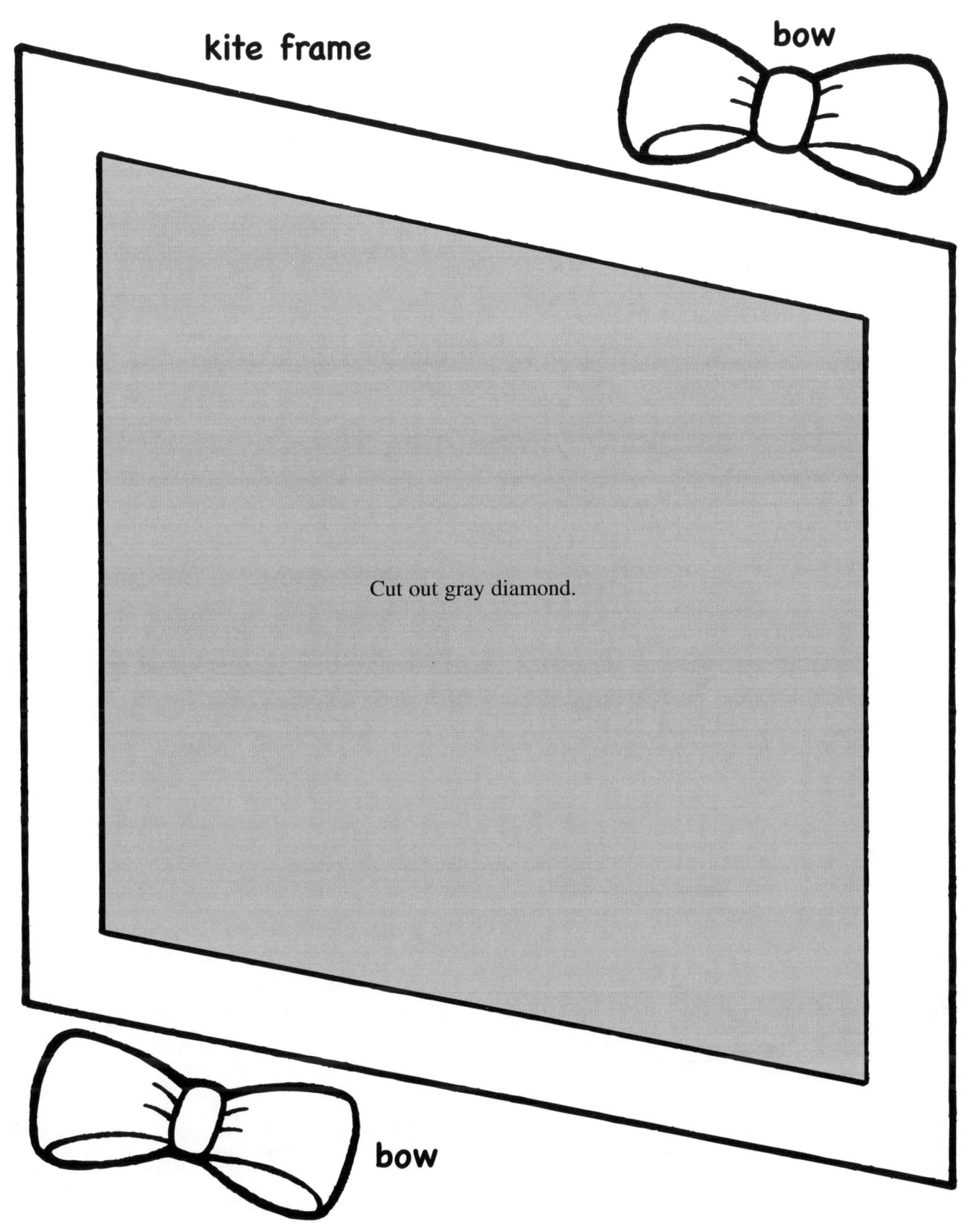

kite frame

bow

Cut out gray diamond.

bow

©Teacher Created Resources, Inc. #2340 Alphabet Treasury

Letter Kk

Kite Template

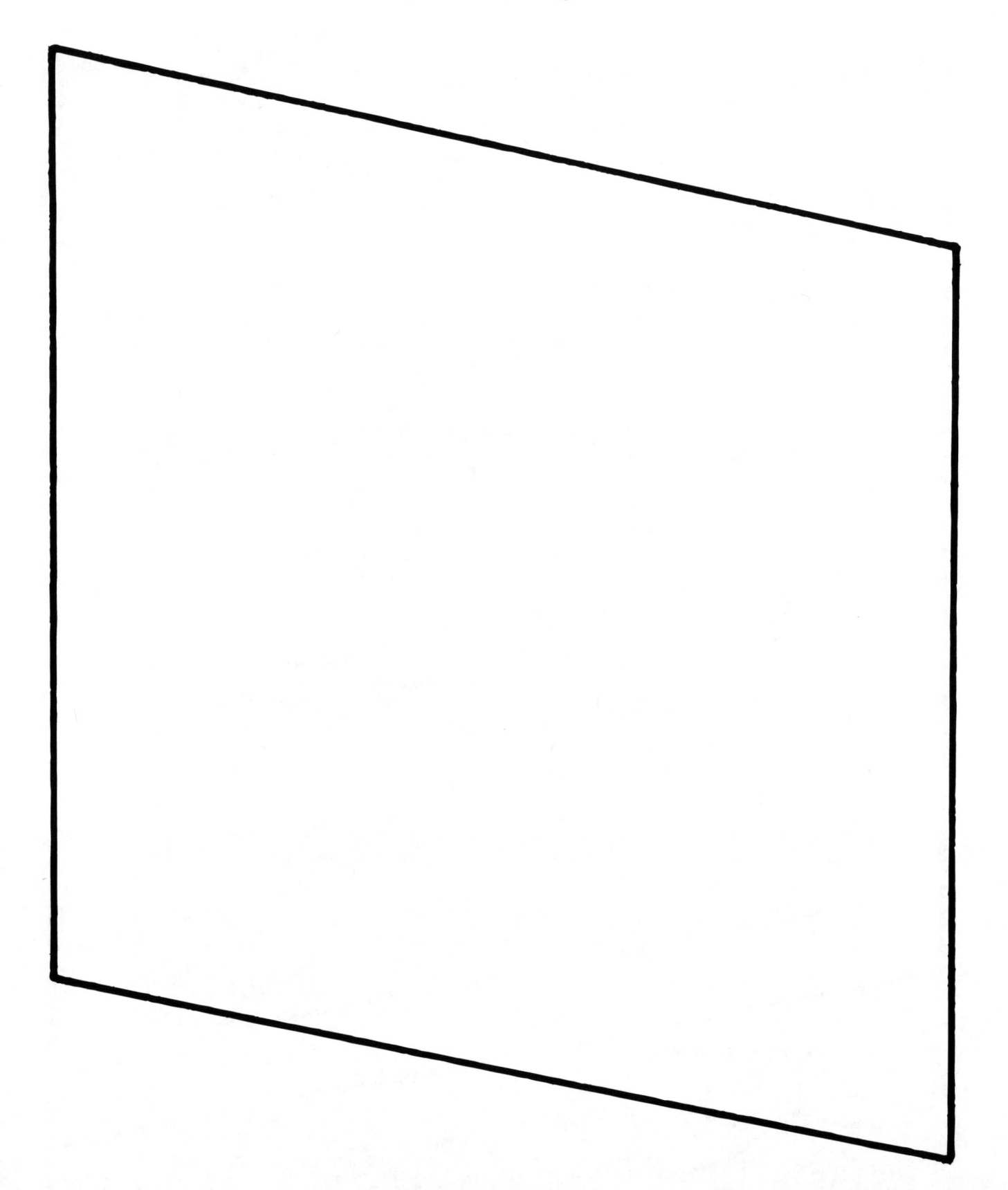

#2340 Alphabet Treasury ©Teacher Created Resources, Inc.

Letter Kk

Kite Pattern

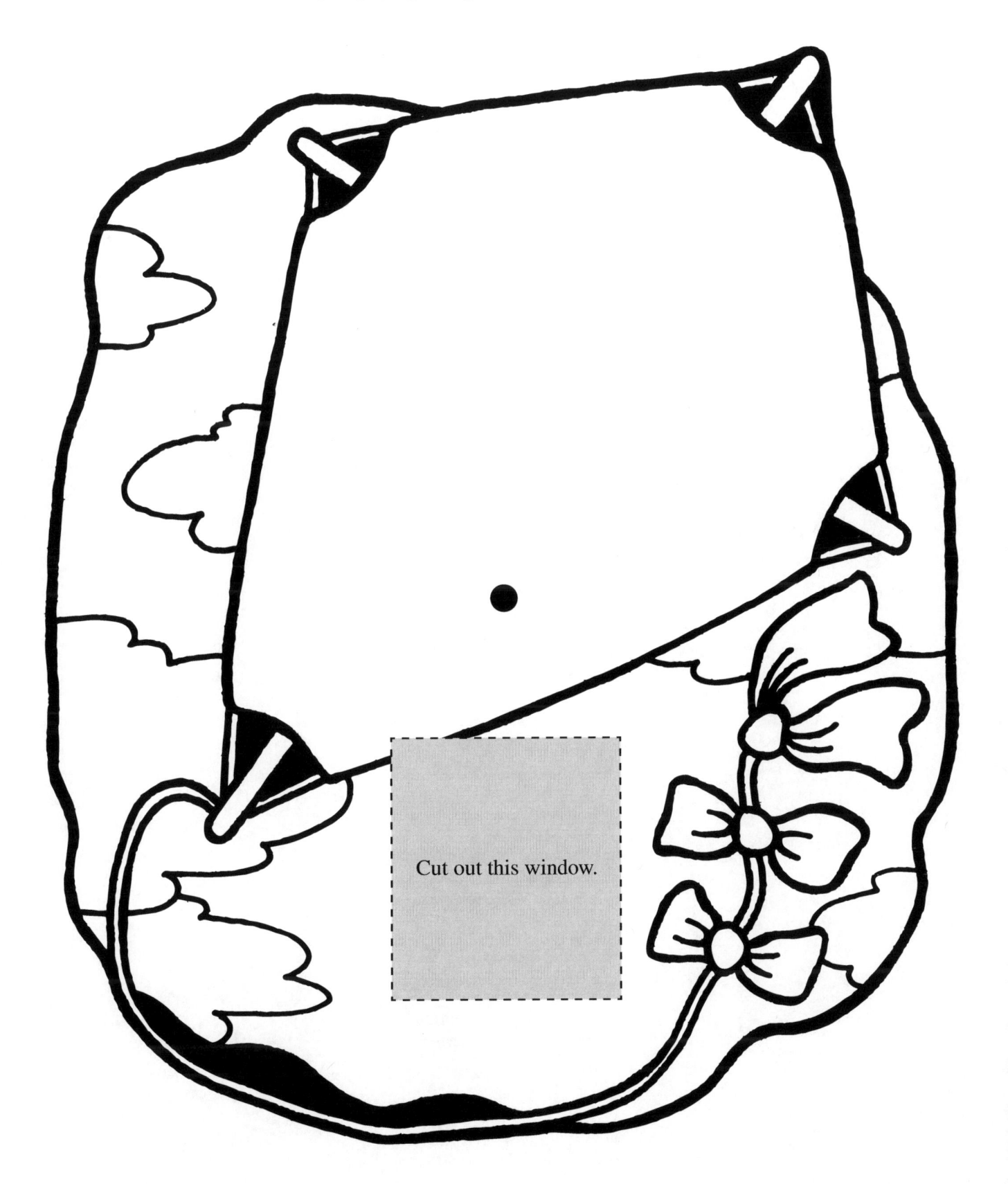

Cut out this window.

©Teacher Created Resources, Inc. 91 #2340 Alphabet Treasury

Letter Kk

Kk Picture Wheel

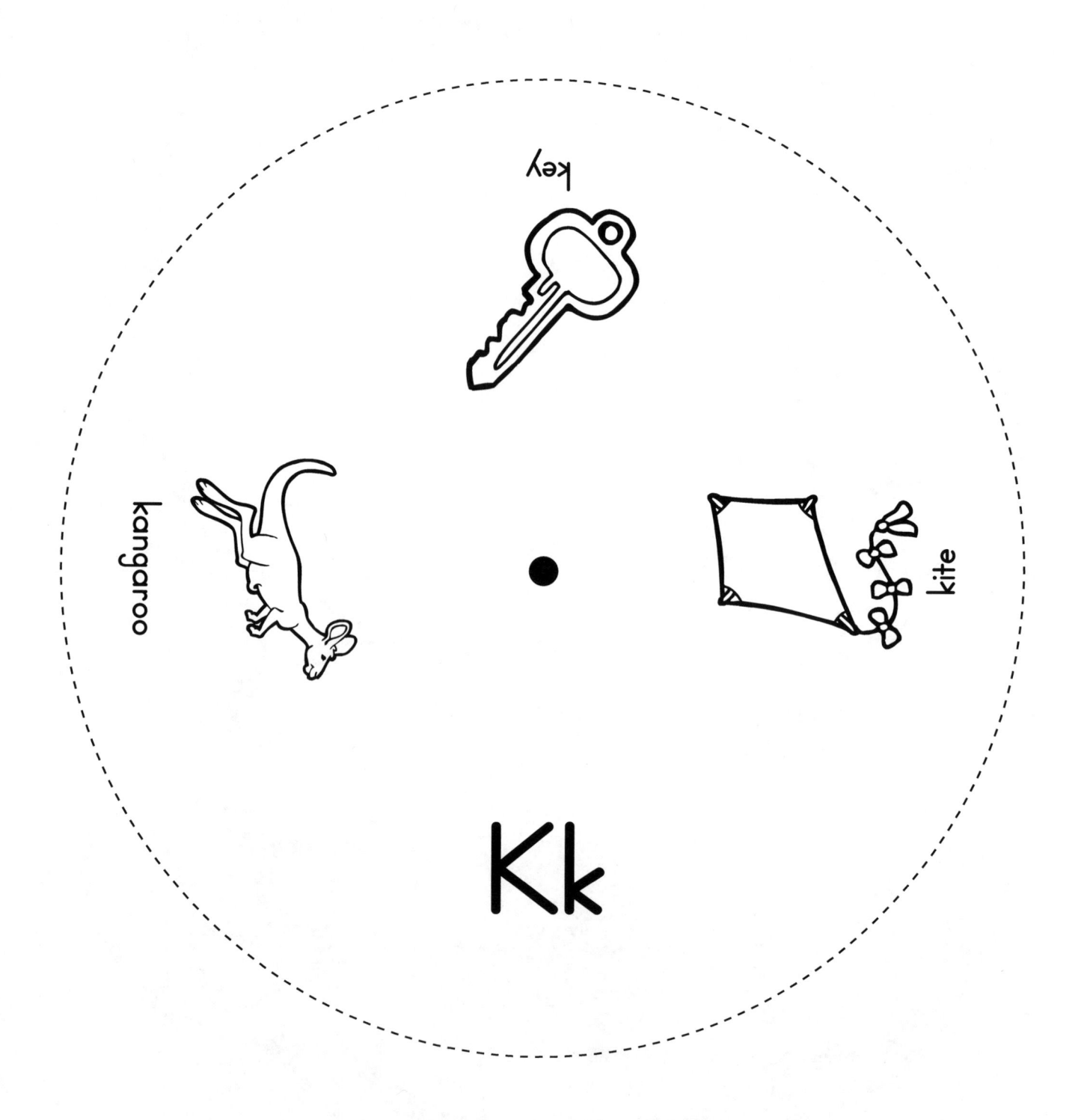

key

kangaroo

kite

Kk

#2340 Alphabet Treasury · 92 · ©Teacher Created Resources, Inc.

Letter Kk

Kk is for a key to unlock a lock.

Kk is for a kangaroo hopping.

Kk is for a kite, flying high.

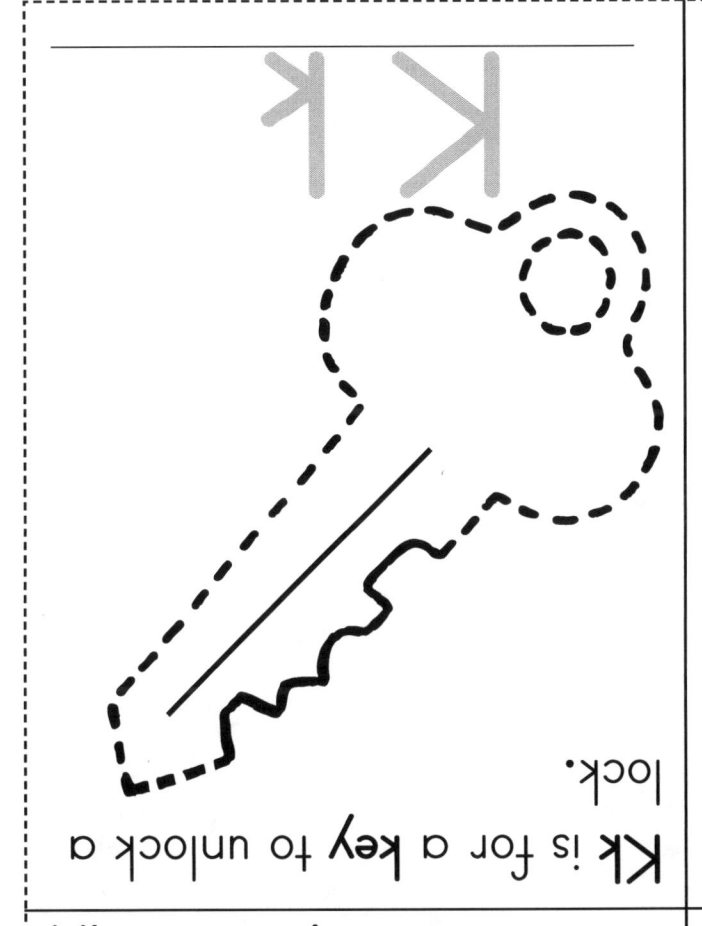

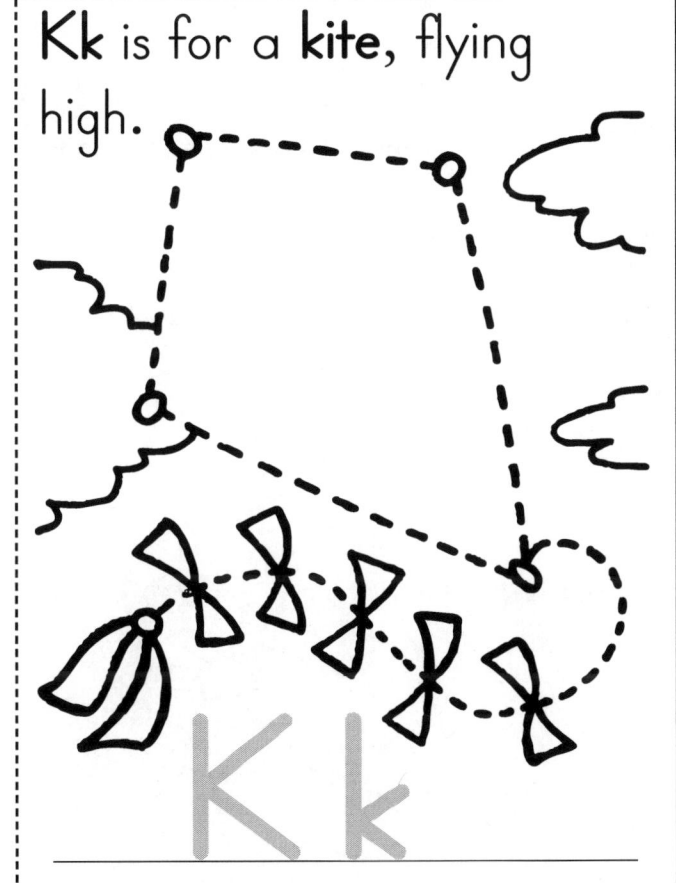

_____'s

Kk

Minibook

©Teacher Created Resources, Inc. 93 #2340 Alphabet Treasury

Letter Ll

Ll

Introduce the letter Ll. Draw and discuss the shape of the letters using chart paper, a white board or a chalkboard. Note any students whose names begin or end with the letter Ll. This will provide opportunities to discuss how and when uppercase and lowercase letters are used.

Introduce the following sentences and accompanying actions. Repeat them often during the week.

Ll is for a **ladder** to climb up.
(Pretend to climb up a ladder.)

Ll is for a **ladybug**, flying around.
(Pretend your little finger is a ladybug and have it fly around.)

Ll is for a **lizard** with a long tongue.
(Pretend to be a lizard and stick your tongue in and out.)

Day 1: Ll Is for Ladder

Materials

- Ll Is for Ladder worksheet (page 97) for each child
- pencils and crayons

Procedure for Child

1. Write your name on the line provided at the top of the page.
2. Trace the ladder and the letters provided.
3. Practice tracing and writing the letter Ll on the lines provided.
4. Finish by coloring the ladder using crayons.

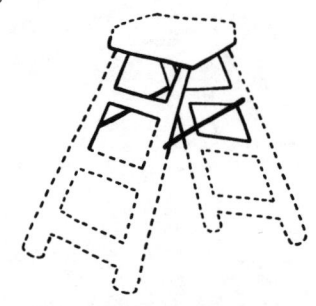

#2340 Alphabet Treasury ©Teacher Created Resources, Inc.

Letter Ll

Ll

Day 2: Ladybug Rock Activity

Materials

- flat, round rock for each child (or Ladybug Craft Pattern on page 98)
- two 2" black pipe cleaners for each child
- 2 wiggle eyes for each child
- red felt (cut to size of rock) for each child
- red and black tempera paint
- paintbrushes
- glue gun (for adult use only)

Procedure for Child

1. Paint a flat, round rock red and set aside to dry. (Or, use the patterns on page 98 to create a paper version of this project. Copy it onto white cardstock for each child. Use markers to color the ladybug in steps 1–3. Then, follow steps 4–5 below to complete the ladybug.)
2. Paint the top 1/3 of the rock black.
3. At this point, explain the term *symmetry*. Tell children that an item that has symmetry is exactly the same on each side. In this case, the dots on the ladybug will be the same on each side of the line down its back.
4. Paint a black stripe down the middle of the red part of the ladybug. Paint symmetrical black dots on each side of the stripe.
5. After the paint dries, an adult can use a glue gun to help attach the eyes, black pipe cleaners (antennae), and red felt (bottom of ladybug).

Day 3: Ladybug Wheel

Materials

- Ladybug Pattern (page 99) for each child
- Ll Picture Wheel (page 100) for each child
- brad for each child
- safety scissors
- markers or crayons
- pencils

Procedure for Child

1. Color the Ladybug Pattern and Ll pictures on the picture wheel page.
2. Cut out the ladybug and the picture wheel. (See page 5 for directions.)
3. Write your name on the back of the wheel.
4. Cut out the picture window on the ladybug. (Note: Adult assistance may be necessary to cut out the picture window.)
5. Place the Ll Picture Wheel behind the Ladybug Pattern. Make certain that one of the pictures is visible in the picture window on the ladybug before going on to the next step.
6. Attach the ladybug to the front of the wheel with a brad. Use the black dot as a guide.

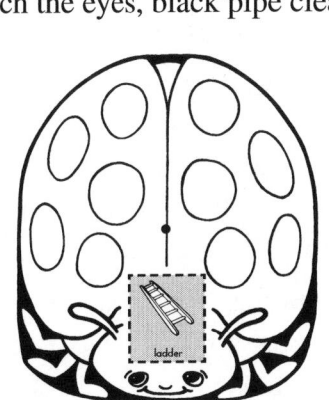

Letter Ll

Ll

Day 4: Ll Minibook

Materials

- Ll Minibook (page 101) for each child
- pencils, colored pencils, crayons or markers

Procedure for Child

1. Trim and fold the page to create the Ll Minibook. (See page 5 for directions.)
2. Write your name in pencil on the line on the minibook cover.
3. Complete each page of the minibook. Trace each picture and then trace the letter Ll on the lines.
4. Color the pictures using the colored pencils, crayons or markers.
5. Read the book as a group. Later, it can be shared at home or with friends.

Day 5: Ladybug Cookies Cooking Project *(serves 10 children)*

Kitchen Implements

- small paper plate for each child
- 2 plastic knives for each child
- small mixing bowl
- cookie sheets
- cooking spray
- mixing spoon

Ingredients

- thirty 3" pieces of thin black licorice
- package of refrigerated sugar cookie dough
- 12 oz. miniature chocolate chips
- 16 oz. chocolate frosting
- 16 oz. white frosting
- red food coloring
- raisins

Preparation

1. Bake the sugar cookies according to package directions. Let cool.
2. In a mixing bowl, add red food coloring to the white frosting. Mix well.
3. Place a cookie on each plate. Frost 3/4 of the cookie with the red frosting using a plastic knife.
4. Using another plastic knife, frost the remaining 1/4 of the cookie with the chocolate frosting.
5. Use the raisins for the ladybug's spots.
6. Use one piece of licorice for the stripe down the ladybug's back. Use the other 2 pieces for the ladybug's antennae.
7. Add two chocolate chips for eyes to complete the ladybug.
8. Practice good table manners.

#2340 Alphabet Treasury

Letter Ll

Ll Is for Ladder

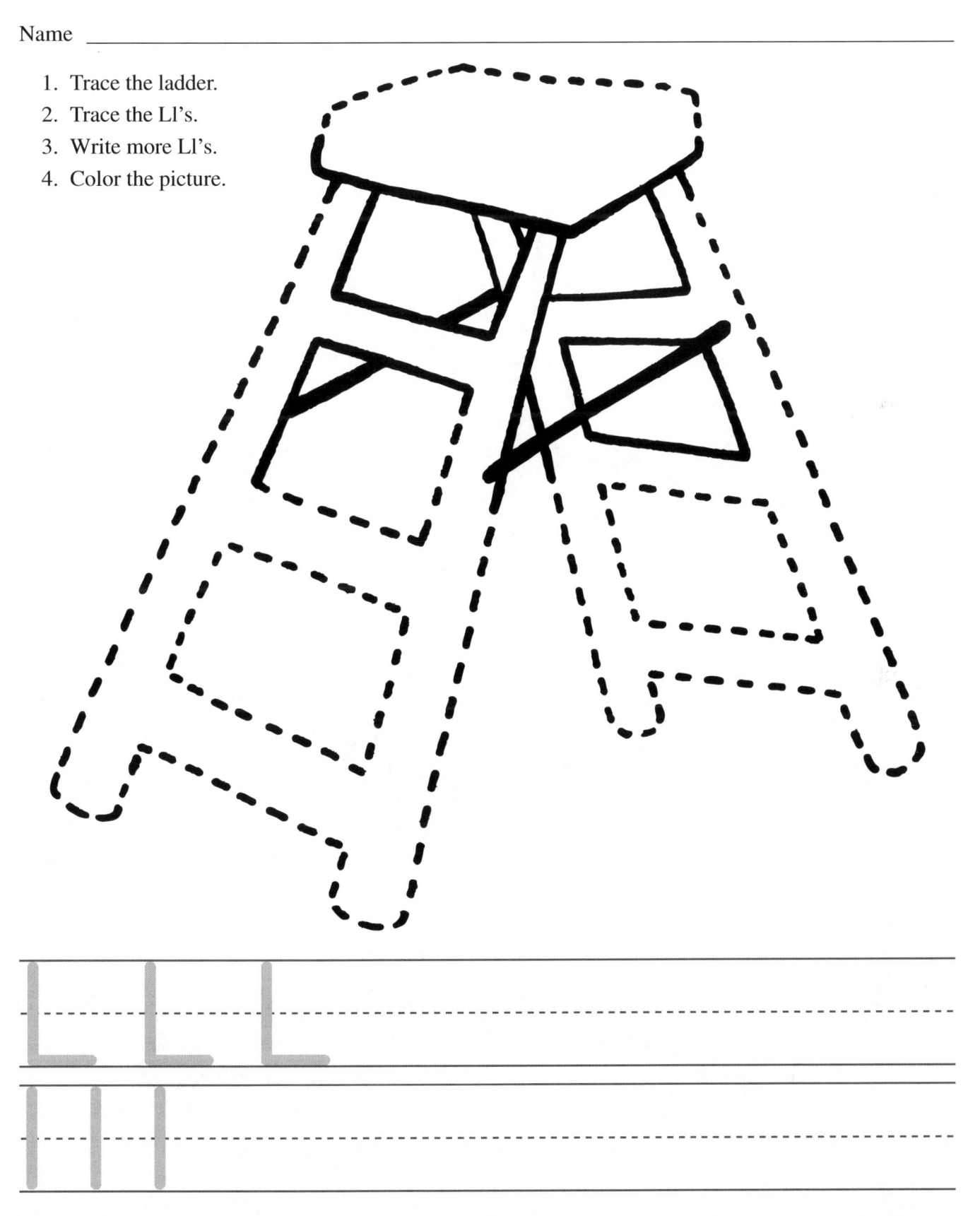

Name _____

1. Trace the ladder.
2. Trace the Ll's.
3. Write more Ll's.
4. Color the picture.

©Teacher Created Resources, Inc.   97   #2340 Alphabet Treasury

Letter Ll

Ladybug Craft Pattern

#2340 Alphabet Treasury ©Teacher Created Resources, Inc.

Letter Ll

Ladybug Pattern

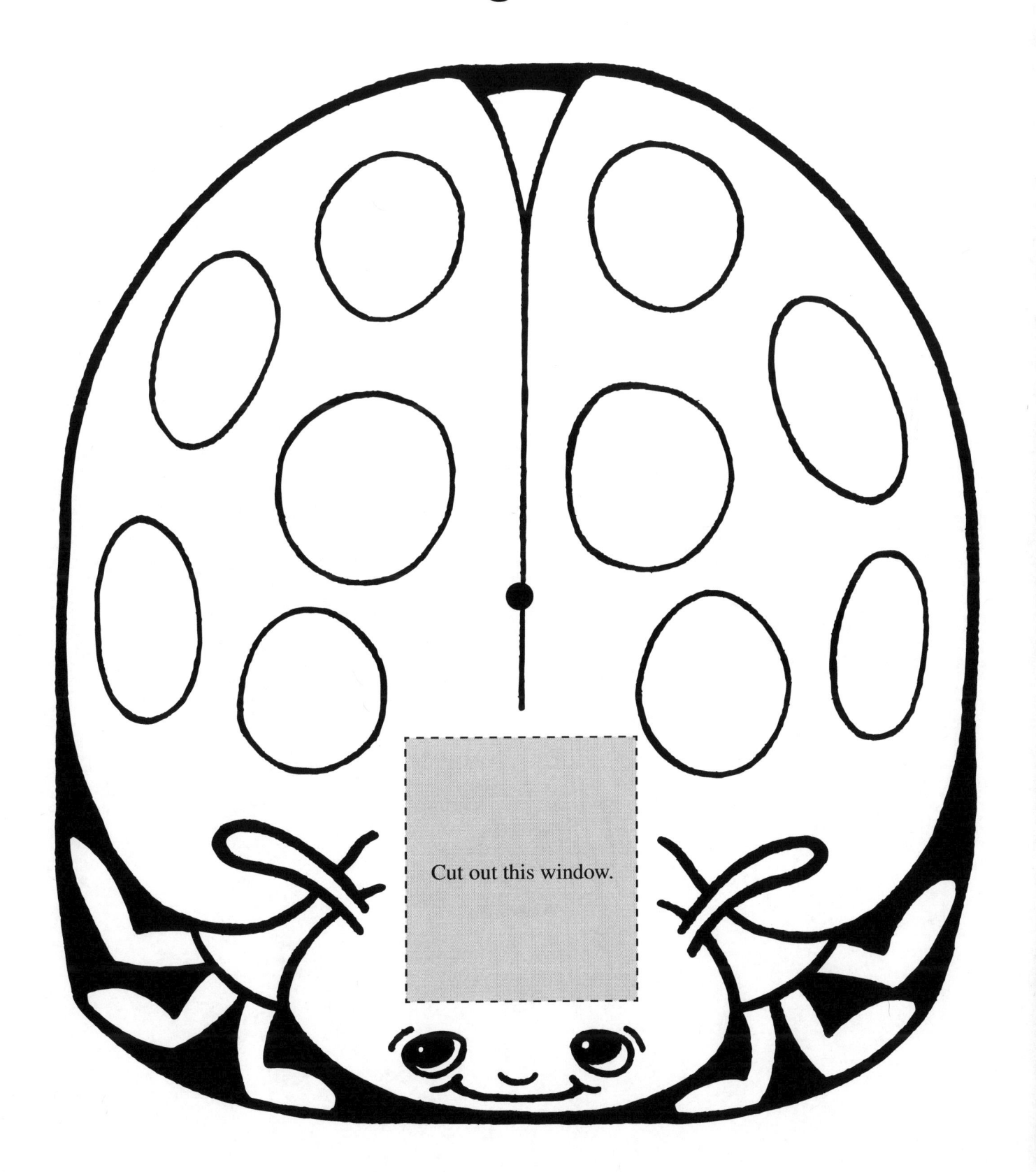

Cut out this window.

©Teacher Created Resources, Inc. 99 #2340 Alphabet Treasury

Letter Ll

Ll Picture Wheel

lizard

ladder

ladybug

Ll

#2340 Alphabet Treasury ©Teacher Created Resources, Inc.

Letter Ll

Ll is for a ladybug, flying around.

Ll is for a ladder to climb.

Ll is for a lizard with a long tongue.

_____'s

Ll

Minibook

©Teacher Created Resources, Inc.   #2340 Alphabet Treasury

Letter Mm

Mm

Introduce the letter Mm. Draw and discuss the shape of the letters using chart paper, a white board or a chalkboard. Note any students whose names begin or end with the letter Mm. This will provide opportunities to discuss how and when uppercase and lowercase letters are used.

Introduce the following sentences and accompanying actions. Repeat them often during the week.

Mm is for a **mouse** saying, "eek, eek."
(Pretend to be a mouse and say, "eek, eek.")

Mm is for a **monkey**, swinging in the trees.
(Pretend to be a monkey swinging in the trees.)

Mm is for a **mitten** to wear when it's cold.
(Pretend to put a mitten on your hand and shiver.)

Day 1: Mm Is for Monkey

Materials

- Mm Is for Monkey worksheet (page 105) for each child
- pencils and crayons

Procedure for Child

1. Write your name on the line provided at the top of the page.
2. Trace the monkey and the letters provided.
3. Practice writing the letter Mm on the lines provided.
4. Finish by coloring the monkey using crayons.

#2340 Alphabet Treasury ©Teacher Created Resources, Inc.

Letter Mm

Mm

Day 2: Mouse and Cheese Activity

Materials

- Mouse and Cheese Patterns (page 106) copied onto cardstock for each child
- 18" length of yarn for each child
- safety scissors
- crayons
- hole punch
- tape (optional)

Procedure for Child

1. Color the mouse and cheese patterns and cut them out.
2. Use the hole punch to punch holes on the cheese and the mouse. Use the black dot as guides.
3. Thread a length of yarn through the hole in the mouse. Secure the yarn. (Note: For additional help, wrap a small piece of tape on the other end of the yarn to form a "needle." The tape will prevent the yarn from fraying.)
4. Lace the free end of the yarn through the the holes in the cheese. Make a loop at the end of the yarn.
5. Pull the loop to have the mouse chase his cheese.

Day 3: Mitten Wheel

Materials

- Mitten Pattern (page 107) for each child
- Mm Picture Wheel (page 108) for each child
- brad for each child
- markers or crayons
- safety scissors
- pencils

Procedure for Child

1. Color the Mitten Pattern and Mm pictures on the picture wheel page.
2. Cut out the mitten and the picture wheel. (See page 5 for directions.)
3. Write your name on the back of the wheel.
4. Cut out the picture window on the mitten. (Note: Adult assistance may be necessary to cut out the picture window.)
5. Place the Mm Picture Wheel behind the Mitten Pattern. Make certain that one of the pictures is visible in the picture window on the mitten before going on to the next step.
6. Attach the mitten to the front of the wheel with a brad.

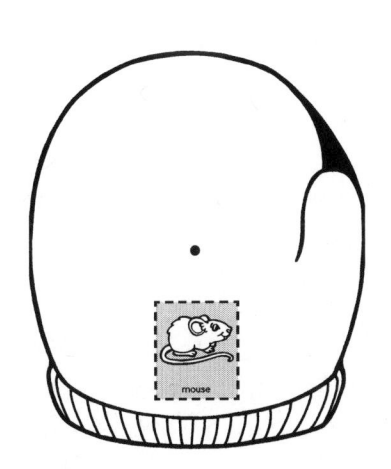

©Teacher Created Resources, Inc. #2340 Alphabet Treasury

Letter Mm

Mm

Day 4: Mm Minibook

Materials

- Mm Minibook (page 109) for each child
- pencils, colored pencils, crayons or markers
- safety scissors

Procedure for Child

1. Trim and fold the page to create the Mm Minibook. (See page 5 for directions.)
2. Write your name in pencil on the line on the minibook cover.
3. Complete each page of the minibook. Trace each picture and then trace the letter Mm on the lines.
4. Color the pictures using the colored pencils, crayons or markers.
5. Read the book as a group. Later, it can be shared at home or with friends.

Day 5: Monkey Faces Cooking Project *(serves 10 children)*

Kitchen Implements

- small paper plate for each child
- plastic knife for each child
- small serving spoon
- shaker for cinnamon and cocoa powder

Ingredients

- 10 rice cakes
- 5 bananas
- 1 cup cream cheese
- 2 tablespoons cocoa powder
- cinnamon
- raisins

Preparation

1. Slice a banana into 1/4" slices using a plastic knife. (See illustration.) Set aside the banana slices.
2. Place a rice cake on a plate. Put a spoonful of cream cheese on the rice cake and spread it out evenly using a plastic knife.
3. Mix the cinnamon and cocoa powder, and pour it into a shaker.
4. Lightly sprinkle the cinnamon and cocoa powder mixture on the cream cheese to make the monkey's face brown.
5. Place a banana slice (nose) on the monkey face. Place 2 banana slices (ears) on the plate near the rice cake.
6. Use raisins to make the monkey's eyes and mouth.
7. Practice good table manners. Don't eat like a monkey!

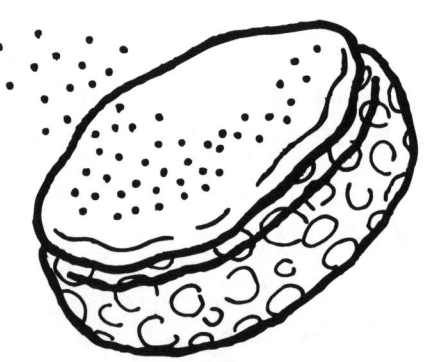

#2340 Alphabet Treasury ©Teacher Created Resources, Inc.

Letter Mm

Mm Is for Monkey

Name _____

1. Trace the monkey.
2. Trace the Mm's.
3. Write more Mm's.
4. Color the picture.

M M M

m m m

©Teacher Created Resources, Inc.   #2340 Alphabet Treasury

Letter Mm

Mouse and Cheese Patterns

#2340 Alphabet Treasury 106 ©Teacher Created Resources, Inc.

Letter Mm

Mitten Pattern

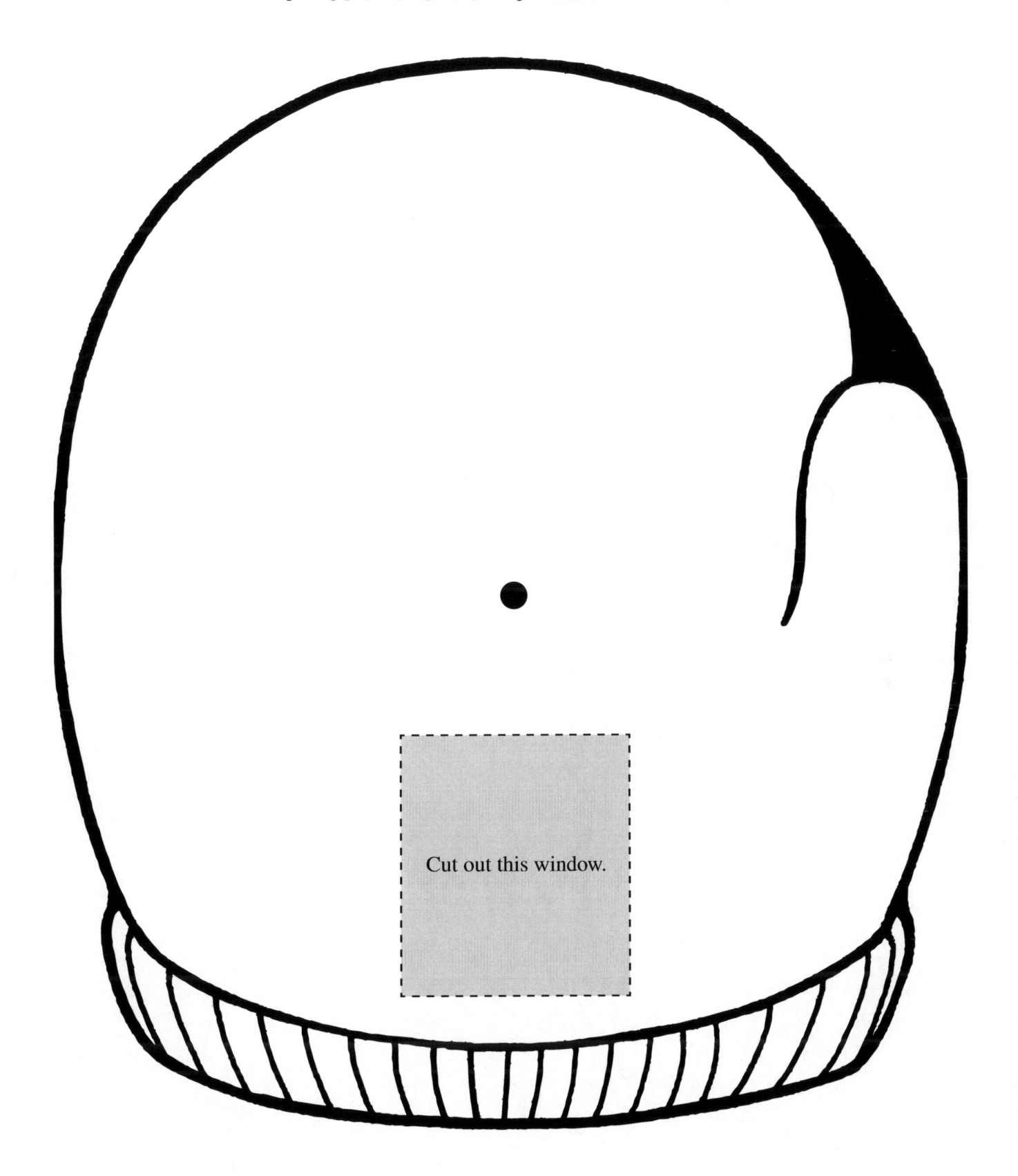

Cut out this window.

©Teacher Created Resources, Inc. 107 #2340 Alphabet Treasury

Letter Mm

Mm Picture Wheel

mouse

monkey

mitten

Mm

#2340 Alphabet Treasury 108 ©Teacher Created Resources, Inc.

Letter Mm

Mm is for a monkey, swinging in the trees.

Mm is for a mouse saying, "eek, eek."

"eek"

Mm is for a mitten to wear when it's cold.

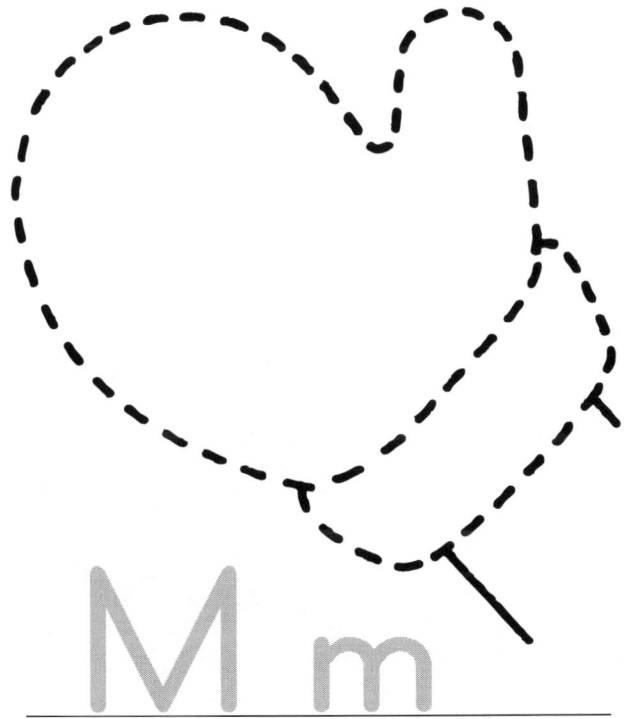

_____'s

Mm

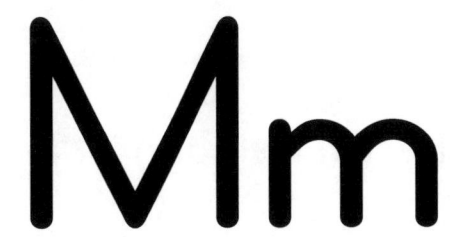

Minibook

©Teacher Created Resources, Inc. #2340 Alphabet Treasury

Letter Nn

Nn

Introduce the letter Nn. Draw and discuss the shape of the letters using chart paper, a white board or a chalkboard. Note any students whose names begin or end with the letter Nn. This will provide opportunities to discuss how and when uppercase and lowercase letters are used.

Introduce the following sentences and accompanying actions. Repeat them often during the week.

Nn is for a **nose** to smell.
(Pretend to smell a flower.)

Nn is for a **nest** of chirping birds.
(Chirp like a bird.)

Nn is for **noodles** to eat—yum!
(Pretend to eat spaghetti.)

Day 1: Nn Is for Nest

Materials

- Nn Is for Nest worksheet (page 113) for each child
- pencils and crayons

Procedure for Child

1. Write your name on the line provided at the top of the page.
2. Trace the nest and the letters provided.
3. Practice writing the letter Nn on the lines provided.
4. Finish by coloring the nest using crayons.

#2340 Alphabet Treasury   ©Teacher Created Resources, Inc.

Letter Nn

Nn

Day 2: Nest with Eggs Activity

Materials

- air-dry clay
- chow mein noodles
- large beads (in a variety of colors)

Procedure for Child

1. Form the clay into a bowl shape to resemble a nest.
2. Arrange the chow mein noodles to resemble sticks sticking out of the nest.
3. Gently press the noodles into the clay. Let the clay dry overnight.
4. Add colored beads (eggs) to complete the nest.

Day 3: Noodles Wheel

Materials

- Noodles Pattern (page 114) for each child
- Nn Picture Wheel (page 115) for each child
- brad for each child
- markers or crayons
- safety scissors
- pencils

Procedure for Child

1. Color the Noodles Pattern and Nn pictures on the picture wheel page.
2. Cut out the noodles and the picture wheel. (See page five for directions.)
3. Write your name on the back of the wheel.
4. Cut out the picture window on the noodles. (Note: Adult assistance may be necessary to cut out the picture window.)
5. Place the Nn Picture Wheel behind the Noodles Pattern. Make certain that one of the pictures is visible in the picture window on the noodles before going on to the next step.
6. Attach the noodles to the front of the wheel with a brad.

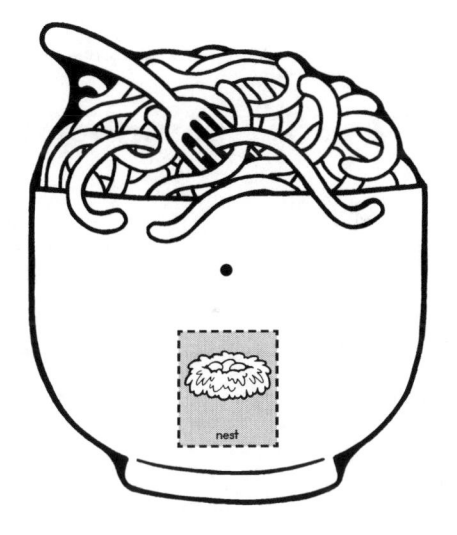

©Teacher Created Resources, Inc. #2340 Alphabet Treasury

Letter Nn

Nn

Day 4: Nn Minibook

Materials

- Nn Minibook (page 116) for each child
- pencils
- colored pencils, crayons or markers
- safety scissors

Procedure for Child

1. Trim and fold the page to create the Nn Minibook. (See page 5 for directions.)
2. Write your name in pencil on the line on the minibook cover.
3. Complete each page of the minibook. Trace each picture and then trace the letter Nn on the lines.
4. Color the pictures using the colored pencils, crayons or markers.
5. Read the book as a group. Later, it can be shared at home or with friends.

Day 5: Noodles Cooking Project *(serves 10 children)*

Kitchen Implements

- bowl for each child
- plastic fork for each child
- large serving spoon
- measuring cup

Ingredients

- 5 cups cooked spaghetti
- spaghetti sauce
- shredded cheese (optional)

Preparation

1. Warm up previously cooked spaghetti noodles and spaghetti sauce in a microwave.
3. Add 1/2 cup of spaghetti noodles to each bowl using a large spoon. Pour sauce over the noodles.
4. Mix the noodles and the sauce together using a plastic fork. Add shredded cheese if desired.
5. Practice good table manners.

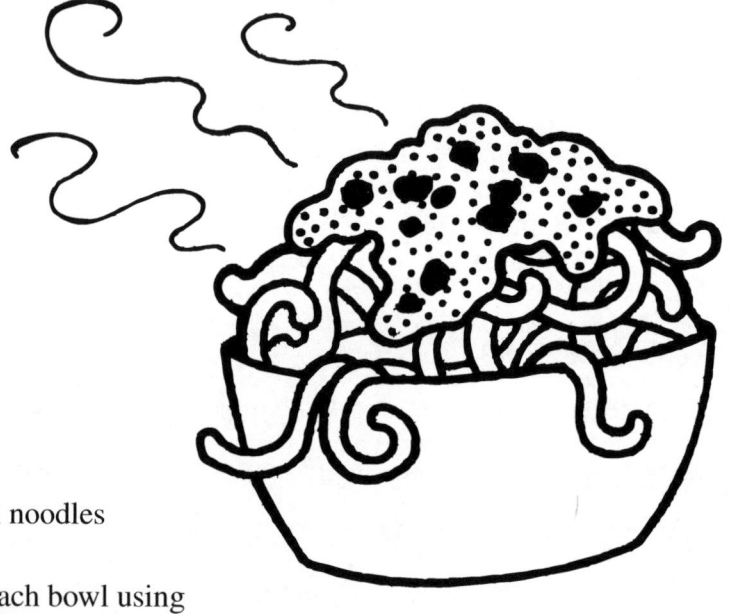

#2340 Alphabet Treasury   112   ©Teacher Created Resources, Inc.

Letter Nn

Nn Is for Nest

Name _____

1. Trace the nest.
2. Trace the Nn's.
3. Write more Nn's.
4. Color the picture.

©Teacher Created Resources, Inc. 113 #2340 Alphabet Treasury

Letter Nn

Noodles Pattern

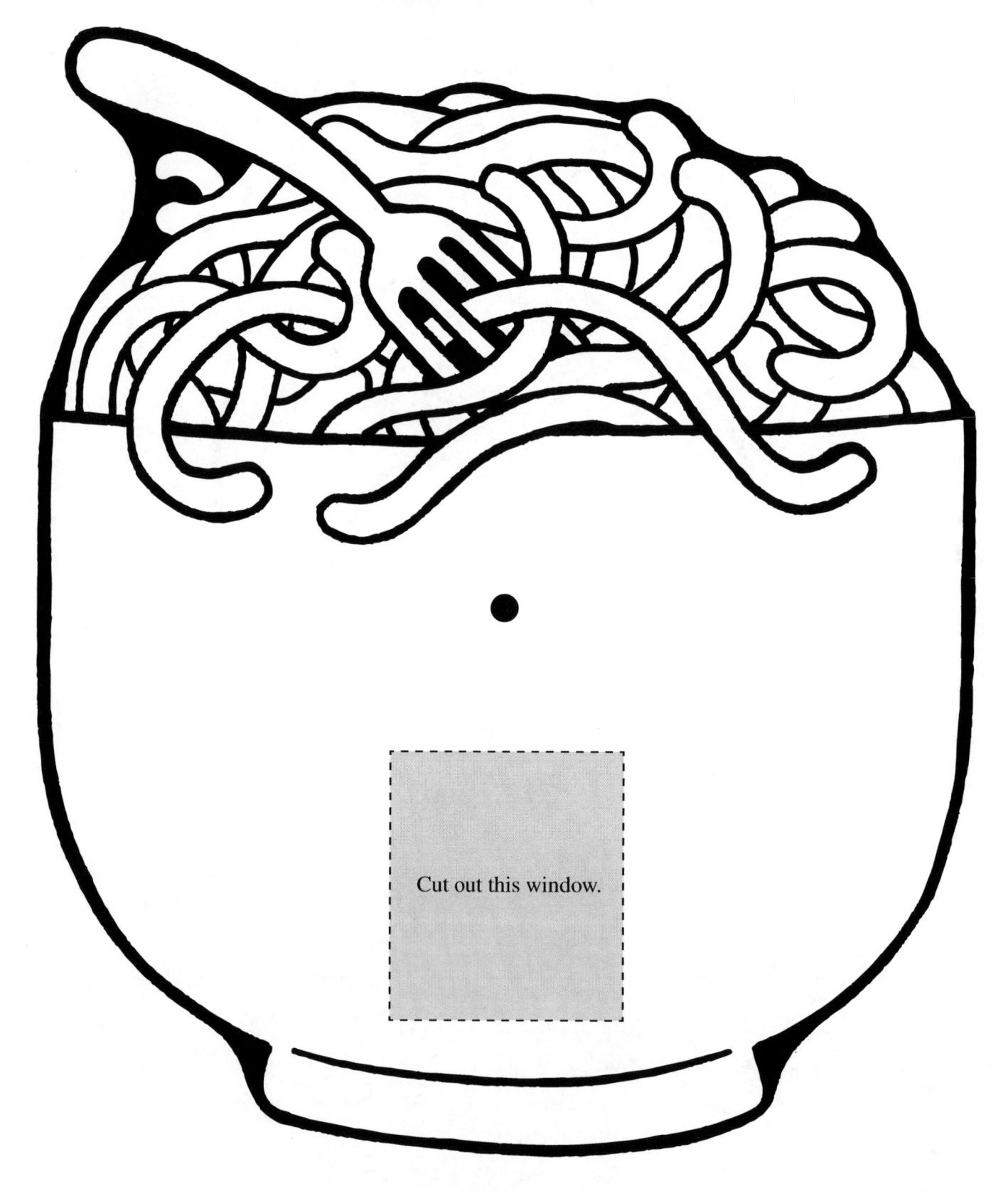

Cut out this window.

#2340 Alphabet Treasury　　　　　114　　　　　©Teacher Created Resources, Inc.

Letter Nn

Nn Picture Wheel

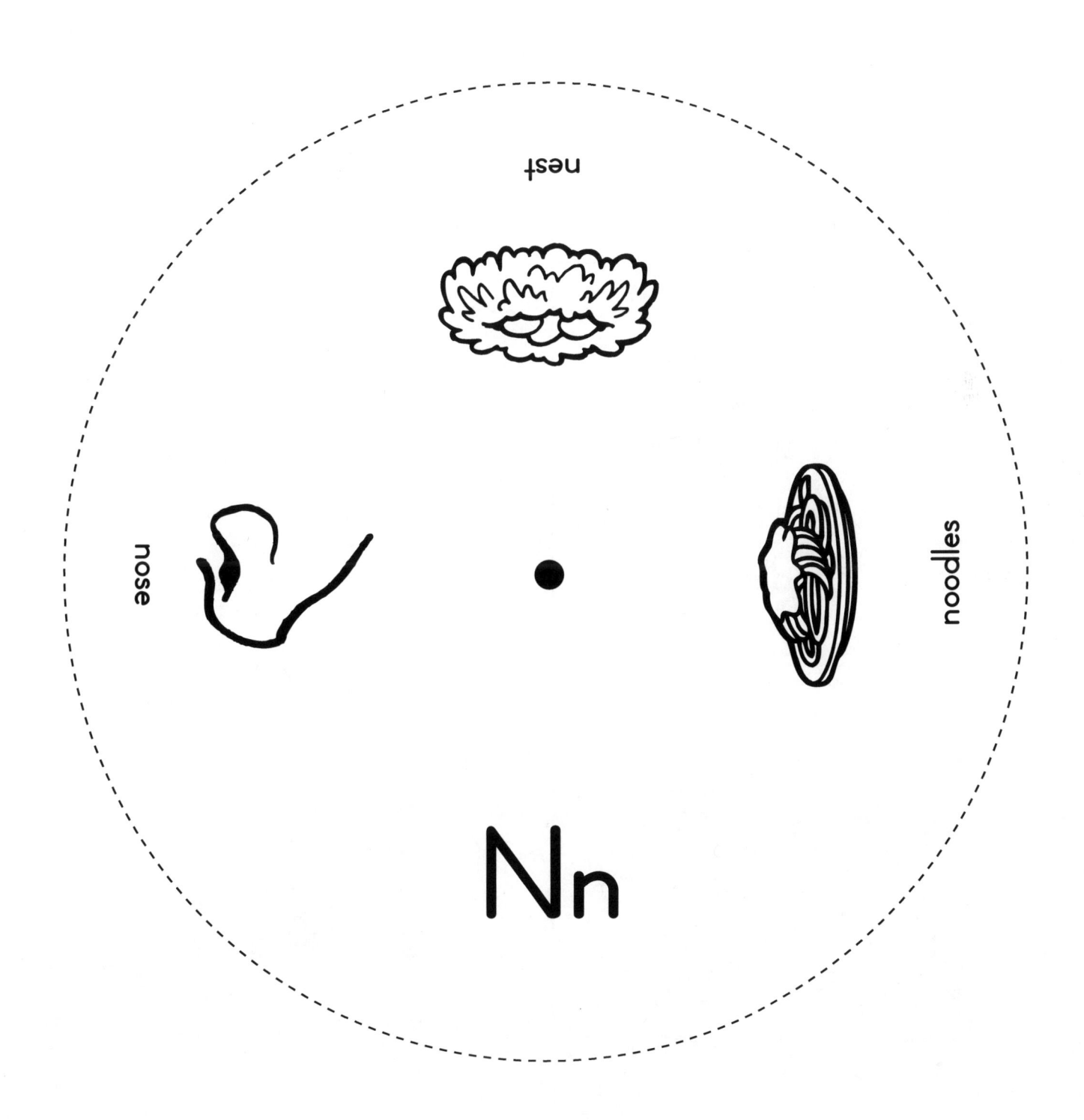

nest

nose

noodles

Nn

©Teacher Created Resources, Inc. 115 #2340 Alphabet Treasury

Letter Nn

Nn is for a nest of chirping birds.

Nn is for a nose to smell.

Nn is for **noodles** to eat— yum!

_____'s

Nn

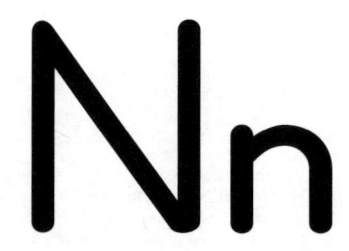

Minibook

#2340 Alphabet Treasury 116 ©Teacher Created Resources, Inc.

Letter Oo

Oo

Introduce the letter Oo. Draw and discuss the shape of the letters using chart paper, a white board or a chalkboard. Note any students whose names begin or end with the letter Oo. This will provide opportunities to discuss how and when uppercase and lowercase letters are used.

Introduce the following sentences and accompanying actions. Repeat them often during the week.

Oo is for an **orange** to eat.
(Pretend to peel and eat an orange.)

Oo is for an **owl** saying, "whoo, whoo."
(Pretend to be an owl. Flap your wings, glide, and say, "whoo, whoo.")

Oo is for an **octopus** with lots of arms.
(Pretend to be an octopus and wave your arms.)

Day 1: Oo Is for Octopus

Materials
- Oo Is for Octopus worksheet (page 120) for each child
- pencils and crayons

Procedure for Child
1. Write your name on the line provided at the top of the page.
2. Trace the octopus and the letters provided.
3. Practice writing the letter Oo on the lines provided.
4. Finish by coloring the octopus using crayons.

©Teacher Created Resources, Inc. 117 #2340 Alphabet Treasury

Letter Oo

Oo

Day 2: Owl Wind Sock Activity

Materials

- Owl Feature Patterns (page 121) for each child
- four 24" lengths of yellow crepe-paper streamers for each child
- four 24" lengths of brown crepe-paper streamers for each child
- one 6" x 18" strip of brown poster board for each child
- four 18" lengths of yarn for each child
- hole punch
- black, brown, and yellow markers
- stapler and glue
- safety scissors

Procedure for Child

1. Color feather tufts using a black marker. Color the eyes and beak yellow. Color the wings and talons brown. Cut out the eyes, feather tufts, beak, wings, and talons.
2. Roll the brown poster-board strip into a cylinder and staple it to create the owl's body.
3. Glue the eyes, feather tufts, and beak to the front of the cylinder. Glue the wings on the sides and the talons below the owl's face.
4. Attach the yellow and brown crepe-paper streamers equal distances around the bottom of the owl's face with a stapler.
5. Use a hole punch to punch 4 holes (equally spaced) around the top of the owl.
6. Tie four 18" lengths of yarn through the holes and tie them together at the top as shown.
7. Hang the owl wind sock where the wind will make it move!

Day 3: Owl Wheel

Materials

- Owl Pattern (page 122) for each child
- Oo Picture Wheel (page 123) for each child
- brad for each child
- safety scissors
- markers or crayons
- pencils

Procedure for Child

1. Color the Owl Pattern and Oo pictures on the picture wheel page.
2. Cut out the owl and the picture wheel. (See page 5 for directions.)
3. Write your name on the back of the wheel.
4. Cut out the picture window on the owl. (Note: Adult assistance may be necessary to cut out the picture window.)
5. Place the Oo Picture Wheel behind the Owl Pattern. Make certain that one of the pictures is visible in the picture window on the owl before going on to the next step.
6. Attach the owl to the front of the wheel with a brad.

Letter Oo

Oo

Day 4: Oo Minibook

Materials

- Oo Minibook (page 124) for each child
- pencils
- colored pencils, crayons or markers

Procedure for Child

1. Trim and fold the page to create the Oo Minibook. (See page 5 for directions.)
2. Write your name in pencil on the line on the minibook cover.
3. Complete each page of the minibook. Trace each picture and then trace the letter Oo on the lines.
4. Color the pictures using the colored pencils, crayons or markers.
5. Read the book as a group. Later, it can be shared at home or with friends.

Day 5: Octopus Cooking Project *(serves 10 children)*

Kitchen Implement

- small paper plate for each child

Ingredients

- 80 baby carrots
- 10 cherry tomatoes
- squeeze bottle of ranch dressing

Preparation

1. Squeeze ranch dressing in the center of a plate.
2. Place the cherry tomato in the dressing (octopus head).
3. Arrange 8 baby carrots around the tomato (octopus tentacles) to complete the octopus.

Presentation

1. Dip the baby carrots and tomato in the dressing.
2. Practice good table manners.

©Teacher Created Resources, Inc. #2340 Alphabet Treasury

Letter Oo

Oo Is for Octopus

Name _____

1. Trace the octopus.
2. Trace the Oo's.
3. Write more Oo's.
4. Color the picture.

#2340 Alphabet Treasury ©Teacher Created Resources, Inc.

Letter Oo

Owl Feature Patterns

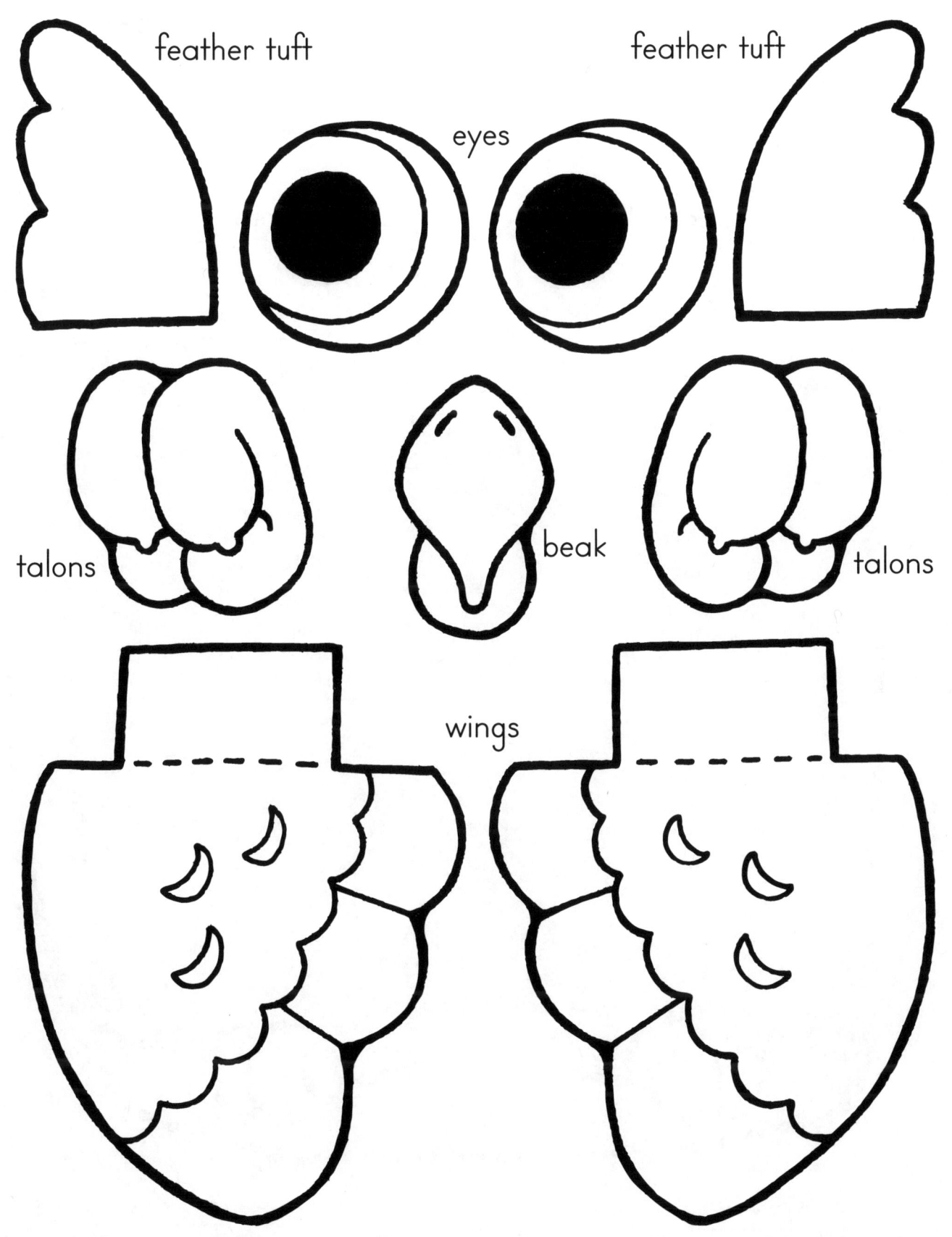

feather tuft

feather tuft

eyes

talons

beak

talons

wings

©Teacher Created Resources, Inc. 121 #2340 Alphabet Treasury

Letter Oo

Owl Pattern

Cut out this window.

Letter Oo

Oo Picture Wheel

octopus

orange

owl

Oo

©Teacher Created Resources, Inc. 123 #2340 Alphabet Treasury

Letter Oo

Oo is for an owl saying, "whoo, whoo."

Oo is for an orange to eat.

Oo is for an octopus with lots of arms.

_____'s

Oo

Minibook

#2340 Alphabet Treasury 124 ©Teacher Created Resources, Inc.

Letter Pp

Pp

Introduce the letter Pp. Draw and discuss the shape of the letters using chart paper, a white board or a chalkboard. Note any students whose names begin or end with the letter Pp. This will provide opportunities to discuss how and when uppercase and lowercase letters are used.

Introduce the following sentences and accompanying actions. Repeat them often during the week.

Pp is for a **pencil** for writing.
(Pretend to write using a pencil.)

Pp is for a **penguin**, walking on the ice.
(Pretend to be a penguin and waddle-walk.)

Pp is for a **pretzel** to munch.
(Pretend to eat a pretzel and say, "crunch.")

Day 1: Pp Is for Pencil

Materials

- Pp Is for Pencil worksheet (page 128) for each child
- pencils and crayons

Procedure for Child

1. Write your name on the line provided at the top of the page.
2. Trace the pencil and the letters provided.
3. Practice writing the letter Pp on the lines provided.
4. Finish by coloring the pencil using crayons.

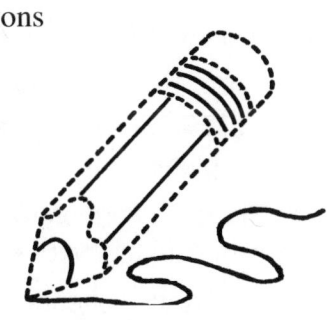

©Teacher Created Resources, Inc. 125 #2340 Alphabet Treasury

Letter Pp

Pp

Day 2: Pencil Topper Activity

Materials

- 6" pipe cleaner for each child (variety of colors)
- 1 1/2" pom-pom for each child (variety of colors)
- 1/4" pom-pom for each child (variety of colors)
- 2 wiggle eyes for each child
- pencil for each child
- safety scissors
- glue gun (adult use only)
- red felt
- glue

Procedure for Child

1. Select a pipe cleaner and a 1 1/2" pom-pom.
2. Attach the wiggle eyes to the large pom-pom using glue. Then attach the 1/4" pom-pom (nose) to the larger pom-pom using glue.
3. Cut a mouth shape from the red felt. Glue the mouth to the large pom-pom.
4. Wrap the pipe cleaner around the end of a pencil to form arms for the creature. Add a dot of glue.
5. Have an adult uses a glue gun to attach the pom-pom head onto the eraser of the pencil.

Day 3: Penguin Wheel

Materials

- Penguin Pattern (page 129) for each child
- Pp Picture Wheel (page 130) for each child
- brad for each child
- markers or crayons
- safety scissors
- pencils

Procedure for Child

1. Color the Penguin Pattern and Pp pictures on the picture wheel page.
2. Cut out the penguin and the picture wheel. (See page 5 for directions.)
3. Write your name on the back of the wheel.
4. Cut out the picture window on the penguin. (Note: Adult assistance may be necessary to cut out the picture window.)
5. Place the Pp Picture Wheel behind the Penguin Pattern. Make certain that one of the pictures is visible in the picture window on the penguin before going on to the next step.
6. Attach the penguin to the front of the wheel with a brad.

#2340 Alphabet Treasury

Letter Pp

Pp

Day 4: Pp Minibook

Materials

- Pp Minibook (page 131) for each child
- pencils, colored pencils, crayons or markers
- safety scissors

Procedure for Child

1. Trim and fold the page to create the Pp Minibook. (See page 5 for directions.)
2. Write your name in pencil on the line on the minibook cover.
3. Complete each page of the minibook. Trace each picture and then trace the letter Pp on the lines.
4. Color the pictures using the colored pencils, crayons or markers.
5. Read the book as a group. Later, it can be shared at home or with friends.

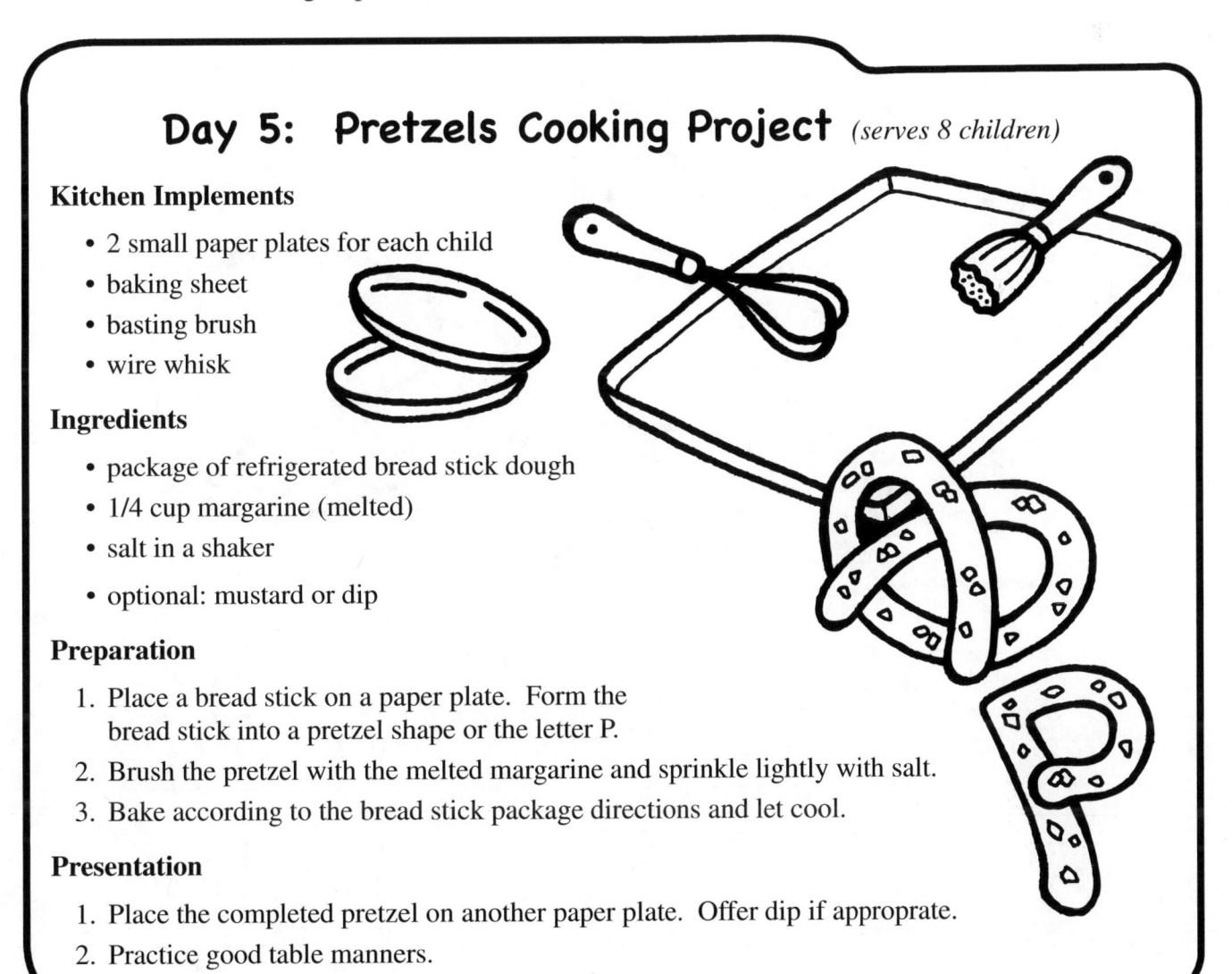

Day 5: Pretzels Cooking Project *(serves 8 children)*

Kitchen Implements

- 2 small paper plates for each child
- baking sheet
- basting brush
- wire whisk

Ingredients

- package of refrigerated bread stick dough
- 1/4 cup margarine (melted)
- salt in a shaker
- optional: mustard or dip

Preparation

1. Place a bread stick on a paper plate. Form the bread stick into a pretzel shape or the letter P.
2. Brush the pretzel with the melted margarine and sprinkle lightly with salt.
3. Bake according to the bread stick package directions and let cool.

Presentation

1. Place the completed pretzel on another paper plate. Offer dip if appropriate.
2. Practice good table manners.

©Teacher Created Resources, Inc. #2340 Alphabet Treasury

Letter Pp

Pp Is for Pencil

Name _____

1. Trace the pencil.
2. Trace the Pp's.
3. Write more Pp's.
4. Color the picture.

#2340 Alphabet Treasury ©Teacher Created Resources, Inc.

Letter Pp

Penguin Pattern

Cut out this window.

©Teacher Created Resources, Inc. 129 #2340 Alphabet Treasury

Letter Pp

Pp Picture Wheel

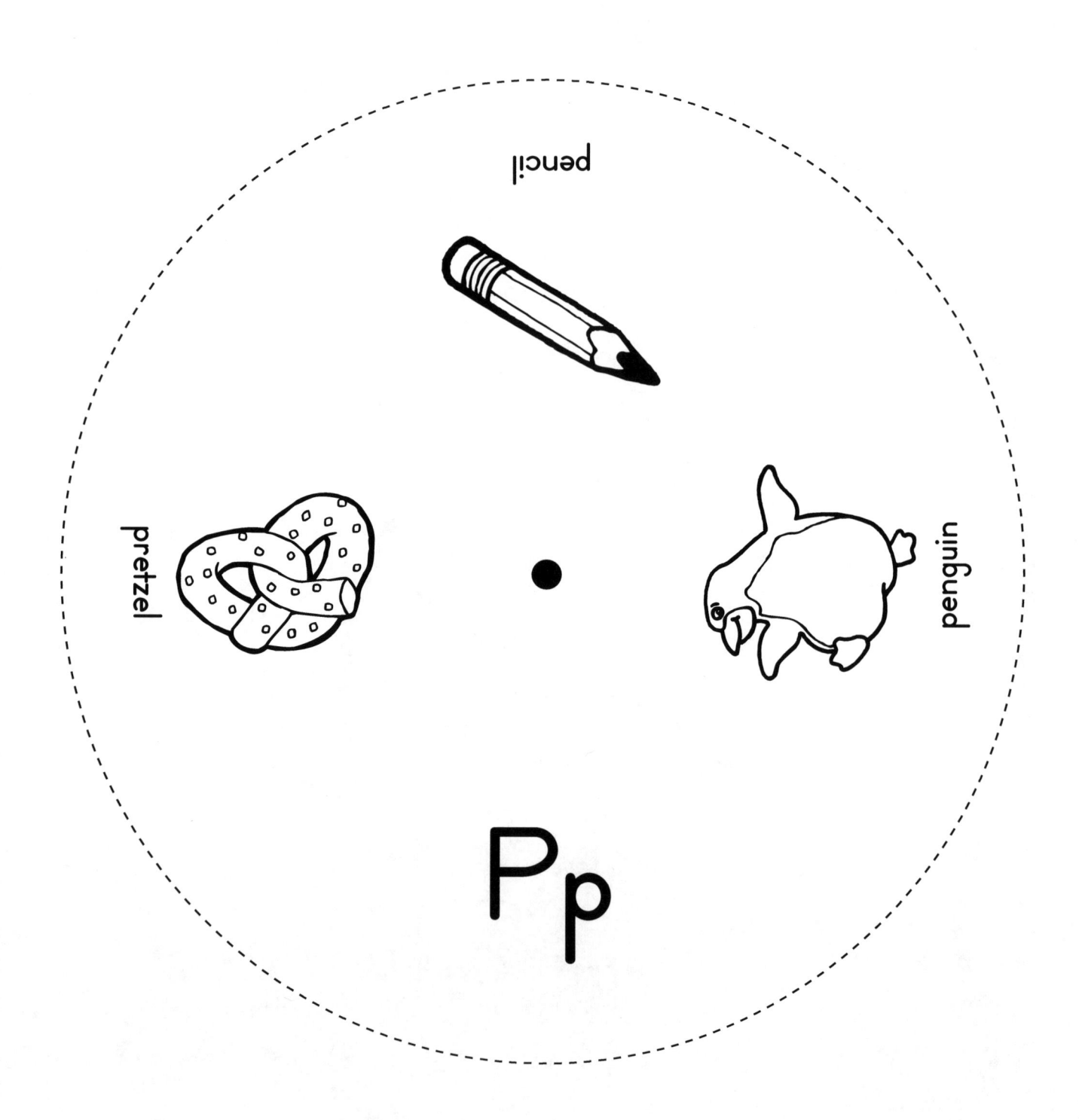

pencil

pretzel

penguin

Pp

#2340 Alphabet Treasury   130   ©Teacher Created Resources, Inc.

Letter Pp

Pp is for a penguin, walking on the ice.

Pp is for a pencil for writing.

Pp is for a pretzel to munch, crunch!

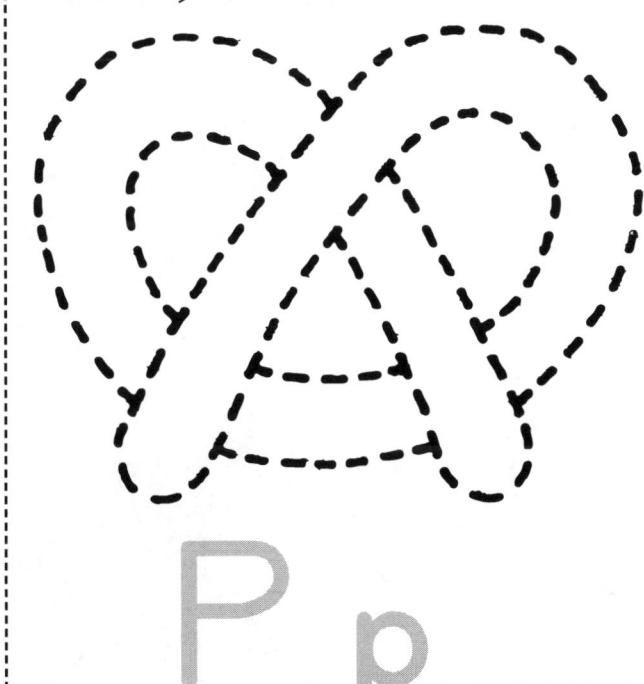

_____'s

Pp

Minibook

©Teacher Created Resources, Inc.   131   #2340 Alphabet Treasury

Letter Qq

Qq

Introduce the letter Qq. Draw and discuss the shape of the letters using chart paper, a white board or a chalkboard. Note any students whose names begin or end with the letter Qq. This will provide opportunities to discuss how and when uppercase and lowercase letters are used.

Introduce the following sentences and accompanying actions. Repeat them often during the week.

Qq is for a **queen** with her crown.
(Pretend to have a crown on your head.)

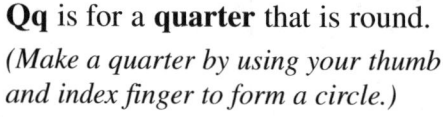

Qq is for a **quarter** that is round.
(Make a quarter by using your thumb and index finger to form a circle.)

Qq is for a **quilt** to cover up with.
(Pretend to cover up with a quilt and go to sleep.)

Day 1: Qq Is for Quilt

Materials
- Qq Is for Quilt worksheet (page 135) for each child
- pencils and crayons

Procedure for Child
1. Write your name on the line provided at the top of the page.
2. Trace the quilt and the letters provided.
3. Practice writing the letter Qq on the lines provided.
4. Finish by coloring the quilt using crayons.

#2340 Alphabet Treasury ©Teacher Created Resources, Inc.

Letter Qq

Qq

Day 2: Queen Puppet Activity

Materials

- Queen Puppet Patterns (page 136) for each child
- small paper bag for each child
- crayons or markers
- safety scissors
- glitter
- glue

Procedure for Child

1. Color the Queen Puppet Patterns and cut them out.
2. Draw a face for the queen on the bag using crayons or markers.
3. Attach glitter to the queen's crown using glue. Glue the crown above the queen's face.
4. Glue the queen's royal robe to the bag.
5. Attach glitter to the queen's scepter using glue. Glue the scepter by one of the queen's hands to complete the queen puppet.

Day 3: Quarter Wheel

Materials

- Quarter Pattern (page 137) for each child
- Qq Picture Wheel (page 138) for each child
- brad for each child
- markers or crayons
- safety scissors
- pencils

Procedure for Child

1. Color the Quarter Pattern and Qq pictures on the picture wheel page.
2. Cut out the quarter and the picture wheel. (See page 5 for directions.)
3. Write your name on the back of the wheel.
4. Cut out the picture window on the quarter. (Note: Adult assistance may be necessary to cut out the picture window.)
5. Place the Qq Picture Wheel behind the Quarter Pattern. Make certain that one of the pictures is visible in the picture window on the quilt before going on to the next step.
6. Attach the quarter to the front of the wheel with a brad. Use the black dot as a guide.

©Teacher Created Resources, Inc. #2340 Alphabet Treasury

Letter Qq

Qq

Day 4: Qq Minibook

Materials

- Qq Minibook (page 139) for each child
- pencils
- colored pencils, crayons or markers

Procedure for Child

1. Trim and fold the page to create the Qq Minibook. (See directions on page 5.)
2. Write your name in pencil on the line on the minibook cover.
3. Complete each page of the minibook. Trace each picture and then trace the letter Qq on the lines.
4. Color the pictures using the colored pencils, crayons or markers.
5. Read the book as a group. Later, it can be shared at home or with friends.

Day 5: Quilts Cooking Project *(serves 10 children)*

Kitchen Implements

- a small plate for each child
- plastic knives and spoons
- small serving bowls

Ingredients

- 10 slices of bread
- 1 cup whipped cream cheese
- diced yellow bell peppers
- sliced cucumbers
- diced tomatoes
- sliced carrots

Preparation

1. Place a slice of bread (quilt) on a plate. Put a spoonful of whipped cream cheese on the bread and spread it evenly using a plastic knife.
2. Choose vegetables and place them on the bread (quilt) in a pattern. (See example.)
3. Use a plastic knife to make dashed lines around the border of the quilt to resemble stitching.
4. Practice good table manners when it's time to eat.

Letter Qq

Qq Is for Quilt

Name _____

1. Trace the quilt.
2. Trace the Qq's.
3. Write more Qq's.
4. Color the picture.

©Teacher Created Resources, Inc. 135 #2340 Alphabet Treasury

Letter Qq

Queen Puppet Patterns

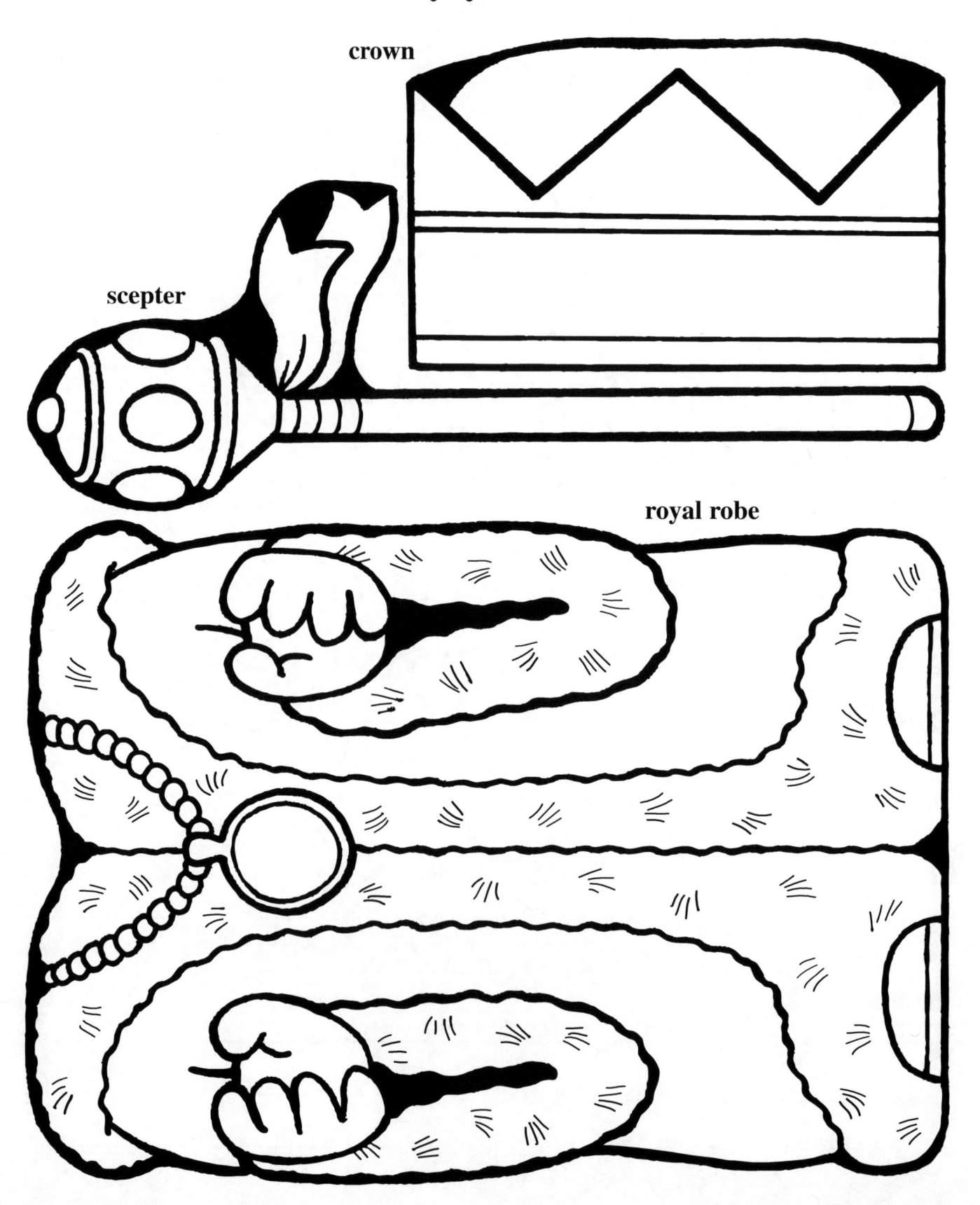

crown

scepter

royal robe

#2340 Alphabet Treasury 136 ©Teacher Created Resources, Inc.

Letter Qq

Quarter Pattern

LIBERTY

IN GOD WE
TRUST

Cut out this window.

P

©Teacher Created Resources, Inc. 137 #2340 Alphabet Treasury

Letter Qq

Qq Picture Wheel

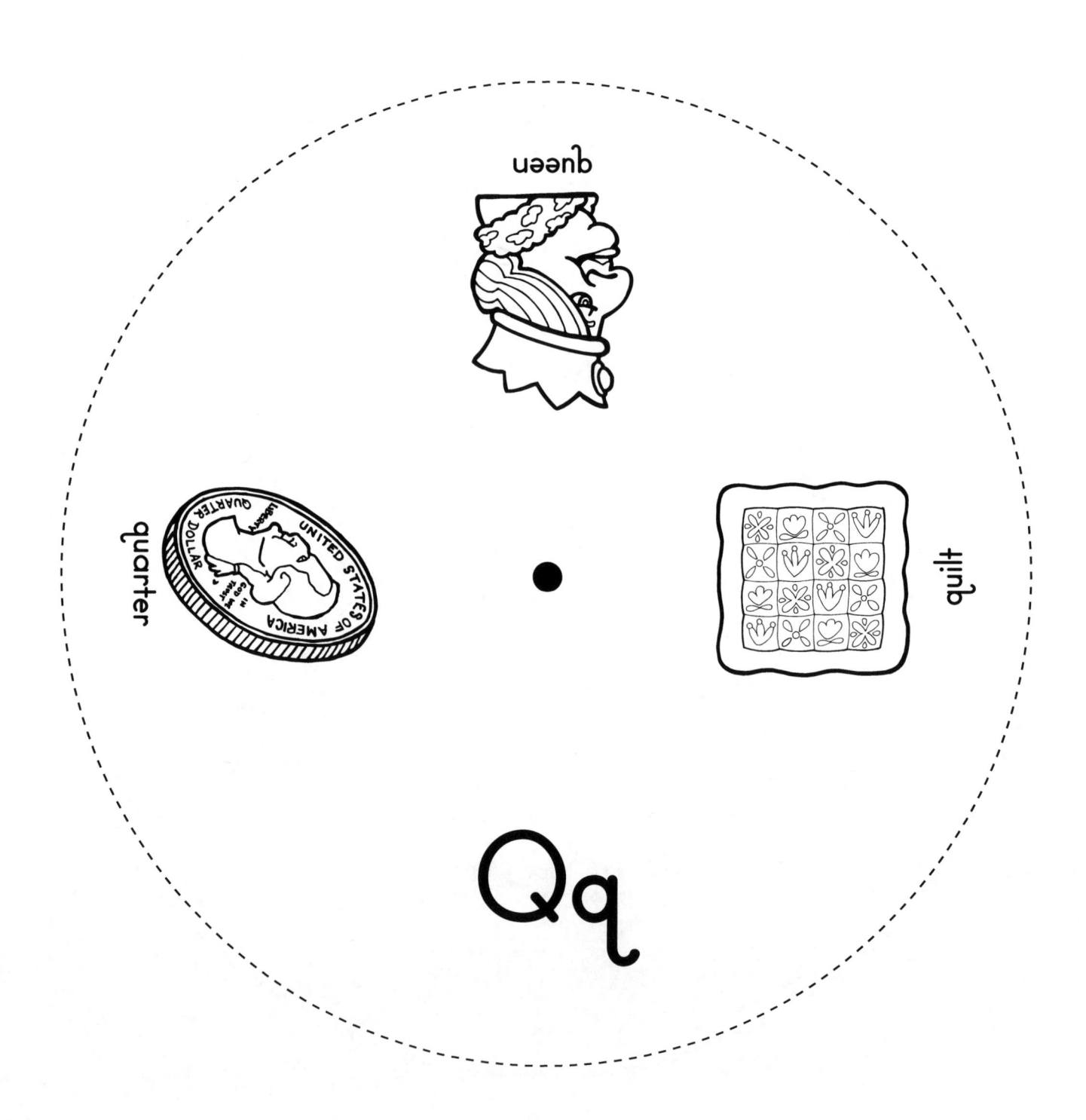

queen

quarter

quilt

Qq

#2340 Alphabet Treasury 138 ©Teacher Created Resources, Inc.

Letter Qq

Qq is for a quarter that is round.

Qq is for a queen with her crown.

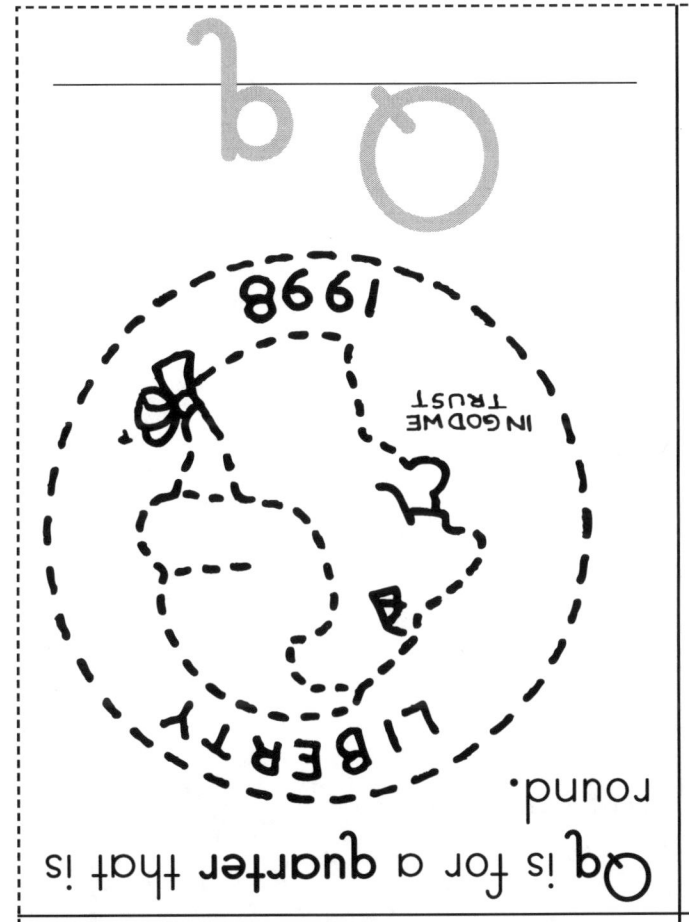

Qq is for a quilt to cover up with.

_____'s

Qq

Minibook

©Teacher Created Resources, Inc. 139 #2340 Alphabet Treasury

Letter Rr

Rr

Introduce the letter Rr. Draw and discuss the shape of the letters using chart paper, a white board or a chalkboard. Note any students whose names begin or end with the letter Rr. This will provide opportunities to discuss how and when uppercase and lowercase letters are used.

Introduce the following sentences and accompanying actions. Repeat them often during the week.

Rr is for a **rose** to smell with your nose.
(Pretend to smell a rose.)

Rr is for a **ring** to wear on your finger.
(Pretend to show a ring on your finger.)

Rr is for a **rabbit**, hopping away.
(Pretend to be a rabbit and hop.)

Day 1: Rr Is for Ring

Materials

- Rr Is for Ring worksheet (page 143) for each child
- pencils and crayons

Procedure for Child

1. Write your name on the line provided at the top of the page.
2. Trace the ring and the letters provided.
3. Practice writing the letter Rr on the lines provided.
4. Finish by coloring the ring using crayons.

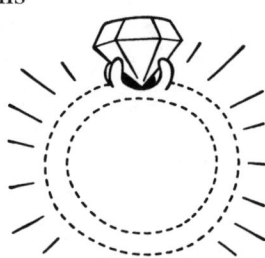

Letter Rr

Rr

Day 2: Rabbit Hide-and-Seek Activity

Materials

- Rabbit Hide-and-Seek Patterns (page 144) for each child
- toilet-paper tube for every 2 children
- 5" craft stick for each child
- green tempera paint
- paintbrushes
- safety scissors
- crayons or markers
- glue

Procedure for Child

1. Cut each toilet-paper tube in half widthwise. Each should be about 2 1/4" tall.
2. Paint the resulting toilet-paper tube green and let it dry.
3. Color the rabbit pattern and cut it out.
4. Attach the rabbit to a craft stick using glue.
5. Hold the toilet-paper tube (grass) in one hand and the rabbit in the other. Move the rabbit puppet up and down in the grass, letting the rabbit play hide and seek!

Day 3: Rabbit Wheel

Materials

- Rabbit Pattern (page 145) for each child
- Rr Picture Wheel (page 146) for each child
- brad for each child
- markers or crayons
- safety scissors
- pencils

Procedure for Child

1. Color the Rabbit Pattern and Rr pictures on the picture wheel page.
2. Cut out the rabbit and the picture wheel. (See page 5 for directions.)
3. Write your name on the back of the wheel.
4. Cut out the picture window on the rabbit. (Note: Adult assistance may be necessary to cut out the picture window.)
5. Place the Rr Picture Wheel behind the Rabbit Pattern. Make certain that one of the pictures is visible in the picture window on the rabbit before going on to the next step.
6. Attach the rabbit to the front of the wheel with a brad.

©Teacher Created Resources, Inc.   141   #2340 Alphabet Treasury

Letter Rr

Rr

Day 4: Rr Minibook

Materials

- Rr Minibook (page 147) for each child
- pencils
- colored pencils, crayons or markers

Procedure for Child

1. Trim and fold the page to create the Rr Minibook. (See page 5 for directions.)
2. Write your name in pencil on the line on the minibook cover.
3. Complete each page of the minibook. Trace each picture and then trace the letter Rr on the lines.
4. Color the pictures using the colored pencils, crayons or markers.
5. Read the book as a group. Later, it can be shared at home or with friends.

Day 5: Rabbit Salad Cooking Project *(serves 10 children)*

Kitchen Implements

- plastic spoon and bowl for each child
- measuring cups
- large mixing bowl and large mixing spoon
- knife (for adult use)

Ingredients

- 1 cup sliced carrots
- 1 cup sliced celery
- 1/2 cup raisins
- 5 cups vanilla yogurt or frozen yogurt (optional)

Preparation

1. Place the carrots, celery, and raisins in a large mixing bowl. Pour the yogurt into the mixing bowl if desired.
2. Take turns stirring the mixture using a large mixing spoon.

Presentation

1. Place a serving of the mixture (rabbit salad) in each child's bowl.
2. Practice good table manners.

Letter Rr

Rr Is for Ring

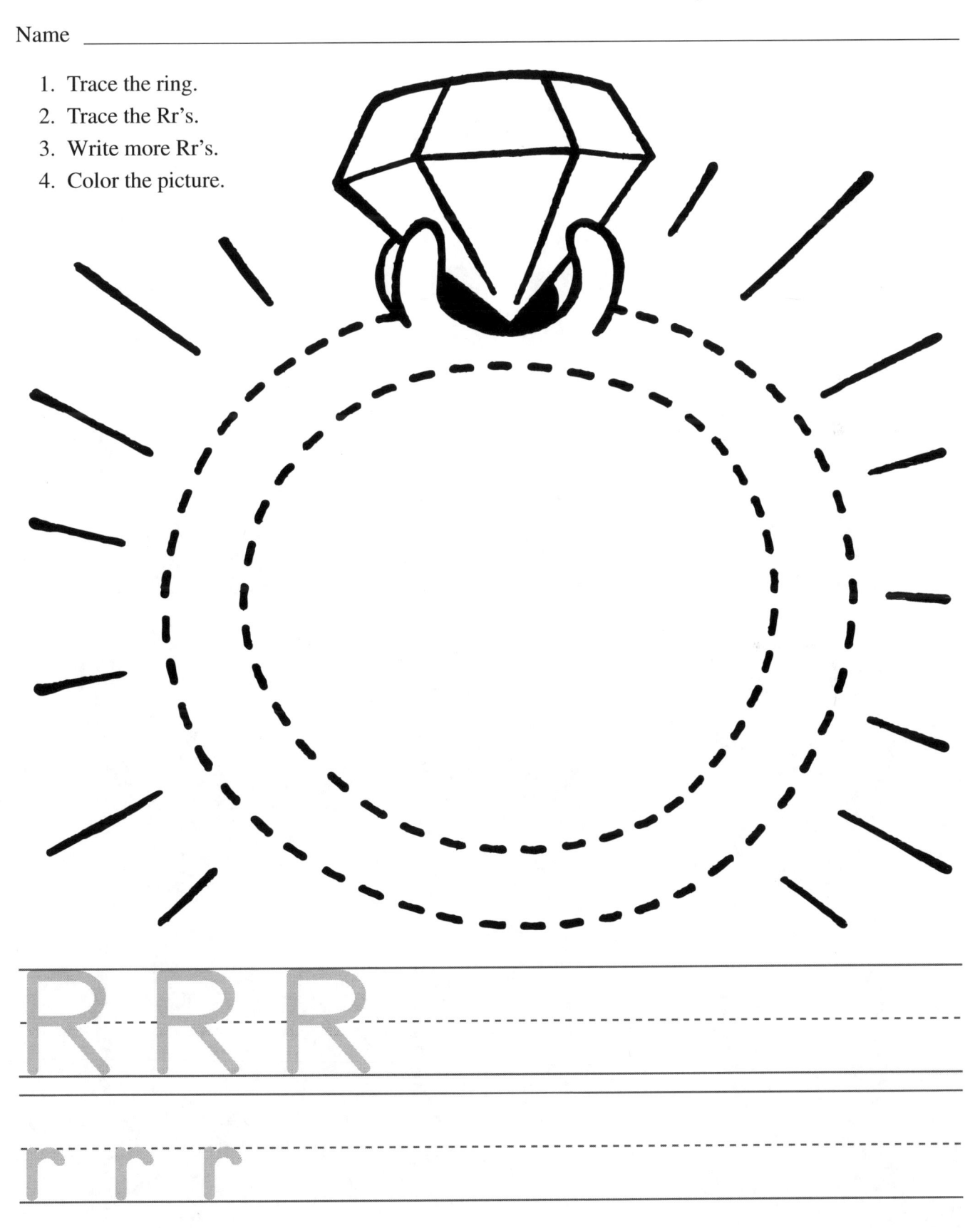

Name _____

1. Trace the ring.
2. Trace the Rr's.
3. Write more Rr's.
4. Color the picture.

R R R

r r r

Letter Rr

Rabbit Hide-and-Seek

Patterns

#2340 Alphabet Treasury 144 ©Teacher Created Resources, Inc.

Letter Rr

Rabbit Pattern

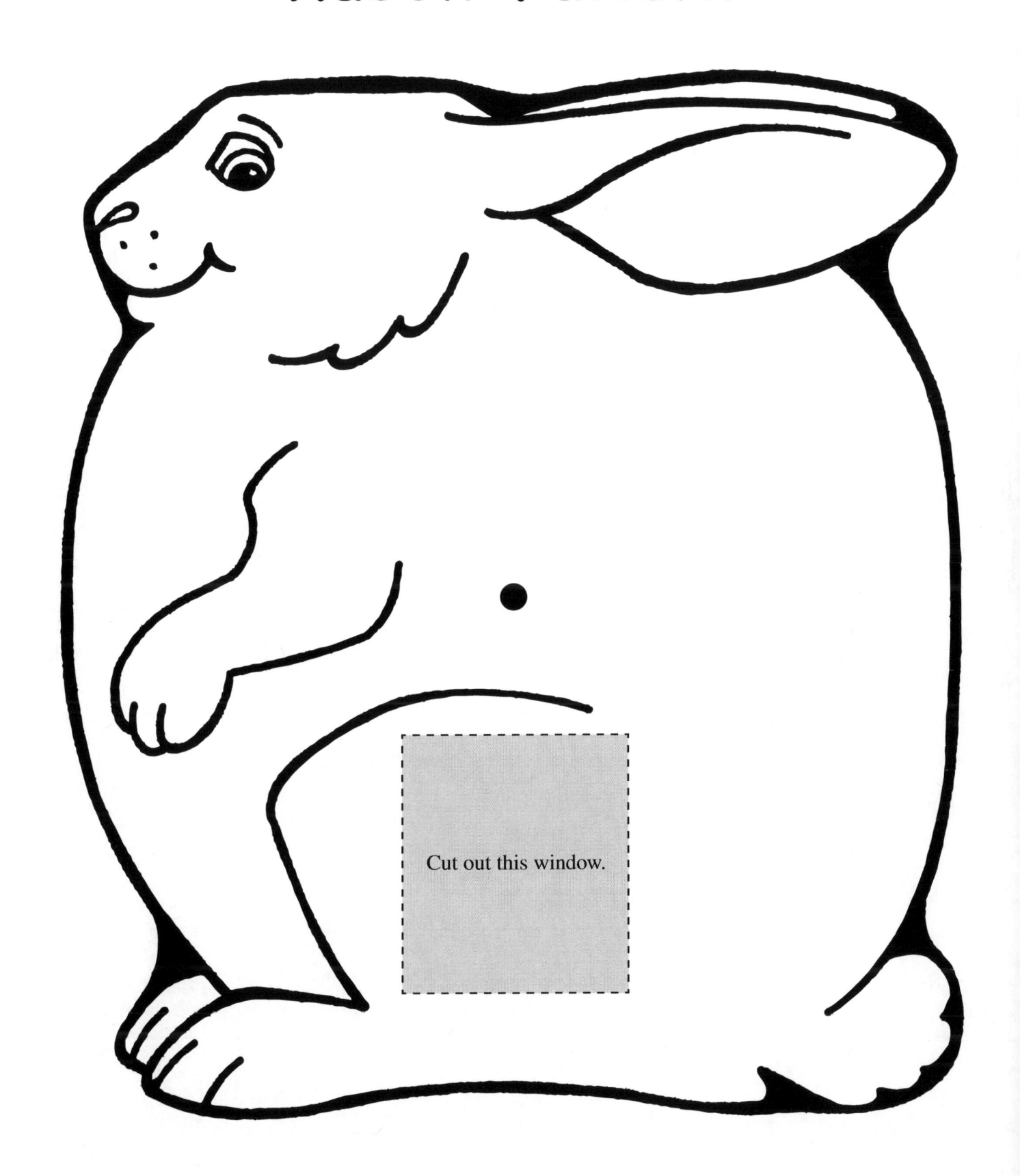

Cut out this window.

©*Teacher Created Resources, Inc.* #2340 *Alphabet Treasury*

Letter Rr

Rr Picture Wheel

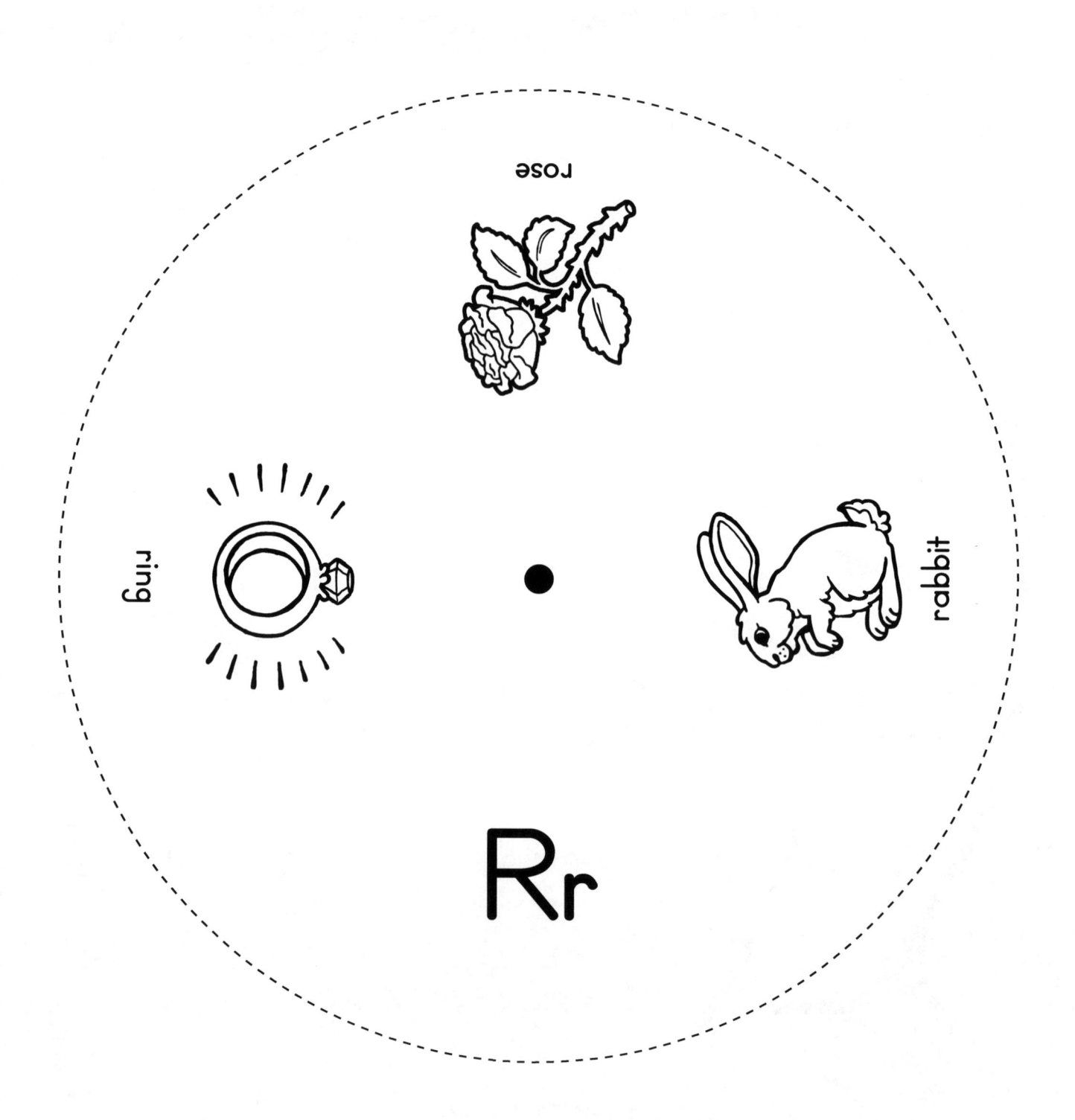

rose

ring

rabbit

Rr

#2340 Alphabet Treasury ©Teacher Created Resources, Inc.

Letter Rr

Rr is for a rose to smell with your nose.

Rr is for a ring to wear on your finger.

Rr is for a rabbit, hopping away.

_____'s

Rr

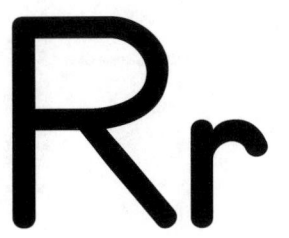

Minibook

©Teacher Created Resources, Inc. 147 #2340 Alphabet Treasury

Letter Ss

Ss

Introduce the letter Ss. Draw and discuss the shape of the letters using chart paper, a white board or a chalkboard. Note any students whose names begin or end with the letter Ss. This will provide opportunities to discuss how and when uppercase and lowercase letters are used.

Introduce the following sentences and accompanying actions. Repeat them often during the week.

Ss is for a **star**, twinkling in the sky.
(Flick your fingers above your head like stars in the sky.)

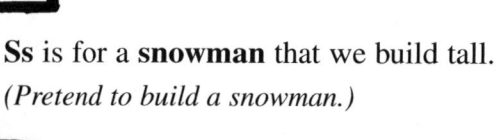

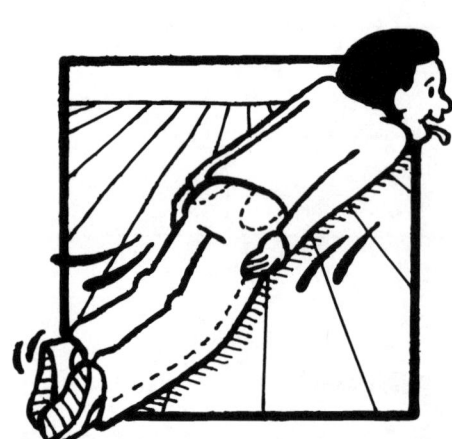

Ss is for a **snowman** that we build tall.
(Pretend to build a snowman.)

Ss is for a **snake**, hissing very softly.
(Slither like a snake and hiss softly.)

Day 1: Ss Is for Snake

Materials

- Ss Is for Snake worksheet (page 151) for each child
- pencils and crayons

Procedure for Child

1. Write your name on the line provided at the top of the page.
2. Trace the snake and the letters provided.
3. Practice writing the letter Ss on the lines provided.
4. Finish by coloring the snake using crayons.

#2340 Alphabet Treasury   148   ©Teacher Created Resources, Inc.

Letter Ss

Ss

Day 2: Star Magnet Activity

Materials

- wooden star for each child (available at craft stores) or Star Pattern (page 152) copied onto cardstock
- self-adhesive magnet for each child
- yellow tempera paint
- paintbrushes
- photo of each child
- glitter and glue

Procedure for Child

1. Paint the front of the star yellow.
2. Sprinkle glitter on the star while the paint is still wet. Let it dry overnight.
3. Glue the photo to the front of the star.
4. Attach a self-adhesive magnet to the back of the star and display the star magnet on any metal surface.

Day 3: Star Wheel

Materials

- Star Pattern (page 153) for each child
- Ss Picture Wheel (page 154) for each child
- brad for each child
- markers or crayons
- safety scissors
- pencils

Procedure for Child

1. Write your name on the back of the picture wheel.
2. Color the Star Pattern and Ss pictures on the picture wheel page.
3. Cut out the star and the picture wheel. (See page 5 for directions.)
4. Cut out the picture window on the star. (Note: Adult assistance may be necessary to cut out the picture window.)
5. Place the Ss Picture Wheel behind the Star Pattern. Make certain that one of the pictures is visible in the picture window on the star before going on to the next step.
6. Attach the star to the front of the wheel with a brad.

©Teacher Created Resources, Inc. #2340 Alphabet Treasury

Letter Ss

Ss

Day 4: Ss Minibook

Materials

- Ss Minibook (page 155) for each child
- pencils, colored pencils, crayons or markers
- safety scissors

Procedure for Child

1. Trim and fold the page to create the Ss Minibook. (See directions on page 5.)
2. Write your name in pencil on the line on the minibook cover.
3. Complete each page of the minibook. Trace each picture and then trace the letter Ss on the lines.
4. Color the pictures using the colored pencils, crayons or markers.
5. Read the book as a group. Later, it can be shared at home or with friends.

Day 5: Star Sandwiches Cooking Project *(serves 10 children)*

Kitchen Implements

- small paper plate for the child
- plastic knife for each child
- star-shaped cookie cutter

Ingredients

- 20 slices of bread
- thin sliced deli meats (chicken, turkey or ham)
- 10 slices of cheese
- small squeeze bottle of mayonnaise (optional)
- small squeeze bottle of mustard (optional)

Preparation

1. Place a slice of bread on the plate. Squirt mustard and mayonnaise on the bread and spread evenly using a plastic knife if desired.
2. Place sliced meat and a slice of cheese on the bread. Add another slice of bread to make a sandwich.
3. Use a star cookie cutter to cut out each star sandwich.
4. Snack on the leftover bread while admiring the star creation!
5. Practice good table manners while eating the star sandwich.

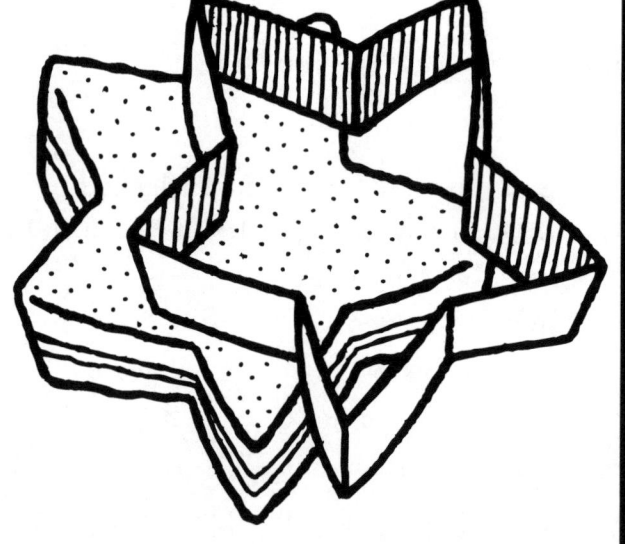

#2340 Alphabet Treasury · ©Teacher Created Resources, Inc.

Letter Ss

Ss Is for Snake

Name _____

1. Trace the snake.
2. Trace the Ss's.
3. Write more Ss's.
4. Color the picture.

©Teacher Created Resources, Inc.   151   #2340 Alphabet Treasury

Letter Ss

Star Patterns

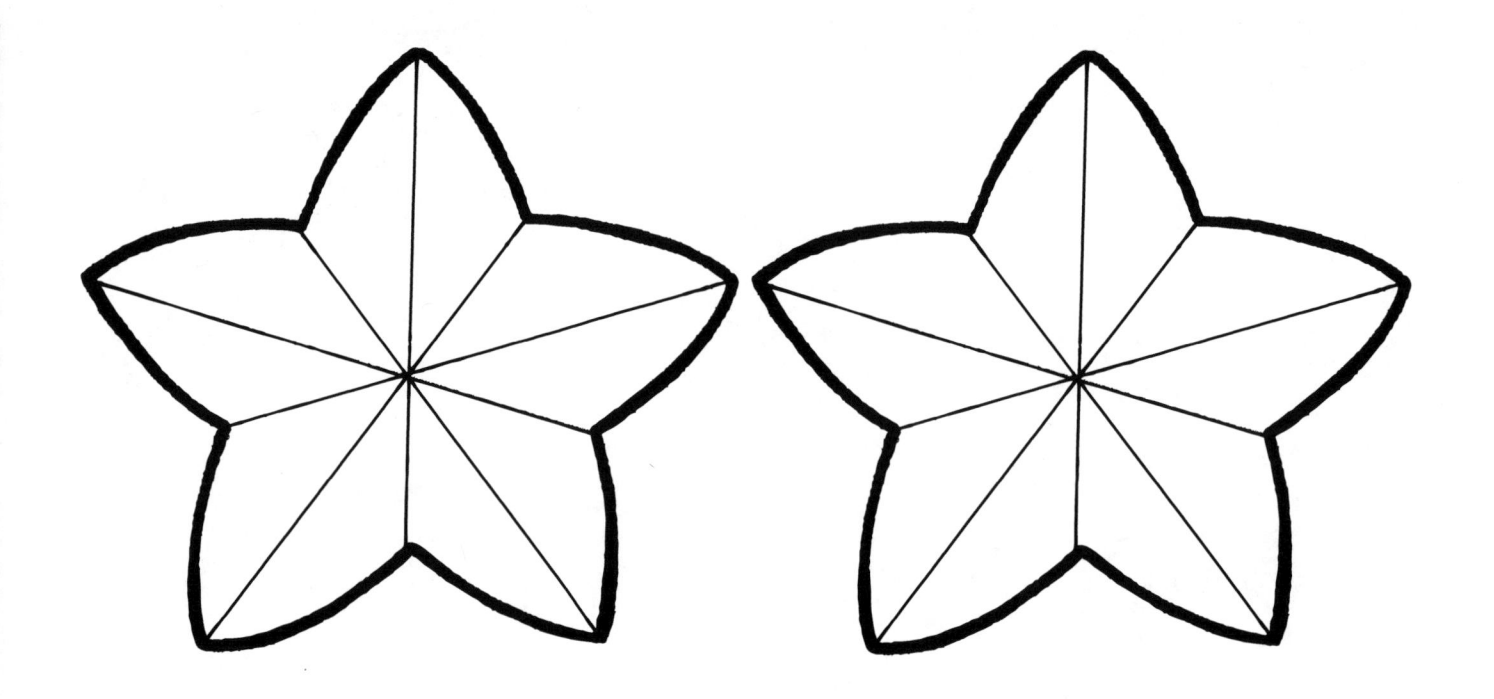

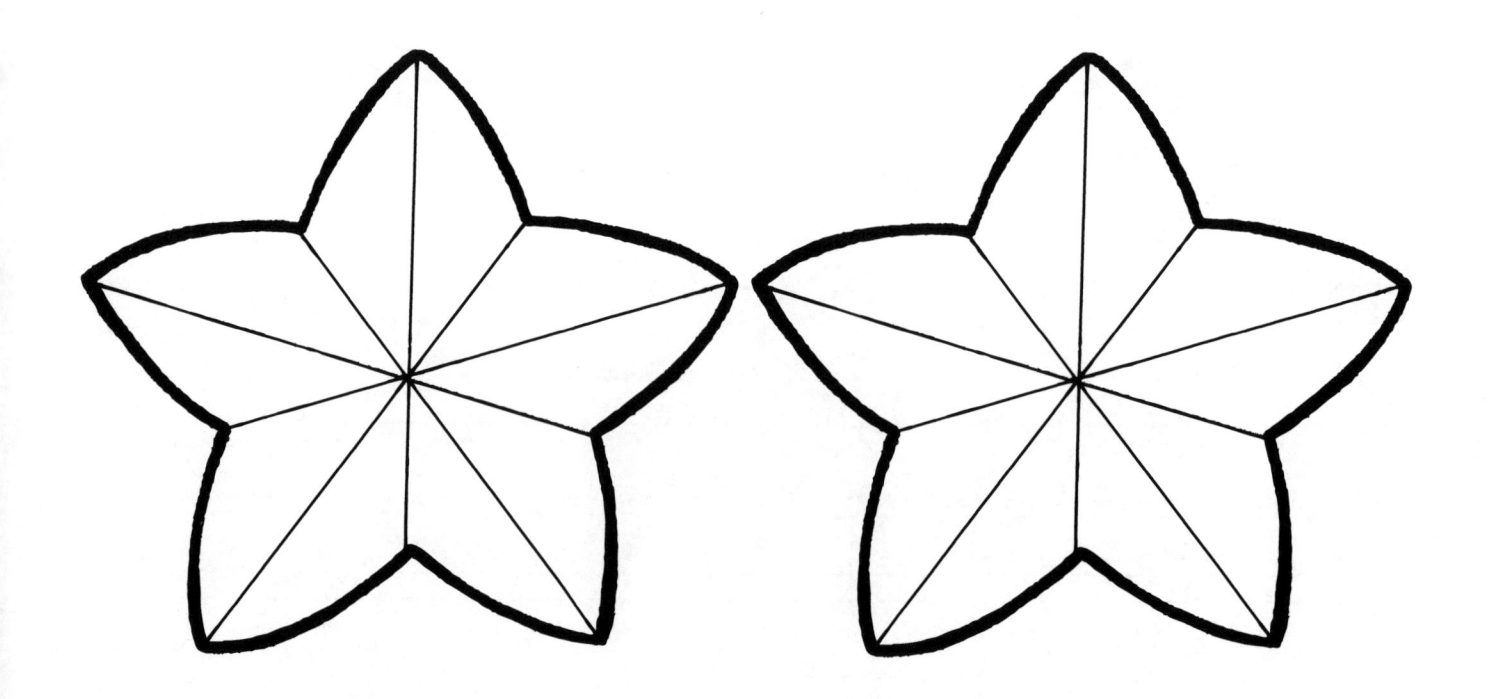

#2340 Alphabet Treasury ©Teacher Created Resources, Inc.

Letter Ss

Star Pattern

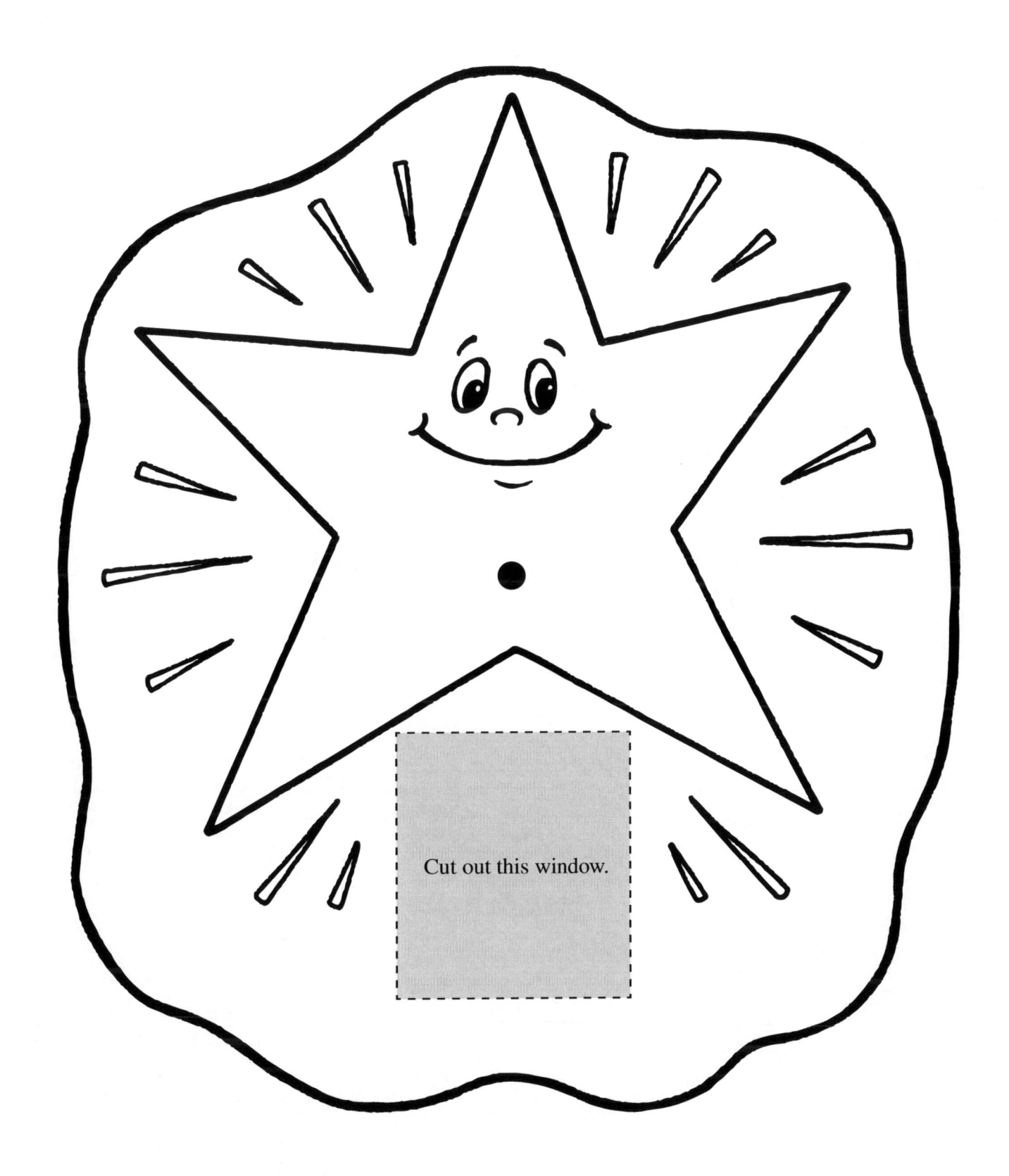

Cut out this window.

©Teacher Created Resources, Inc. 153 #2340 Alphabet Treasury

Letter Ss

Ss Picture Wheel

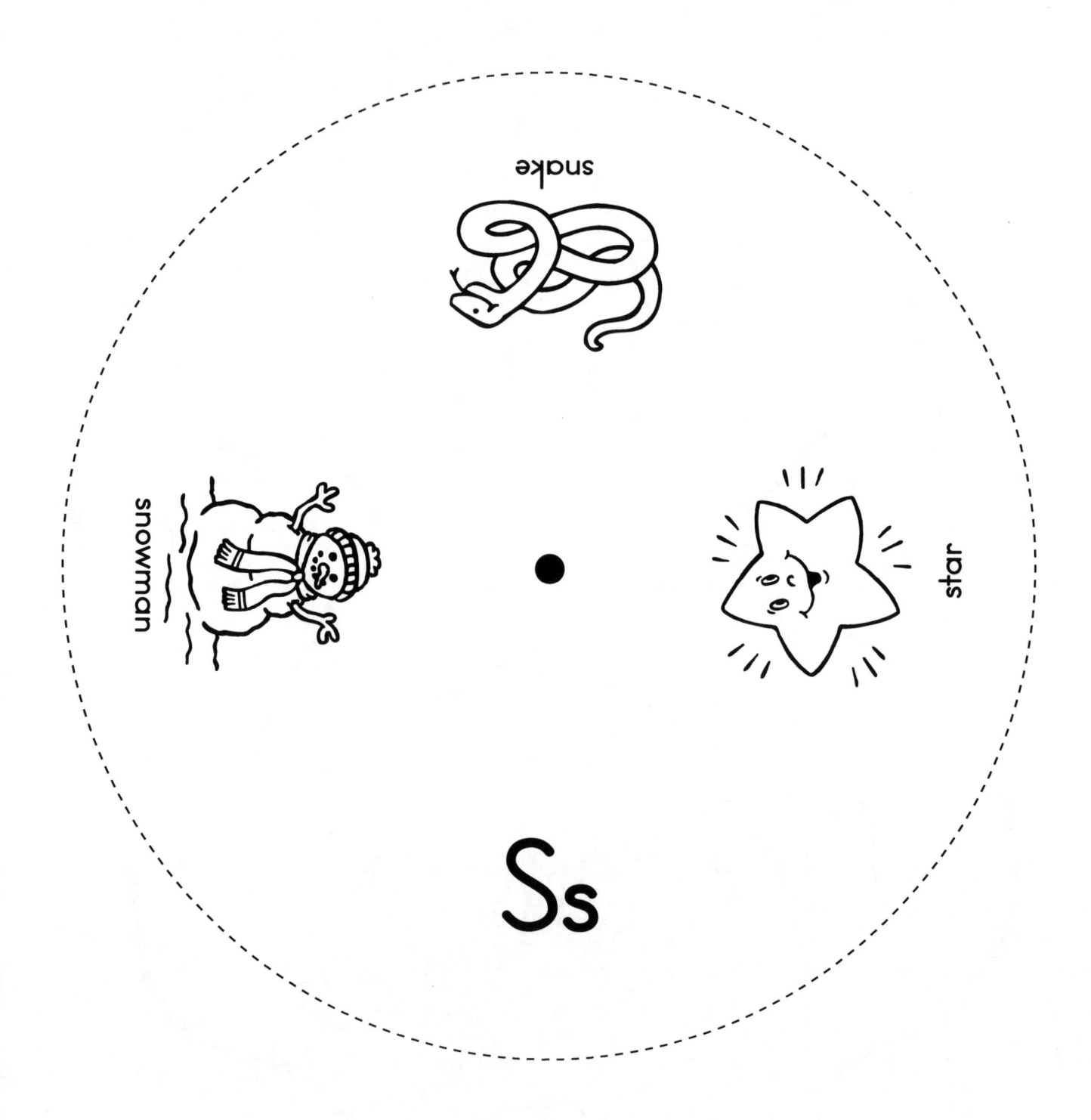

snake

snowman

star

Ss

Letter Ss

Ss is for a star, twinkling in the sky.

Ss is for a snowman that we build tall.

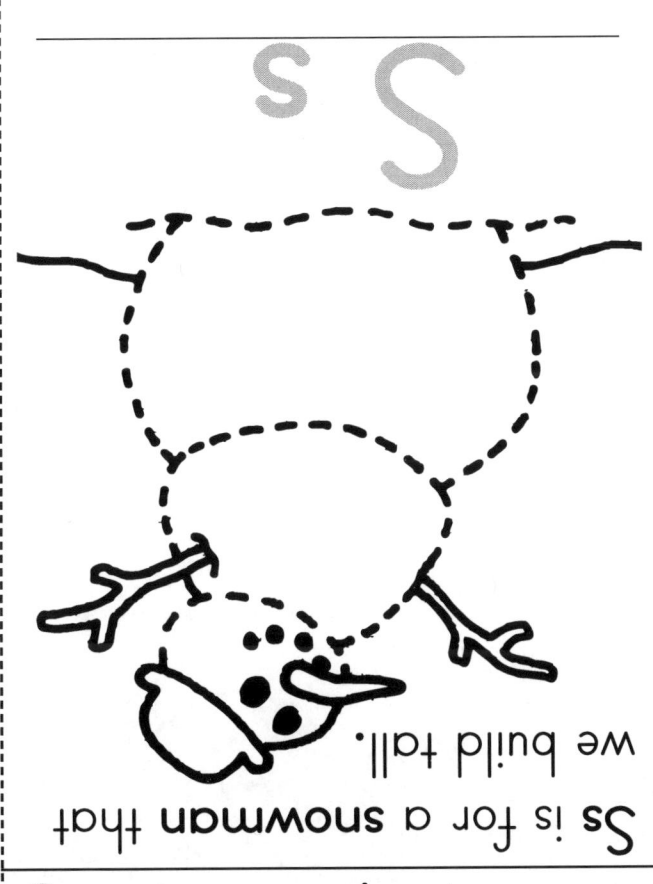

Ss is for a snake, hissing very softly.

_____'s

Ss

Minibook

©Teacher Created Resources, Inc. 155 #2340 Alphabet Treasury

Letter Tt

Tt

Introduce the letter Tt. Draw and discuss the shape of the letters using chart paper, a white board or a chalkboard. Note any students whose names begin or end with the letter Tt. This will provide opportunities to discuss how and when uppercase and lowercase letters are used.

Introduce the following sentences and accompanying actions. Repeat them often during the week.

Tt is for a **tree**, swaying in the wind.
(Sway back and forth.)

Tt is for a **turtle**, moving slowly.
(Pretend to be a turtle, moving slowly.)

Tt is for a **turkey** saying, "gobble, gobble."
(Pretend to be a turkey gobbling.)

Day 1: Tt Is for Tree

Materials

- Tt Is for Tree worksheet (page 159) for each child
- pencils and crayons

Procedure for Child

1. Write your name on the line provided at the top of the page.
2. Trace the tree and the letters provided.
3. Practice writing the letter Tt on the lines provided.
4. Finish by coloring the tree using crayons.

Letter Tt

Tt

Day 2: Tree of Many Colors Activity

Materials

- Copy of Tree Pattern, (page 160) copied onto cardstock for each child
- red, orange, yellow, brown, and purple tempera paint
- crayons
- paper towels

Procedure for Child

1. Color the tree trunk and branches using crayons.
2. Dip one fingertip into the desired color of tempera paint. Make prints on the tree branches to resemble colored leaves.
3. Wash the fingertip and pat dry, then use a different color paint to create additional leaves on the tree.
4. Repeat step #3 for additional colors of leaves, if desired.

Day 3: Turtle Wheel

Materials

- Turtle Pattern (page 161) for each child
- Tt Picture Wheel (page 162) for each child
- brad for each child
- markers or crayons
- safety scissors
- pencils

Procedure for Child

1. Color the Turtle Pattern and Tt pictures on the picture wheel page.
2. Cut out the turtle and the picture wheel. (See page 5 for directions.)
3. Write your name on the back of the wheel.
4. Cut out the picture window on the turtle. (Note: Adult assistance may be necessary to cut out the picture window.)
5. Place the Tt Picture Wheel behind the Turtle Pattern. Make certain that one of the pictures is visible in the picture window on the turtle before going on to the next step.
6. Attach the turtle to the front of the wheel with a brad. Use the black dot as a guide.

©Teacher Created Resources, Inc.   #2340 Alphabet Treasury

Letter Tt

Tt

Day 4: Tt Minibook

Materials

- Tt Minibook (page 163) for each child
- pencils, colored pencils, crayons or markers
- safety scissors

Procedure for Child

1. Trim and fold the page to create the Tt Minibook. (See directions on page 5.)
2. Write your name in pencil on the line on the minibook cover.
3. Complete each page of the minibook. Trace each picture and then trace the letter Tt on the lines.
4. Color the pictures using the colored pencils, crayons or markers.
5. Read the book as a group. Later, it can be shared at home or with friends.

Day 5: Turkey Toast Cooking Project *(serves 10 children)*

Kitchen Implements

- toaster
- turkey-shaped cookie cutter
- plastic knife for each child
- small paper plate for each child

Ingredients

- 10 slices of whole wheat bread
- peanut butter (or cream cheese mixed with cinnamon)
- fruit-flavored, o-shaped cereal
- tube of red gel icing

Preparation

1. Toast the slice of bread. (Dark brown toast works best.)
2. Use the turkey cookie cutter to cut a turkey from the toast.
3. Place the turkey on a plate. Spread peanut butter on the back part of the turkey using a plastic knife.
4. Place the o-shaped cereal on top of the peanut butter to decorate the turkey's feathers. Use one piece of cereal with a little peanut butter on it to make an eye for the turkey.

Presentation

1. Add red gel icing to the turkey's head to make its wattle.
2. Practice good table manners. Gobble, gobble, gobble!

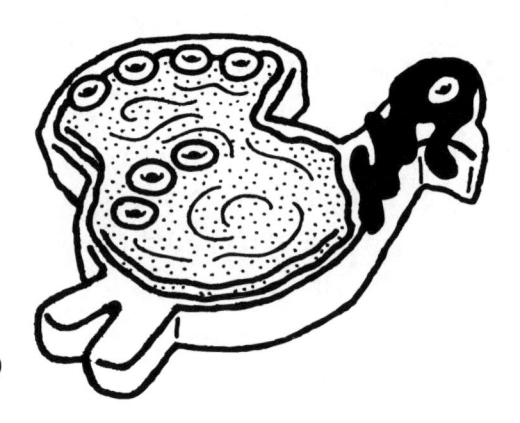

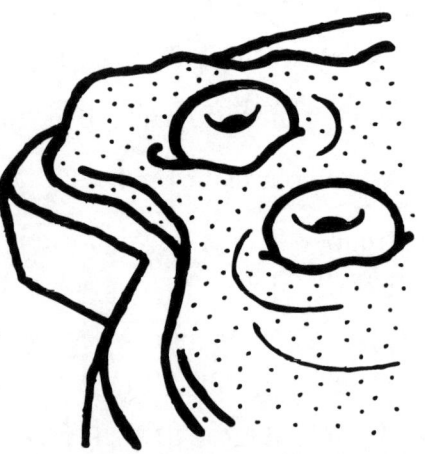

Letter Tt

Tt Is for Tree

Name _____

1. Trace the tree.
2. Trace the Tt's.
3. Write more Tt's.
4. Color the picture.

©Teacher Created Resources, Inc.   159   #2340 Alphabet Treasury

Letter Tt

Tree Pattern

#2340 Alphabet Treasury 160 ©Teacher Created Resources, Inc.

Letter Tt

Turtle Pattern

Cut out this window.

Letter Tt

Tt Picture Wheel

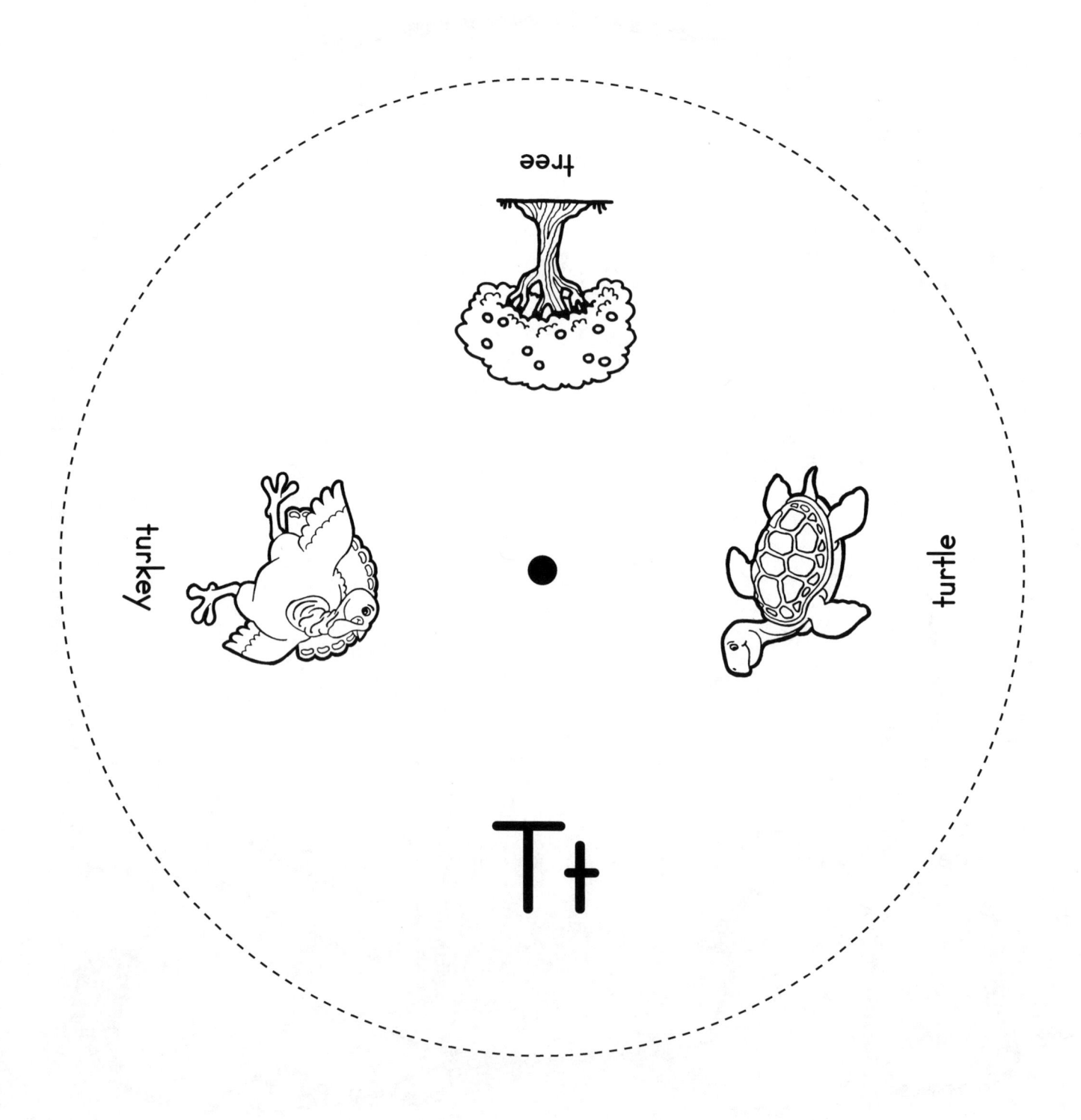

tree

turkey

turtle

Tt

#2340 Alphabet Treasury 162 ©Teacher Created Resources, Inc.

Letter Tt

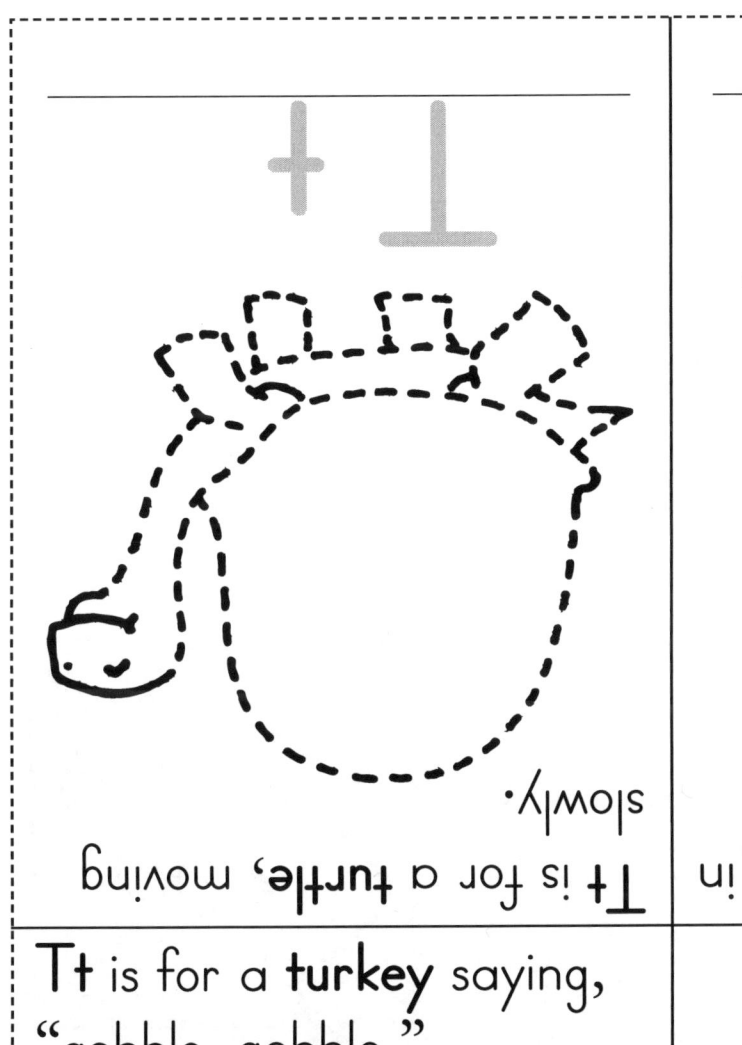

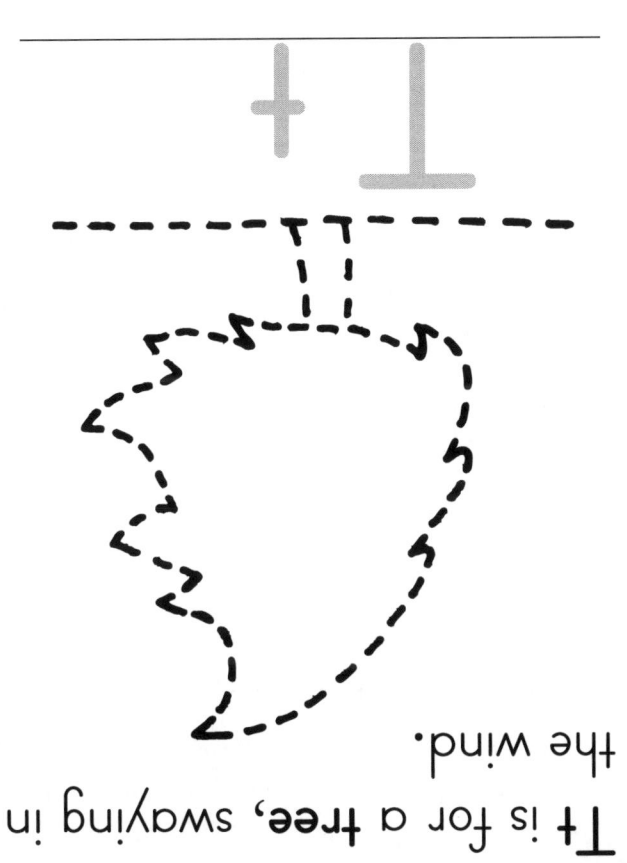

Tt is for a tree, swaying in the wind.

Tt is for a turtle, moving slowly.

Tt is for a turkey saying, "gobble, gobble."

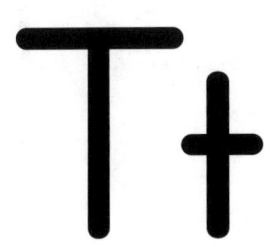

gobble

_____'s

Tt

Minibook

©Teacher Created Resources, Inc. 163 #2340 Alphabet Treasury

Letter Uu

Uu

Introduce the letter Uu. Draw and discuss the shape of the letters using chart paper, a white board or a chalkboard. Note any students whose names begin or end with the letter Uu. This will provide opportunities to discuss how and when uppercase and lowercase letters are used.

Introduce the following sentences and accompanying actions. Repeat them often during the week.

Uu is for a **unicycle**, going round and round.
(Pretend to pedal a unicycle.)

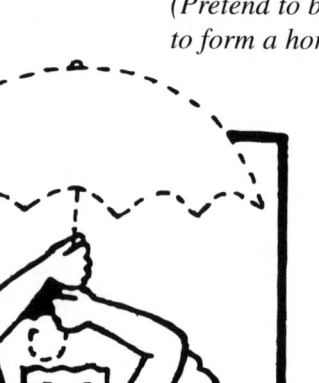

Uu is for a **unicorn** with a magic horn.
(Pretend to be a unicorn by using your hand to form a horn in the middle of your forehead.)

Uu is for an **umbrella** to keep the rain off your head.
(Pretend to hold an umbrella over your head.)

Day 1: Uu Is for Umbrella

Materials

- Uu Is for Umbrella worksheet (page 167) for each child
- pencils and crayons

Procedure for Child

1. Write your name on the line provided at the top of the page.
2. Trace the umbrella and the letters provided.
3. Practice writing the letter Uu on the lines provided.
4. Finish by coloring the umbrella using crayons.

Letter Uu

Uu

Day 2: Unicorn Horn Activity

Materials

- 12" x 15" sheet of aluminum foil for each child
- 4" x 22" poster-board strip for each child
- markers or crayons
- safety scissors
- stapler
- glitter
- glue

Procedure for Child

1. Cut the 4" x 22" poster-board strip as needed to fit around your head.
2. Decorate the resulting poster-board strip using glue and glitter, markers or crayons. Allow time to dry.
3. Fit the strip around your head and staple the strip together to create a headband.
4. Fold the sheet of aluminum foil in half lengthwise and roll it into a unicorn horn shape.
5. Cut a slit in the front of the headband and place the horn through the slit.
6. Bend back the end of the horn inside the headband. Then, staple it to the inside of the headband.
7. Show off your new creation by participating in a Unicorn Parade!

Day 3: Unicycle Wheel

Materials

- Unicycle Pattern (page 168) for each child
- Uu Picture Wheel (page 169) for each child
- brad for each child
- markers or crayons
- safety scissors
- pencils

Procedure for Child

1. Color the Unicycle Pattern and Uu pictures on the picture wheel page.
2. Cut out the unicycle and the picture wheel. (See page 5 for directions.)
3. Write your name on the back of the wheel.
4. Cut out the picture window on the unicycle. (Note: Adult assistance may be necessary to cut out the picture window.)
5. Place the Uu Picture Wheel behind the Unicycle Pattern. Make certain that one of the pictures is visible in the picture window on the unicycle before going on to the next step.
6. Attach the unicycle to the front of the wheel with a brad.

Letter Uu

Uu

Day 4: Uu Minibook

Materials

- Uu Minibook (page 170) for each child
- pencils, colored pencils, crayons or markers
- safety scissors

Procedure for Child

1. Trim and fold the page to create the Uu Minibook. (See page 5 for directions.)
2. Write your name in pencil on the line on the minibook cover.
3. Complete each page of the minibook. Trace each picture and then trace the letter Uu on the lines.
4. Color the pictures using the colored pencils, crayons or markers.
5. Read the book as a group. Later, it can be shared at home or with friends.

Day 5: Umbrellas Cooking Project *(serves 10 children)*

Kitchen Implements

- small paper plate and plastic knife for each child
- measuring cups
- small serving spoons

Ingredients

- 5 English muffins
- 10 pretzel sticks
- 1 cup jam or jelly (may use sugar-free)
- dried fruit (e.g., apples, bananas)

Preparation

1. Cut an English muffin in half using a plastic knife. Place the "umbrella shape" on a plate.
2. Place a spoonful of jam or jelly on the plate. Spread the jam evenly on the muffin (umbrella) using a plastic knife.
3. Place a pretzel stick (handle) under the umbrella muffin.
4. Decorate the umbrella using dried fruit as desired.
5. Practice good table manners.

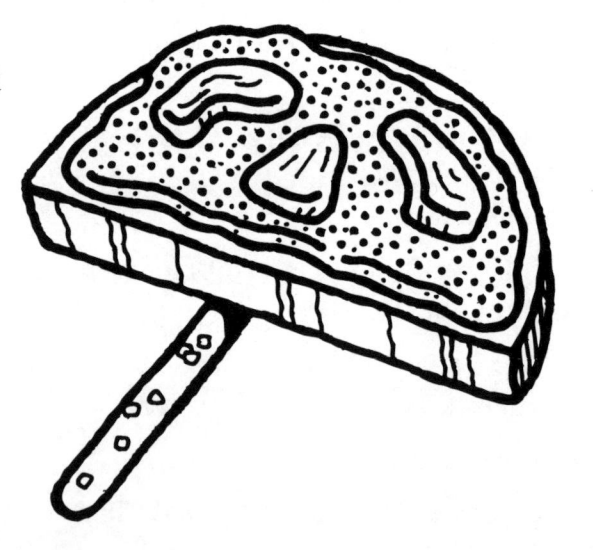

Letter Uu

Uu Is for Umbrella

Name _____

1. Trace the umbrella.
2. Trace the Uu's.
3. Write more Uu's.
4. Color the picture.

©Teacher Created Resources, Inc.   167   #2340 Alphabet Treasury

Letter Uu

Unicycle Pattern

Cut out this window.

#2340 Alphabet Treasury 168 ©Teacher Created Resources, Inc.

Letter Uu

Uu Picture Wheel

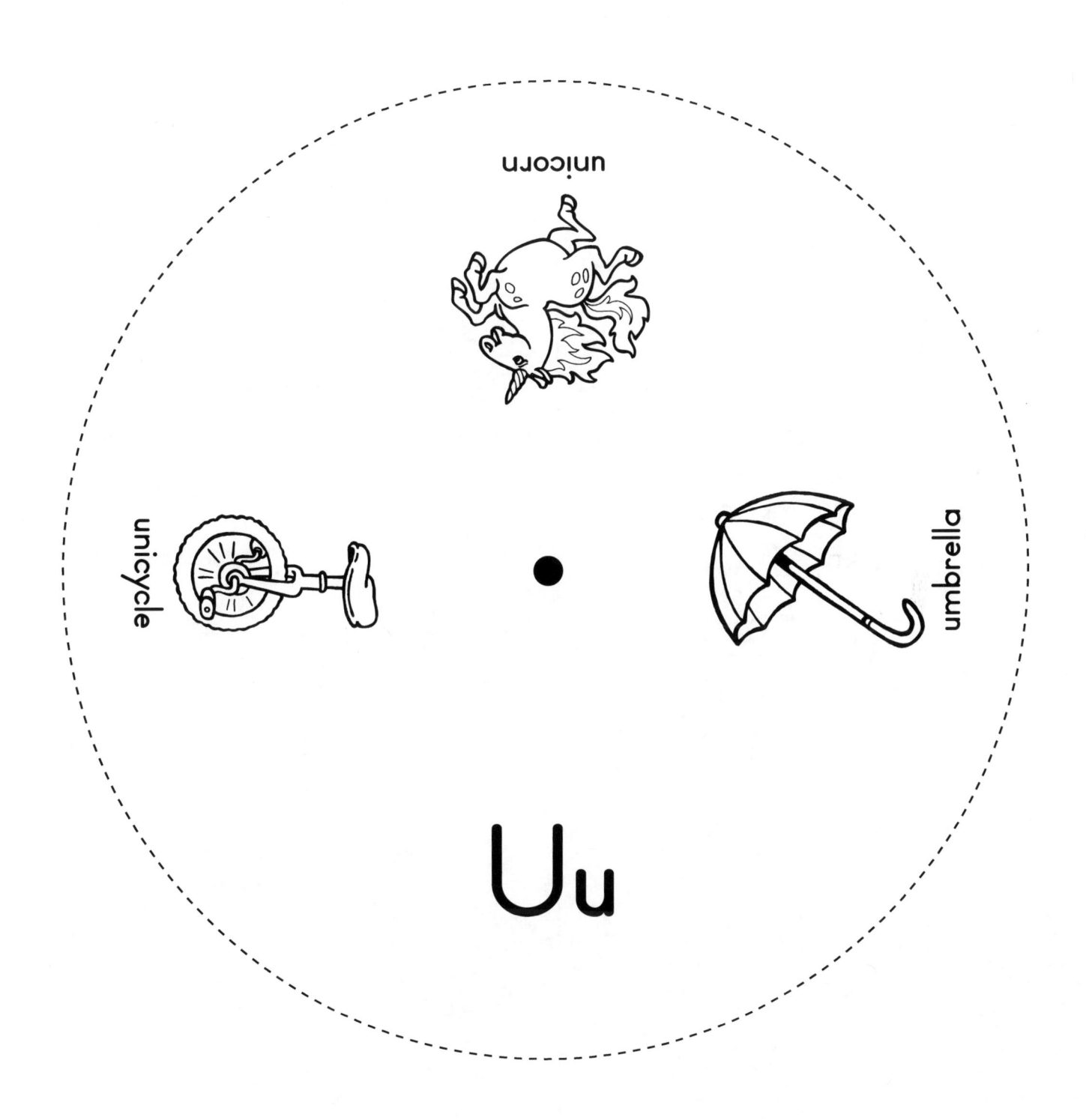

unicorn

unicycle

umbrella

Uu

©Teacher Created Resources, Inc. 169 #2340 Alphabet Treasury

Letter Uu

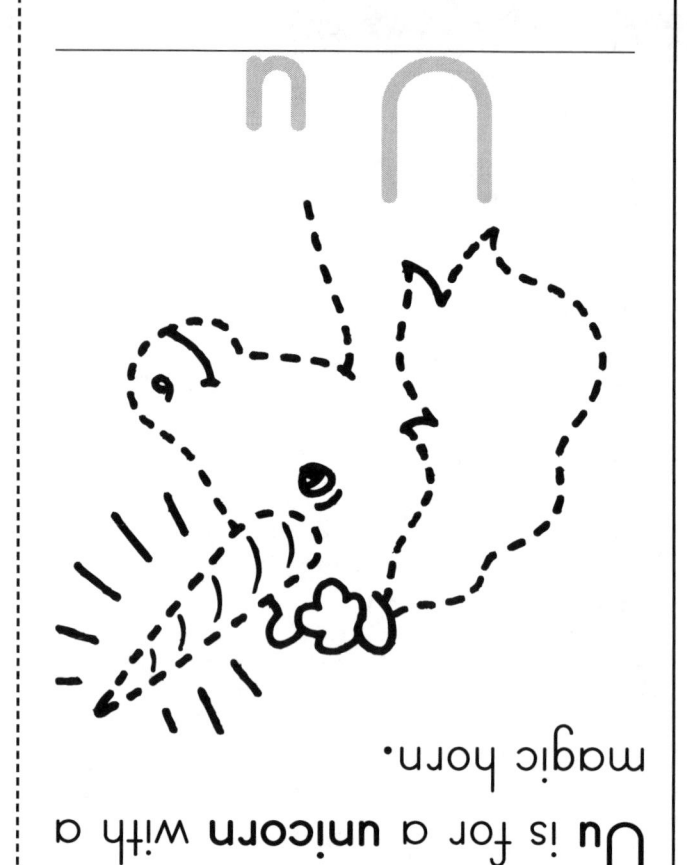

Uu is for a unicorn with a magic horn.

Uu is for a unicycle, going round and round.

Uu is for an umbrella to keep the rain off your head.

_____'s

Uu

Minibook

#2340 Alphabet Treasury 170 ©Teacher Created Resources, Inc.

Letter Vv

Vv

Introduce the letter Vv. Draw and discuss the shape of the letters using chart paper, a white board or a chalkboard. Note any students whose names begin or end with the letter Vv. This will provide opportunities to discuss how and when uppercase and lowercase letters are used.

Introduce the following sentences and accompanying actions. Repeat them often during the week.

Vv is for a vase to put flowers in.
(Pretend to put flowers in a vase.)

Vv is for a van honking, "beep, beep."
(Pretend to honk horn and say, "beep, beep.")

Vv is for a valentine for you.
(Make a heart shape with your hands and pretend to give a valentine to someone.)

Day 1: Vv Is for Vase of Violets

Materials
- Vv Is for Vase of Violets worksheet (page 174) for each child
- pencils and crayons

Procedure for Child
1. Write your name on the line provided at the top of the page.
2. Trace the Vase of Violets and the letters provided.
3. Practice writing the letter Vv on the lines provided.
4. Finish by coloring the Vase of Violets using crayons.

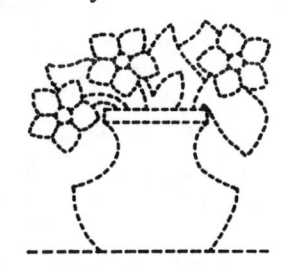

©Teacher Created Resources, Inc.   171   #2340 Alphabet Treasury

Letter Vv

Vv

Day 2: Violet Vase Activity

Materials

- Violet Patterns (page 175) for each child
- clean, plastic bottle or empty metal can for each child (ensure there are no sharp edges)
- light purple crayons or markers
- light purple tissue paper
- assortment of stickers
- safety scissors
- glue

Procedure for Child

1. Color the violets using light purple crayons or markers and cut them out.
2. Tear the light purple tissue paper into small pieces.
3. Cover the outside of the can (vase) with glue. (Do not put glue on the bottom of the can.)
4. Apply the tissue pieces to the glue and let dry.
5. Attach the violet patterns to the vase using glue.

Day 3: Van Wheel

Materials

- Van Pattern (page 176) for each child
- Vv Picture Wheel (page 177) for each child
- brad for each child
- markers or crayons
- safety scissors
- pencils

Procedure for Child

1. Write your name on the back of the picture wheel.
2. Color the Van Pattern and Vv pictures on the picture wheel page.
3. Cut out the van and the picture wheel. (See page 5 for directions.)
4. Cut out the picture window on the van. (Note: Adult assistance may be necessary to cut out the picture window.)
5. Place the Vv Picture Wheel behind the Van Pattern. Make certain that one of the pictures is visible in the picture window on the van before going on to the next step.
6. Attach the van to the front of the wheel with a brad.

#2340 Alphabet Treasury ©Teacher Created Resources, Inc.

Letter Vv

Vv

Day 4: Vv Minibook

Materials

- Vv Minibook (page 178) for each child
- pencils, colored pencils, crayons or markers

Procedure for Child

1. Trim and fold the page to create the Vv Minibook. (See page 5 for directions.)
2. Have students write their names in pencil on the line on the minibook cover.
3. Complete each page of the minibook. Trace each picture and then trace the letter Vv on the lines.
4. Color the pictures using the colored pencils, crayons or markers.
5. Read the book as a group. Later it can be shared at home or with friends.

Day 5: Valentine Veggies with Heart-Smart Dip Cooking Project *(serves 10 children)*

Kitchen Implements

- small paper plate for each child
- medium-sized mixing bowl
- measuring cups
- mixing spoon
- small serving spoon

Ingredients

- assorted bite-sized vegetables (carrots, broccoli, cucumbers, celery)
- 1/2 cup low-fat mayonnaise
- 1 cup low-fat sour cream
- 1 teaspoon lemon juice
- 2 T chopped dill

Preparation

1. In a medium-sized mixing bowl, combine the sour cream, mayonnaise, dill, and lemon juice using a mixing spoon.
2. Take turns stirring the dill dip mixture until mixed well.
3. Chill the dill dip in a refrigerator for several hours.
4. Place desired vegetables on a plate.
5. Add a spoonful of dill dip to the plate.

Presentation

1. Discuss how eating vegetables and a low-fat, salt-free dip is like giving a valentine to your body because healthful foods can be nutritious and delicious!
2. Practice good table manners.

Letter Vv

Vv Is for Vase of Violets

Name _____

1. Trace the vase of violets.
2. Trace the Vv's.
3. Write more Vv's.
4. Color the picture.

#2340 Alphabet Treasury ©Teacher Created Resources, Inc.

Letter Vv

Violet Patterns

Letter Vv

Van Pattern

Cut out this window.

#2340 Alphabet Treasury 176 ©Teacher Created Resources, Inc.

Letter Vv

Vv Picture Wheel

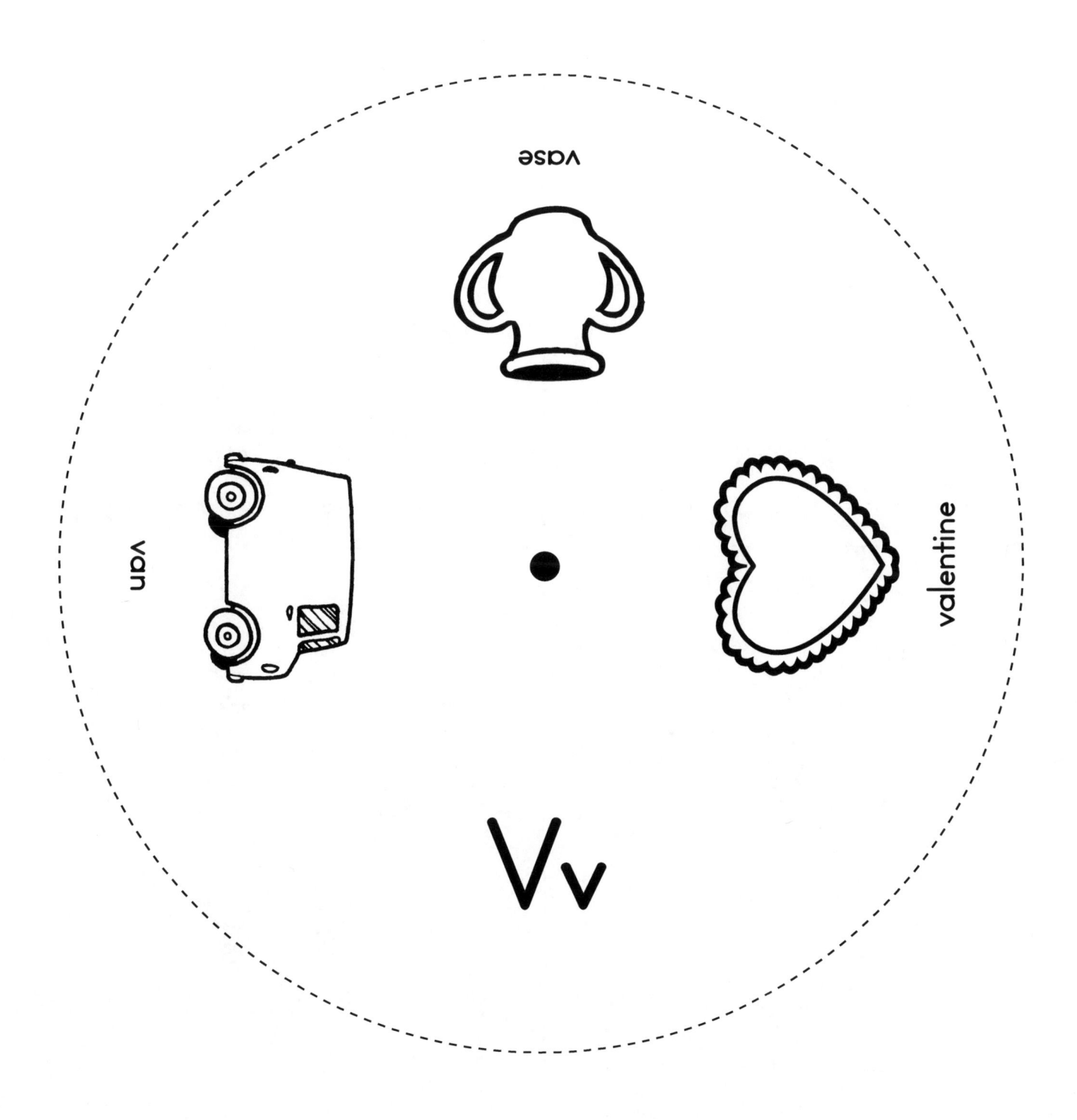

vase

van

valentine

Vv

©Teacher Created Resources, Inc. 177 #2340 Alphabet Treasury

Letter Vv

Vv

Vv is for a van honking, "beep, beep."

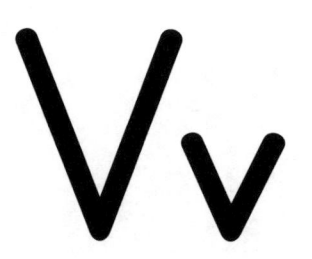

Vv

Vv is for a vase to put flowers in.

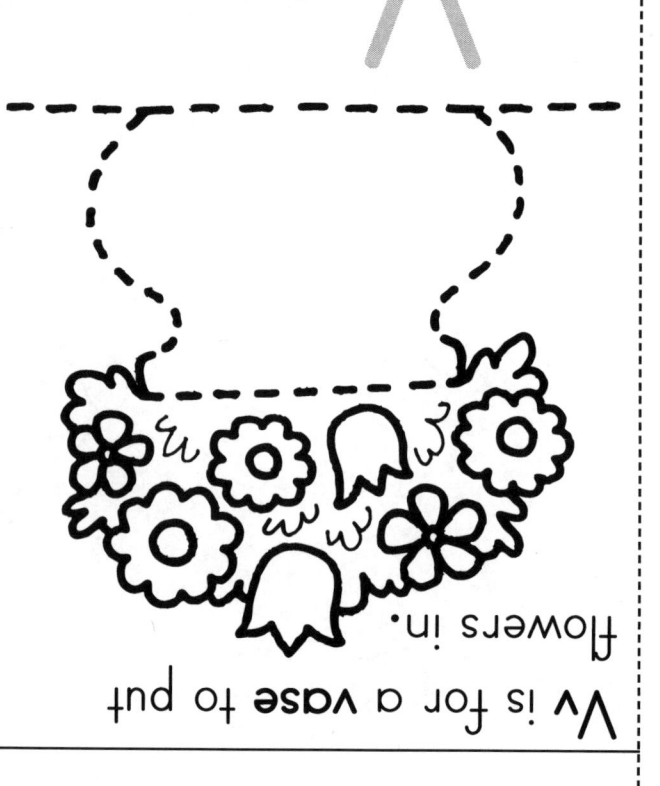

Vv is for a valentine for you.

My Best Friend

Vv

_____'s

Vv

Minibook

#2340 Alphabet Treasury

Letter Ww

Ww

Introduce the letter Ww. Draw and discuss the shape of the letters using chart paper, a white board or a chalkboard. Note any students whose names begin or end with the letter Ww. This will provide opportunities to discuss how and when uppercase and lowercase letters are used.

Introduce the following sentences and accompanying actions. Repeat them often during the week.

Ww is for a **watch** to tell the time.
(Pretend to look at a watch and point to the time.)

Ww is for a **wagon** to pull.
(Pretend to pull a heavy wagon behind you.)

Ww is for a **whale**, swimming in the ocean.
(Pretend to be a whale moving up and down in the ocean to get air.)

Day 1: Ww Is for Watch

Materials

- Ww Is for Watch worksheet (page 182) for each child
- pencils and crayons

Procedure for Child

1. Write your name on the line provided at the top of the page.
2. Trace the watch and the letters provided.
3. Practice writing the letter Ww on the lines provided.
4. Finish by coloring the watch using crayons.

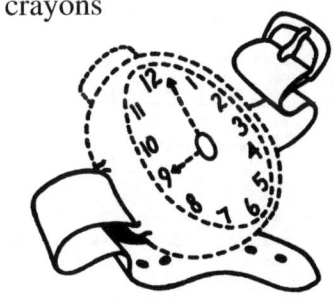

©Teacher Created Resources, Inc.   #2340 Alphabet Treasury

Letter Ww

Ww

Day 2: Whale Activity

Materials

- three 4" lengths of blue curling ribbon for each child
- 6" blue pipe cleaner for each child
- small paper bag for each child
- crayons or markers
- masking tape
- old newspapers
- glue
- safety scissors
- yarn

Procedure for Child

1. Draw a face for the whale on the base of a paper bag using crayons or markers.
2. Push a pipe cleaner through the paper bag as shown. Bend the end of the pipe cleaner inside the bag and tape it down.
3. Crumple the old newspapers into small balls and stuff the bag with newspaper balls until it is full.
4. Wrap a piece of yarn around the open end of the bag and tie it closed.
5. Tie 3 pieces of curling ribbon to the pipe cleaner. Curl the ribbon using scissors to resemble water spouting out of the whale. (Note: An adult needs to curl the ribbon.)

Day 3: Whale Wheel

Materials

- Whale Pattern (page 183) for each child
- Ww Picture Wheel (page 184) for each child
- brad for each child
- safety scissors
- markers or crayons
- pencils

Procedure for Child

1. Color the Whale Pattern and Ww pictures on the picture wheel page.
2. Cut out the whale and the picture wheel. (See page 5 for directions.)
3. Write your name on the back of the wheel.
4. Cut out the picture window on the whale. (Note: Adult assistance may be necessary to cut out the picture window.)
5. Place the Ww Picture Wheel behind the Whale Pattern. Make certain that one of the pictures is visible in the picture window on the whale before going on to the next step.
6. Attach the whale to the front of the wheel with a brad.

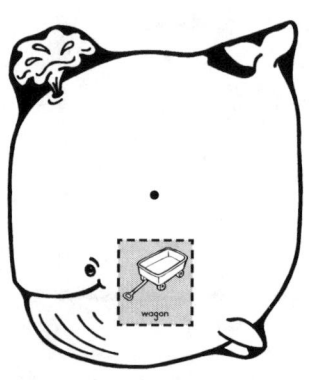

#2340 Alphabet Treasury ©Teacher Created Resources, Inc.

Letter Ww

Ww

Day 4: Ww Minibook

Materials

- Ww Minibook (page 185) for each child
- pencils, colored pencils, crayons or markers
- safety scissors

Procedure for Child

1. Trim and fold the page to create the Ww Minibook. (See directions on page 5.)
2. Write your name in pencil on the line on the minibook cover.
3. Complete each page of the minibook. Trace each picture and then trace the letter Ww on the lines.
4. Color the pictures using the colored pencils, crayons or markers.
5. Read the book as a group. Later, it can be shared at home or with friends.

Day 5: Watch Pizza Cooking Project *(serves 10 children)*

Kitchen Implements

- 1 small paper plate for each child
- plastic knife
- spatula
- baking sheet
- measuring cup
- knife (adult use only)

Ingredients

- refrigerated pizza dough package
- 8 oz. finely shredded cheese
- 2 cups pizza sauce
- 12 pepperoni slices
- bell pepper strips

Preparation

1. Unroll the pizza dough. Cut off 2 thin pieces of dough using a plastic knife to form 2 long strands (wristband).
2. Stretch the remaining dough to resemble a pizza (clock face).
3. Place the clock face on a baking sheet. Place a wristband strand on each side of the clock face.
4. Pour the pizza sauce on the clock face and spread it out evenly using a plastic knife.
5. Add pepperoni slices to resemble the 12 numbers on a clock face. Use bell pepper strips for the watch hands.
6. Lightly sprinkle shredded cheese on top of the watch and bake in the oven according to the pizza dough package instructions. Let the watch cool.

Presentation

1. Cut the pizza watch into slices. Use a spatula to place a slice on each child's plate.
2. Practice good table manners.

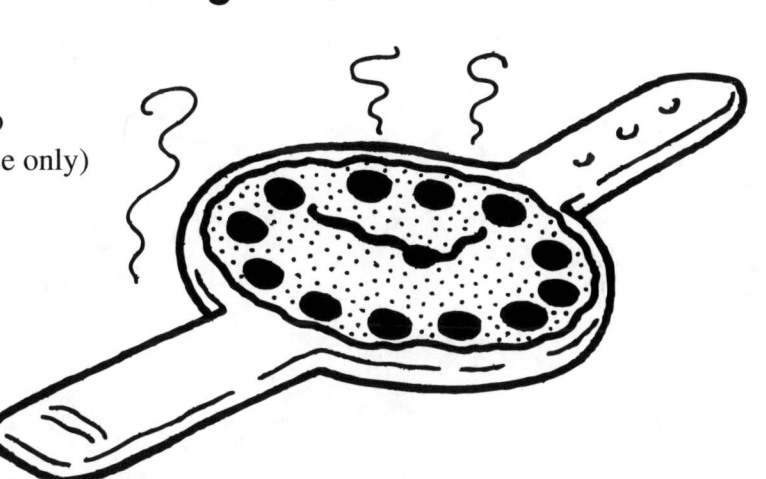

Letter Ww

Ww Is for Watch

Name _____

1. Trace the watch.
2. Trace the Ww's.
3. Write more Ww's.
4. Color the picture.

#2340 Alphabet Treasury 182 ©Teacher Created Resources, Inc.

Letter Ww

Whale Pattern

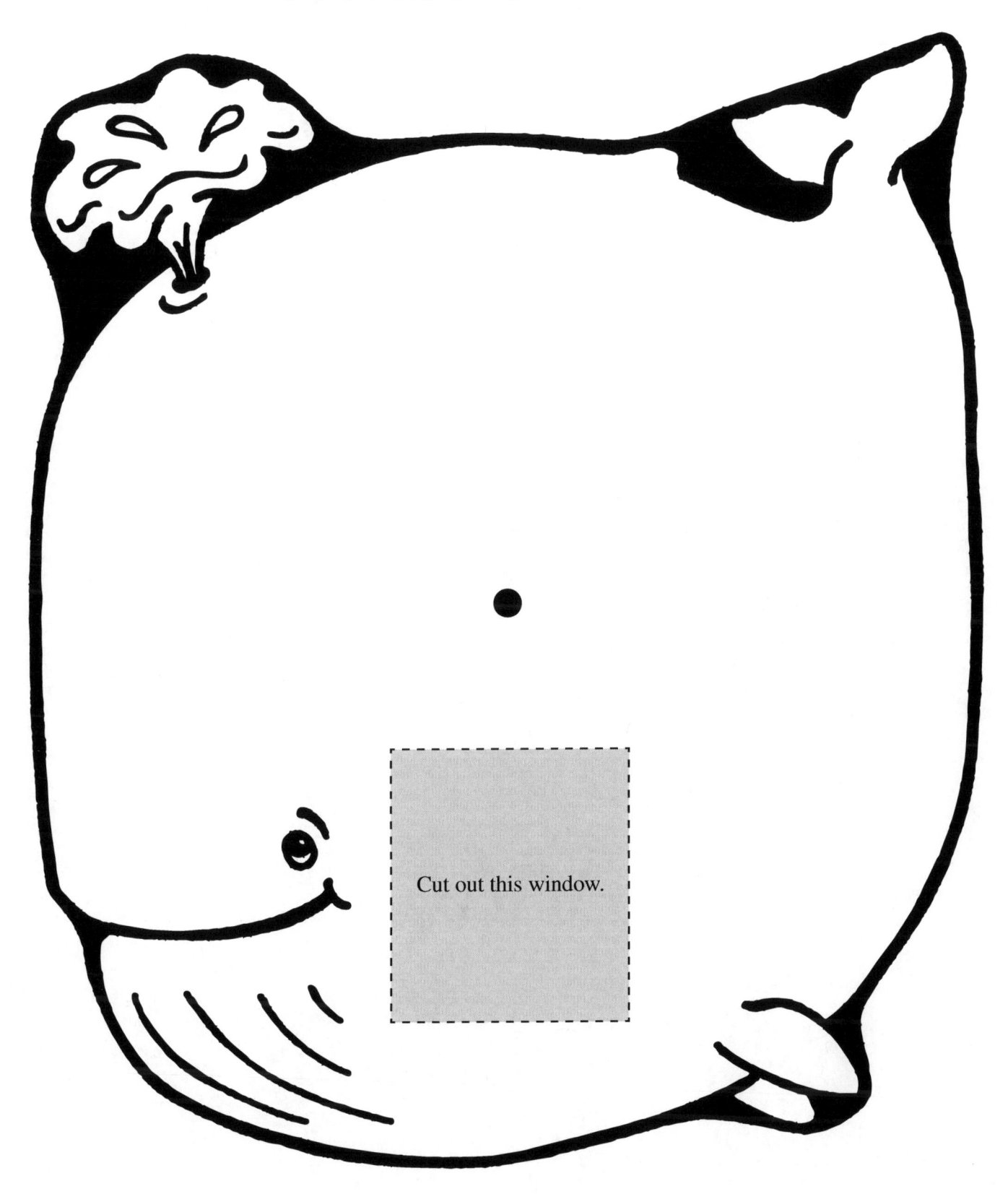

Cut out this window.

Letter Ww

Ww Picture Wheel

watch

wagon

whale

Ww

#2340 Alphabet Treasury ©Teacher Created Resources, Inc.

Letter Ww

Ww is for a watch to tell the time.

Ww is for a wagon to pull.

Ww is for a whale, swimming in the ocean.

_____'s

Ww

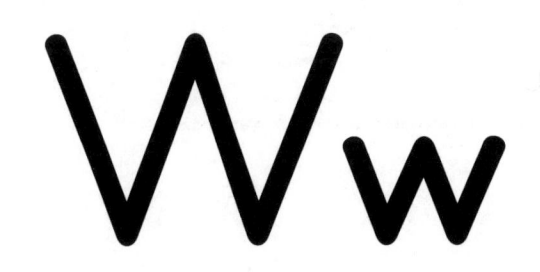

Minibook

©Teacher Created Resources, Inc.   185   #2340 Alphabet Treasury

Letter Xx

Xx

Introduce the letter Xx. Draw and discuss the shape of the letters using chart paper, a white board or a chalkboard. Note any students whose names begin or end with the letter Xx. This will provide opportunities to discuss how and when uppercase and lowercase letters are used.

Introduce the following sentences and accompanying actions. Repeat them often during the week.

Xx is for an **x-ray** of my hand.
(Hold up one hand and keep it still. Use the other hand to pretend to take a picture of the still hand.)

Xx is for a **fox**, moving from tree to tree.
(Crawl back and forth, pretending to stop behind trees.)

Xx is for a **box** to play hide-and-seek in.
(Crouch down like you are hiding in a box.)

Day 1: Xx Is for Fox

Materials

- Xx Is for Fox worksheet (page 189) for each child
- pencils and crayons

Procedure for Child

1. Write your name on the line provided at the top of the page.
2. Trace the fox and the letters provided.
3. Practice writing the letter Xx on the lines provided.
4. Finish by coloring the fox using crayons.

#2340 Alphabet Treasury ©Teacher Created Resources, Inc.

Letter Xx

Xx

Day 2: Fox Mask Activity

Materials

- Fox Mask Pattern (page 190) copied onto cardstock for each child
- one 12" dowel (1/4" thick) for each child
- glue gun (adult use only) or tape
- safety scissors
- brown and red watercolor paints
- red or gold glitter
- paintbrushes
- glue

Procedure for Child

1. Cut out the mask. (An adult needs to cut out the eye holes.)
2. Paint the fox mask using brown and red watercolor paints. Allow time to dry.
3. Write your name on the back of the mask.
4. Decorate the mask by attaching glitter using glue.
5. After the mask is dry, tape or glue a dowel to the back of the mask. (Aa adult needs to complete this step if using a glue gun.)

Day 3: X-ray Wheel

Materials

- X-ray Pattern (page 191) for each child
- Xx Picture Wheel (page 192) for each child
- brad for each child
- safety scissors
- markers or crayons
- pencils

Procedure for Child

1. Color the X-ray Pattern and Xx pictures on the picture wheel page.
2. Cut out the x-ray and the picture wheel. (See page 5 for directions.)
3. Write your name on the back of the wheel.
4. Cut out the picture window on the x-ray. (Note: Adult assistance may be necessary to cut out the picture window.)
5. Place the Xx Picture Wheel behind the X-ray Pattern. Make certain that one of the pictures is visible in the picture window on the x-ray before going on to the next step.
6. Attach the x-ray to the front of the wheel with a brad.

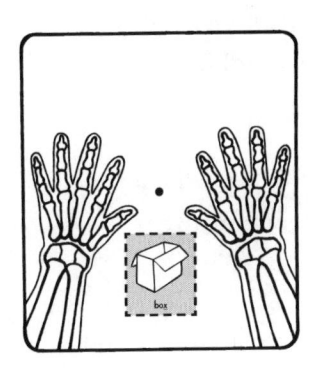

©Teacher Created Resources, Inc.   187   #2340 Alphabet Treasury

Letter Xx

Xx

Day 4: Xx Minibook

Materials

- Xx Minibook (page 193) for each child
- pencils, colored pencils, crayons or markers
- safety scissors

Procedure for Child

1. Trim and fold the page to create the Xx Minibook. (See page 5 for directions.)
2. Write your name in pencil on the line on the minibook cover.
3. Complete each page of the minibook. Trace each picture and then trace the letter Xx on the lines.
4. Color the pictures using the colored pencils, crayons or markers.
5. Read the book as a group. Later, it can be shared at home or with friends.

Day 5: X-ray Sandwiches Cooking Project *(serves 10 children)*

Kitchen Implements

- small paper plate for each child
- plastic knife for each child
- hand-shaped cookie cutter

Ingredients

- 20 slices of whole wheat bread
- whipped cream cheese

Preparation

1. Place a slice of bread on your plate. Use the cutter to cut out a hand shape in the middle of the bread. You can eat the hand shape later.
2. On another slice of bread, spread cream cheese evenly using a plastic knife.
3. Put the 2 slices of bread together to make a sandwich.

Presentation

1. Set the sandwich on the plate so that the hand cutout slice is on top. Admire the x-ray of the hand before eating it!
2. Practice good table manners.

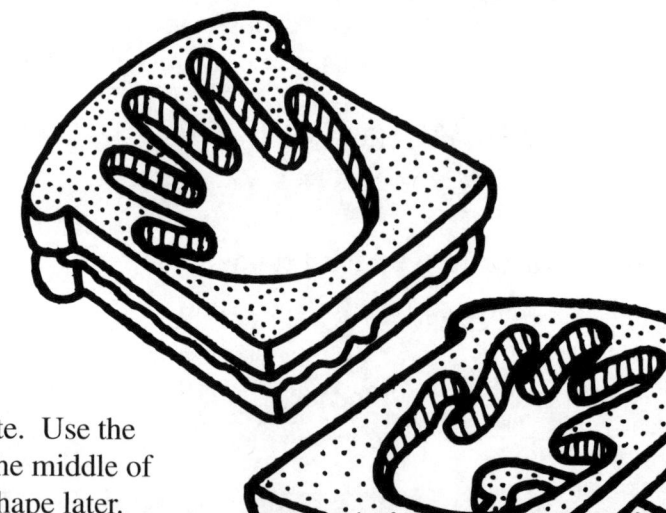

Letter Xx

Xx Is for Fox

Name _____

1. Trace the fox.
2. Trace the Xx's.
3. Write more Xx's.
4. Color the picture.

©Teacher Created Resources, Inc.   189   #2340 Alphabet Treasury

Letter Xx

Fox Mask Pattern

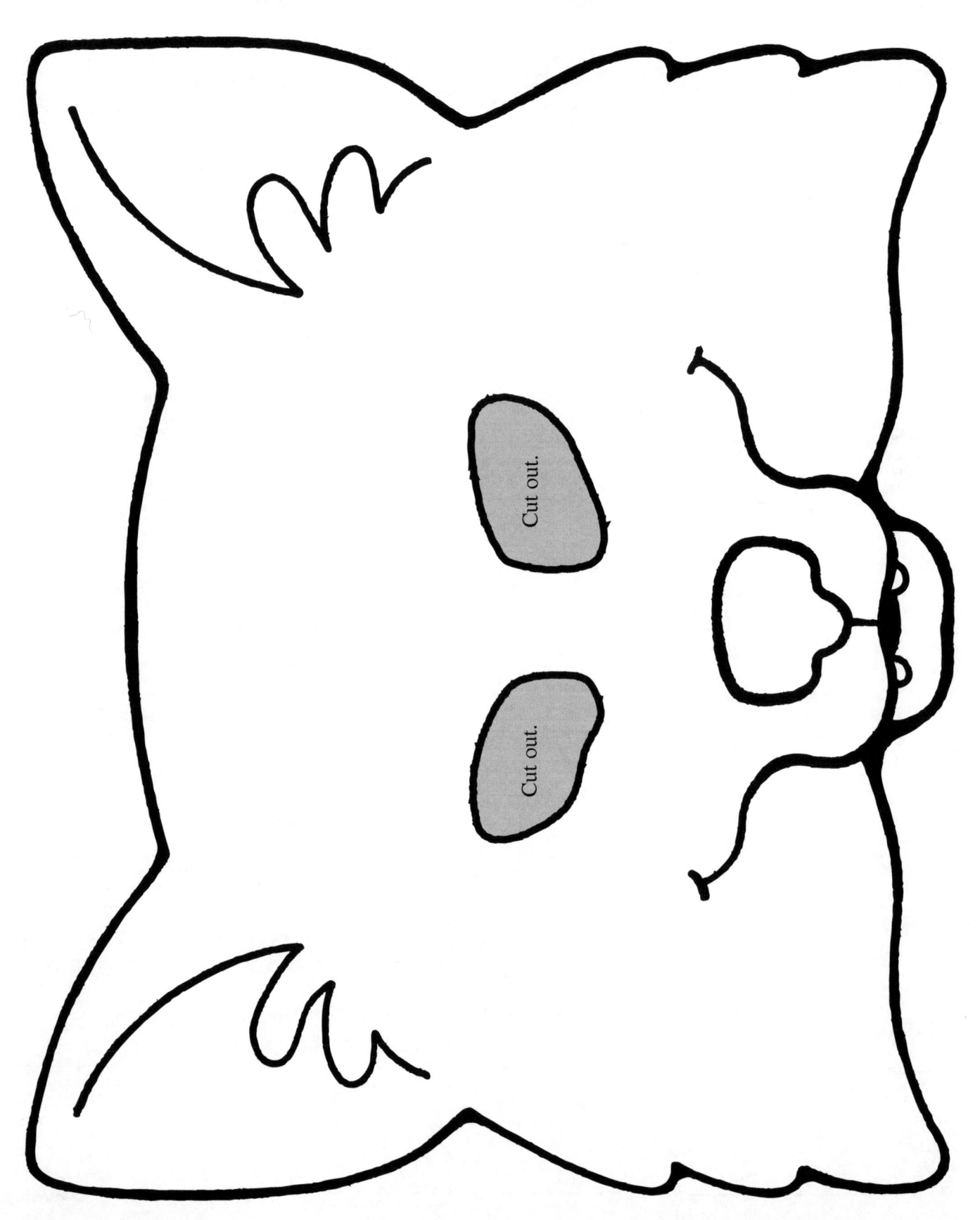

Cut out.

Cut out.

#2340 Alphabet Treasury ©Teacher Created Resources, Inc.

Letter Xx

X-ray Pattern

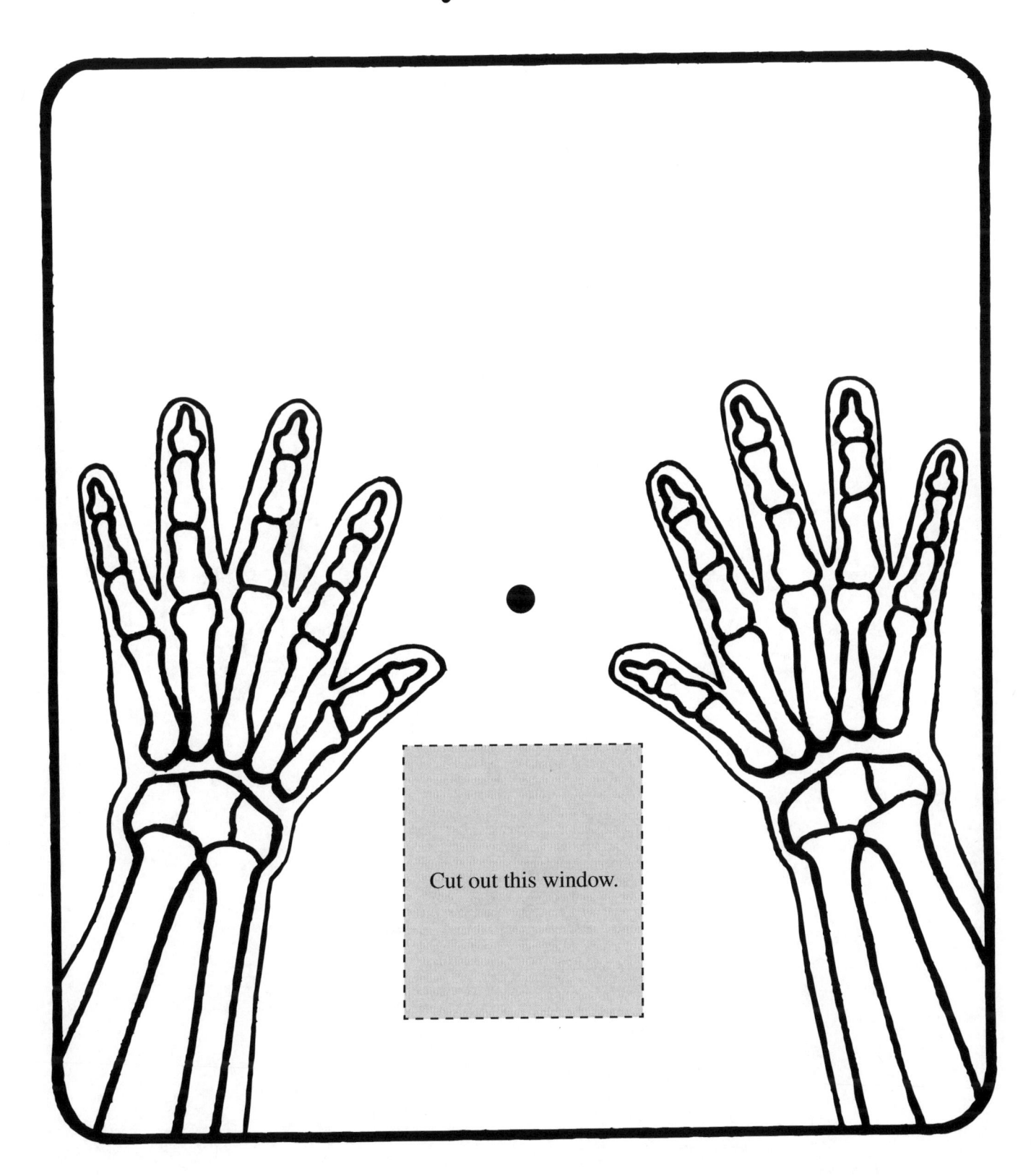

Cut out this window.

©Teacher Created Resources, Inc. 191 #2340 Alphabet Treasury

Letter Xx

Xx Picture Wheel

fox

box

x-ray

Xx

#2340 Alphabet Treasury 192 ©Teacher Created Resources, Inc.

Letter Xx

Xx is for an x-ray of my hand.

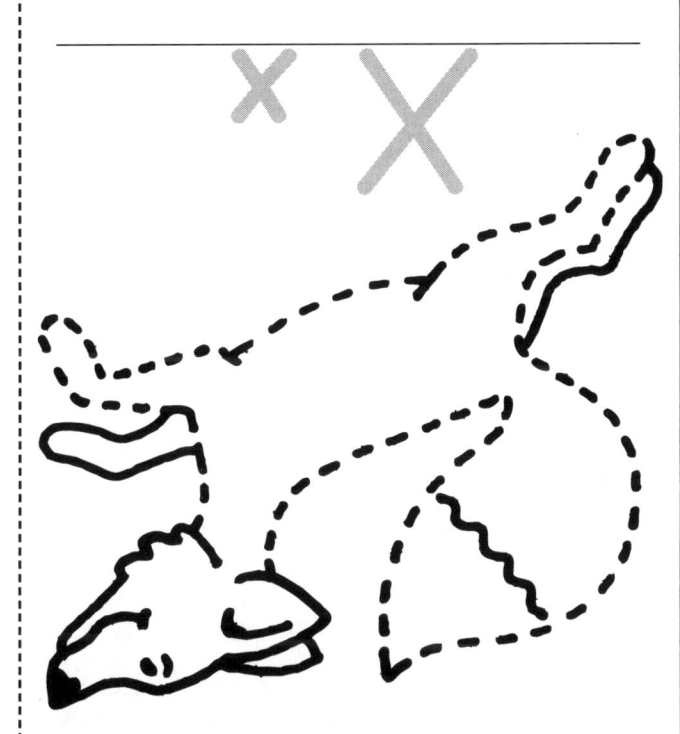

Xx is for a fox, running from tree to tree.

Xx is for a box to play hide-and-seek in.

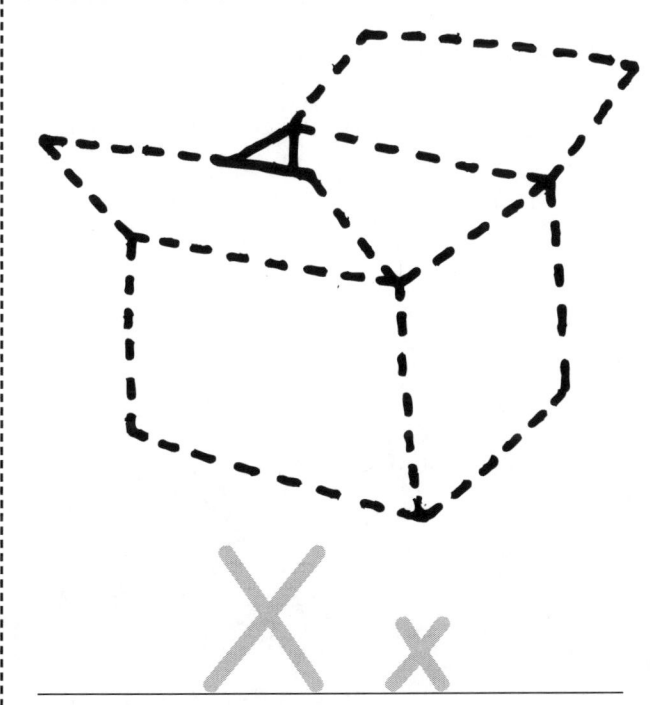

_____'s

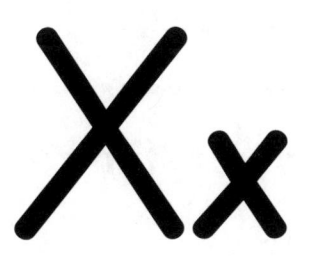

Xx

Minibook

©Teacher Created Resources, Inc.   193   #2340 Alphabet Treasury

Letter Yy

Yy

Introduce the letter Yy. Draw and discuss the shape of the letters using chart paper, a white board or a chalkboard. Note any students whose names begin or end with the letter Yy. This will provide opportunities to discuss how and when uppercase and lowercase letters are used.

Introduce the following sentences and accompanying actions. Repeat them often during the week.

Yy is for **yarn** to knit with.
(Pretend to knit using yarn.)

Yy is for a **yo-yo**, going up and down.
(Pretend you are playing with a yo-yo.)

Yy is for a **yucca** plant blooming.
(Crouch, then slowly stand.)

Day 1: Yy Is for Yo-Yo

Materials

- Yy Is for Yo-Yo worksheet (page 197) for each child
- pencils and crayons

Procedure for Child

1. Write your name on the line provided at the top of the page.
2. Trace the yo-yo and the letters provided.
3. Practice writing the letter Yy on the lines provided.
4. Finish by coloring the yo-yo using crayons.

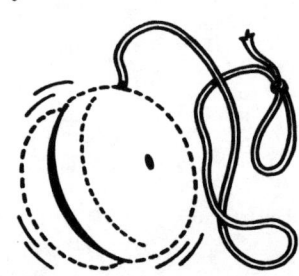

#2340 Alphabet Treasury 194 ©Teacher Created Resources, Inc.

Letter Yy

Yy

Day 2: Yucca Plant Activity

Materials

- 10 pieces of popped popcorn for each child
- sheet of white paper for each child
- green tempera paint
- paintbrushes
- glue

Procedure for Child

1. Paint your palm with green tempera paint.
2. Place the painted palm onto the white paper and set aside to dry.
3. Wash your palm.
4. Glue popcorn (blooms) onto the handprint (yucca tree) and let dry.

Day 3: Yarn Wheel

Materials

- Yarn Pattern (page 198) for each child
- Yy Picture Wheel (page 199) for each child
- brad for each child
- markers or crayons
- safety scissors
- pencils

Procedure for Child

1. Color the Yarn Pattern and Yy pictures on the picture wheel page.
2. Cut out the yarn and the picture wheel. (See page 5 for directions.)
3. Write your name on the back of the wheel.
4. Cut out the picture window on the yarn. (Note: Adult assistance may be necessary to cut out the picture window.)
5. Place the Yy Picture Wheel behind the Yarn Pattern. Make certain that one of the pictures is visible in the picture window on the yarn before going on to the next step.
6. Attach the yarn to the front of the wheel with a brad.

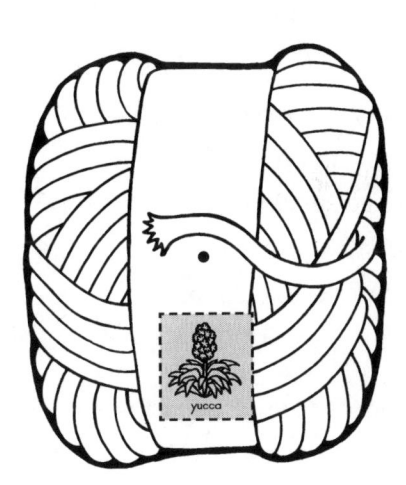

Letter Yy

Yy

Day 4: Yy Minibook

Materials

- Yy Minibook (page 200) for each child
- pencils, colored pencils, crayons or markers

Procedure for Child

1. Trim and fold the page to create the Yy Minibook. (See page 5 for directions.)
2. Write your name in pencil on the line on the minibook cover.
3. Complete each page of the minibook. Trace each picture and then trace the letter Yy on the lines.
4. Color the pictures using the colored pencils, crayons or markers.
5. Read the book as a group. Later, it can be shared at home or with friends.

Day 5: Yummy Yogurt Cooking Project *(serves 10 children)*

Kitchen Implements

- small plastic bowl for each child
- plastic spoon for each child
- serving bowls
- large serving spoon
- small serving spoons
- knife (adult use only)

Ingredients

- 5 cups vanilla yogurt or frozen yogurt
- sliced strawberries
- sliced bananas
- diced apples
- grapes

Preparation

1. Using a large serving spoon, place 1/2 cup of yogurt in each plastic bowl.
2. Add fruit to the yogurt as desired using small serving spoons.

Presentation

1. Stir the fruit into the yogurt with a plastic spoon to make it yummy!
2. Practice good table manners.

Letter Yy

Yy Is for Yo-Yo

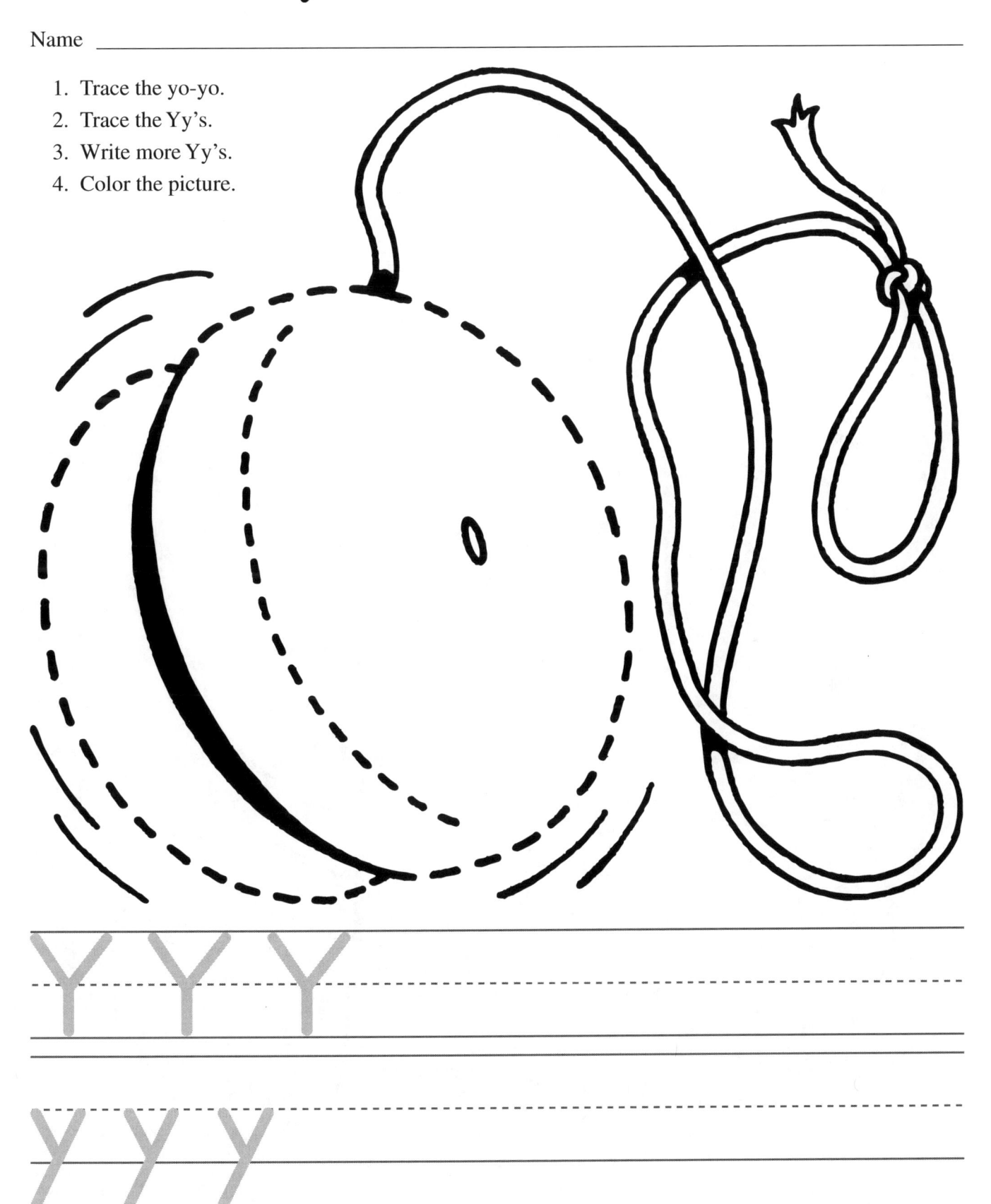

Name _____

1. Trace the yo-yo.
2. Trace the Yy's.
3. Write more Yy's.
4. Color the picture.

©Teacher Created Resources, Inc.   197   #2340 Alphabet Treasury

Letter Yy

Yarn Pattern

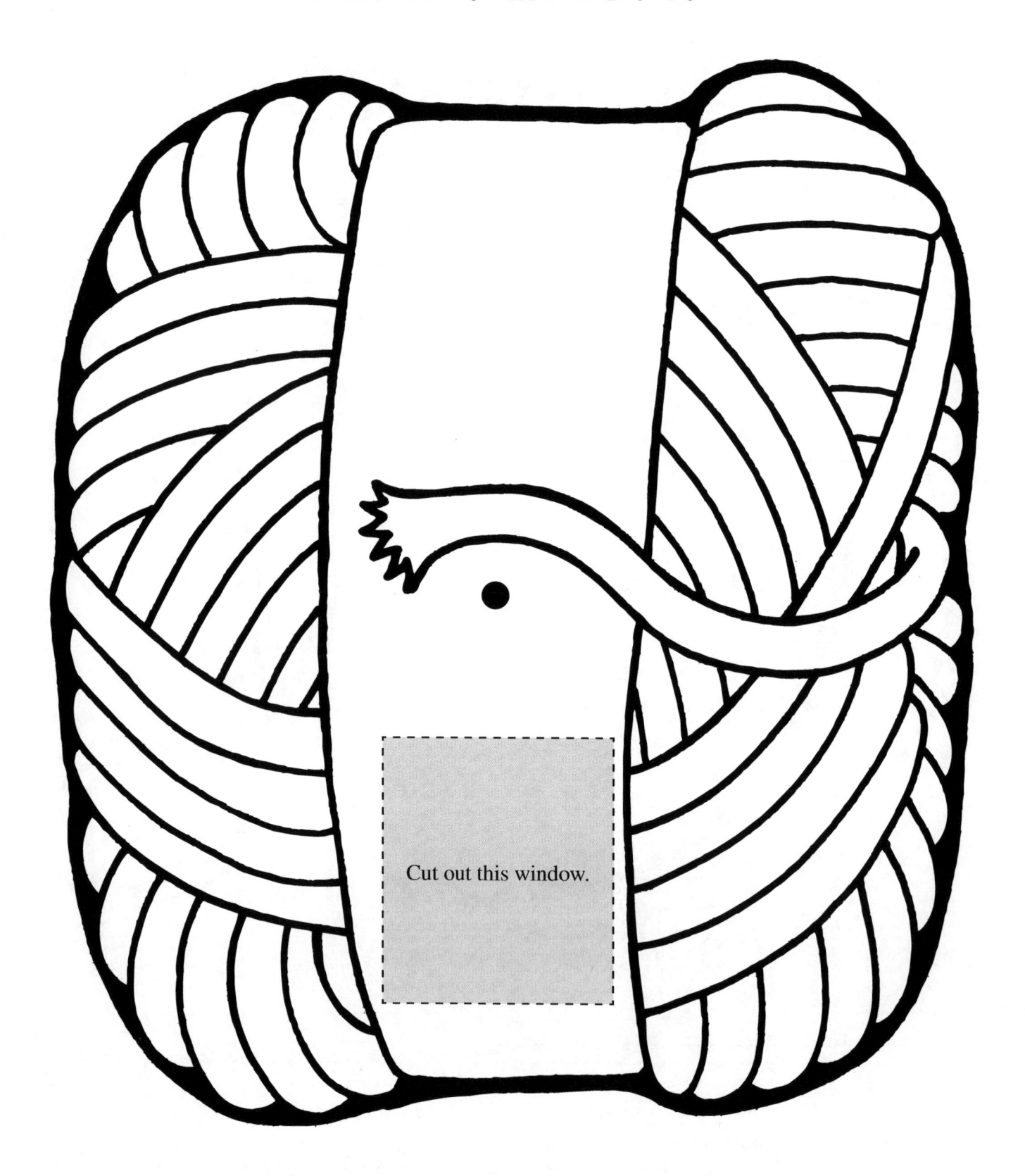

Cut out this window.

#2340 Alphabet Treasury 198 ©Teacher Created Resources, Inc.

Letter Yy

Yy Picture Wheel

yo-yo

yucca

yarn

Yy

Letter Yy

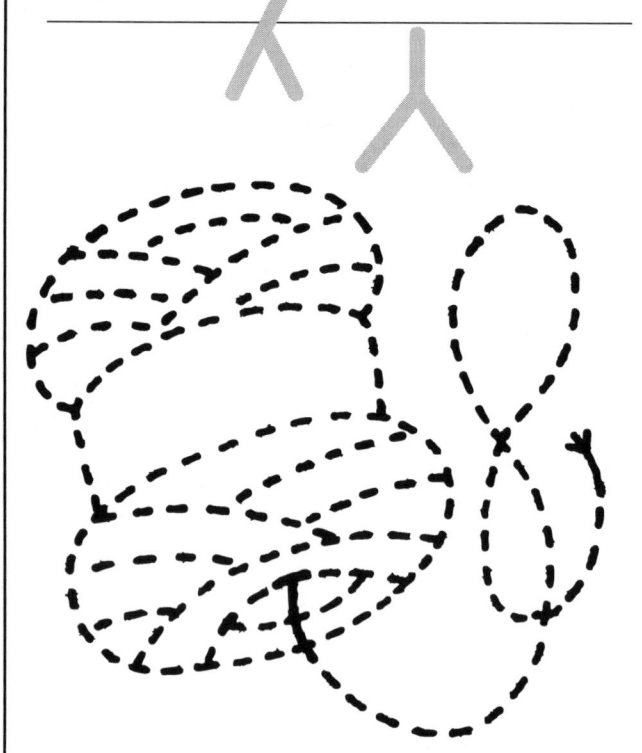

Yy is for yarn to knit with.

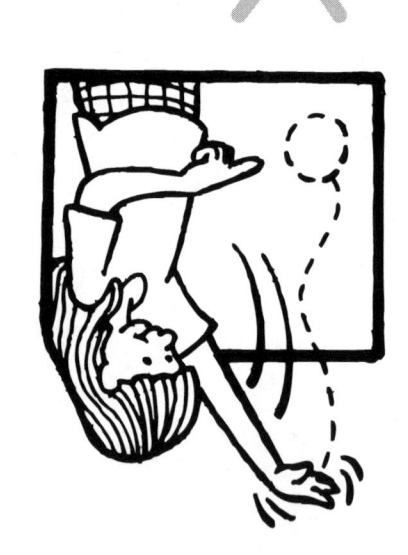

Yy is for a yo-yo, going up and down.

Yy is for a yucca plant blooming.

_____'s

Yy

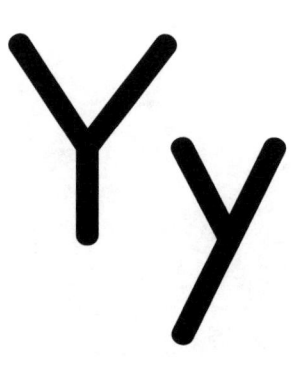

Minibook

#2340 Alphabet Treasury

Letter Zz

Zz

Introduce the letter Zz. Draw and discuss the shape of the letters using chart paper, a white board or a chalkboard. Note any students whose names begin or end with the letter Zz. This will provide opportunities to discuss how and when uppercase and lowercase letters are used.

Introduce the following sentences and accompanying actions. Repeat them often during the week.

Zz is for a **zero**, big and curved.
(Make a zero using both hands.)

Zz is for a **zipper**, going up and down.
(Pretend to make a zipper go up and down.)

Zz is for a **zebra**, running through the grasslands.
(Pretend to be a zebra running.)

Day 1: Zz Is for Zebra

Materials
- Zz Is for Zebra worksheet (page 204) for each child
- pencils and crayons

Procedure for Child
1. Write your name on the line provided at the top of the page.
2. Trace the zebra and the letters provided.
3. Practice writing the letter Zz on the lines provided.
4. Finish by coloring the zebra using crayons.

©Teacher Created Resources, Inc.   201   #2340 Alphabet Treasury

Letter Zz

Zz

Day 2: Zany Zero Lacing Activity

Materials

- Zany Zero Lacing Pattern (page 205) copied onto cardstock for each child.
- 43" length of yarn for each child (variety of colors)
- crayons or markers
- confetti
- tape
- safety scissors
- glitter
- hole punch
- glue

Procedure for Child

1. Write your name on the back of the zero.
2. Color the Zero Pattern and cut it out. (Note: An adult may need to cut out the section in the middle of the zero.)
3. Punch holes around the outer border of the zero using a hole punch. Slide the zero into the hole punch as far as it will go before punching. Doing so should ensure that the holes are placed away from the edge of the cardstock.
4. Choose a piece of yarn. Tape the yarn to the back of the zero so that it will stay in place. (Note: For additional help, wrap a small piece of tape on the other end to form a "needle." The tape will prevent the yarn from fraying.)
5. Lace the yarn in and out of the holes around the zero. Tie or tape the ends of the yarn together on the back.
6. Attach confetti and glitter using glue to decorate the Zany Zero.

Day 3: Zipper Wheel

Materials

- Zipper Pattern (page 206) for each child
- Zz Picture Wheel (page 207) for each child
- brad for each child
- safety scissors
- markers or crayons
- pencils

Procedure for Child

1. Color the Zipper Pattern and Zz pictures on the picture wheel page.
2. Cut out the zipper and the picture wheel. (See page 5 for directions.)
3. Write your name on the back of the wheel.
4. Cut out the picture window on the zipper. (Note: Adult assistance may be necessary to cut out the picture window.)
5. Place the Zz Picture Wheel behind the Zipper Pattern. Make certain that one of the pictures is visible in the picture window on the zipper before going on to the next step.
6. Attach the zipper to the front of the wheel with a brad.

Letter Zz

Zz

Day 4: Zz Minibook

Materials

- Zz Minibook (page 208) for each child
- pencils, colored pencils, crayons or markers
- safety scissors

Procedure for Child

1. Trim and fold the page to create the Zz Minibook. (See page 5 for directions.)
2. Write your name in pencil on the line on the minibook cover.
3. Complete each page of the minibook. Trace each picture and then trace the letter Zz on the lines.
4. Color the pictures using the colored pencils, crayons or markers.
5. Read the book as a group. Later, it can be shared at home or with friends.

Day 5: Zebra Stripes Cooking Project *(serves 10 children)*

Kitchen Implements

- 5 oz. clear plastic cup for each child
- plastic spoon for each child
- 2 large mixing bowls
- 2 whisks
- 2 large serving spoons
- measuring cups

Ingredients

- 5 oz. chocolate instant pudding mix (may use sugar-free)
- 5 oz. vanilla instant pudding mix (may use sugar-free)
- 6 cups milk

Preparation

1. Mix chocolate instant pudding mix and 3 cups milk in a large mixing bowl using a whisk.
2. Mix vanilla instant pudding mix and 3 cups milk in a different large mixing bowl using a whisk.
3. Refrigerate the pudding for at least 10 minutes.
4. Layer vanilla pudding and chocolate pudding, alternating the flavors (zebra stripes), in a clear plastic cup.
5. Practice good table manners and enjoy the treat!

Letter Zz

Zz Is for Zebra

Name _____

1. Trace the zebra.
2. Trace the Zz's.
3. Write more Zz's.
4. Color the picture.

Z z Z z

Z z Z z

#2340 Alphabet Treasury   204   ©Teacher Created Resources, Inc.

Letter Zz

Zany Zero Lacing Pattern

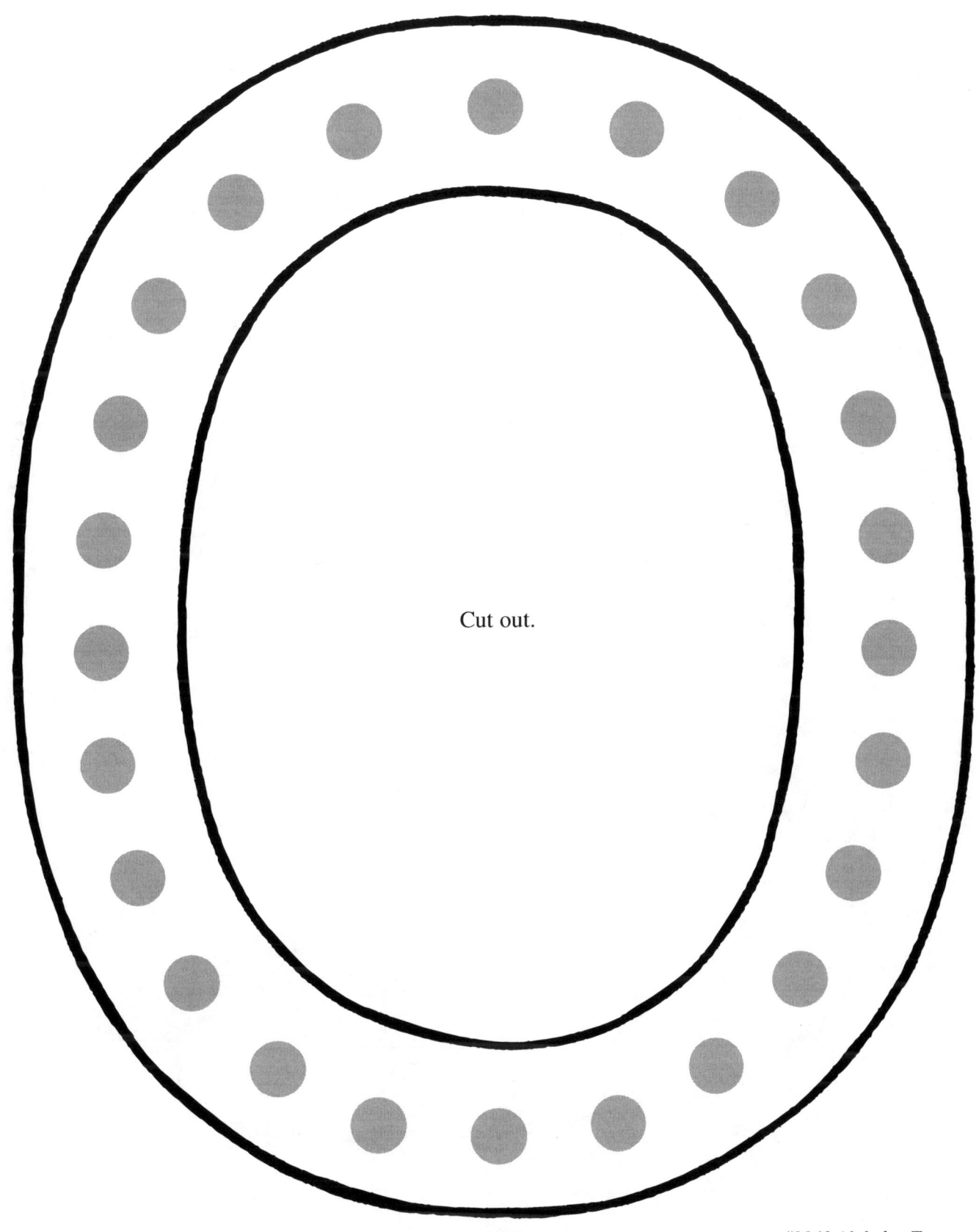

Cut out.

©*Teacher Created Resources, Inc.* 205 #2340 *Alphabet Treasury*

Letter Zz

Zipper Pattern

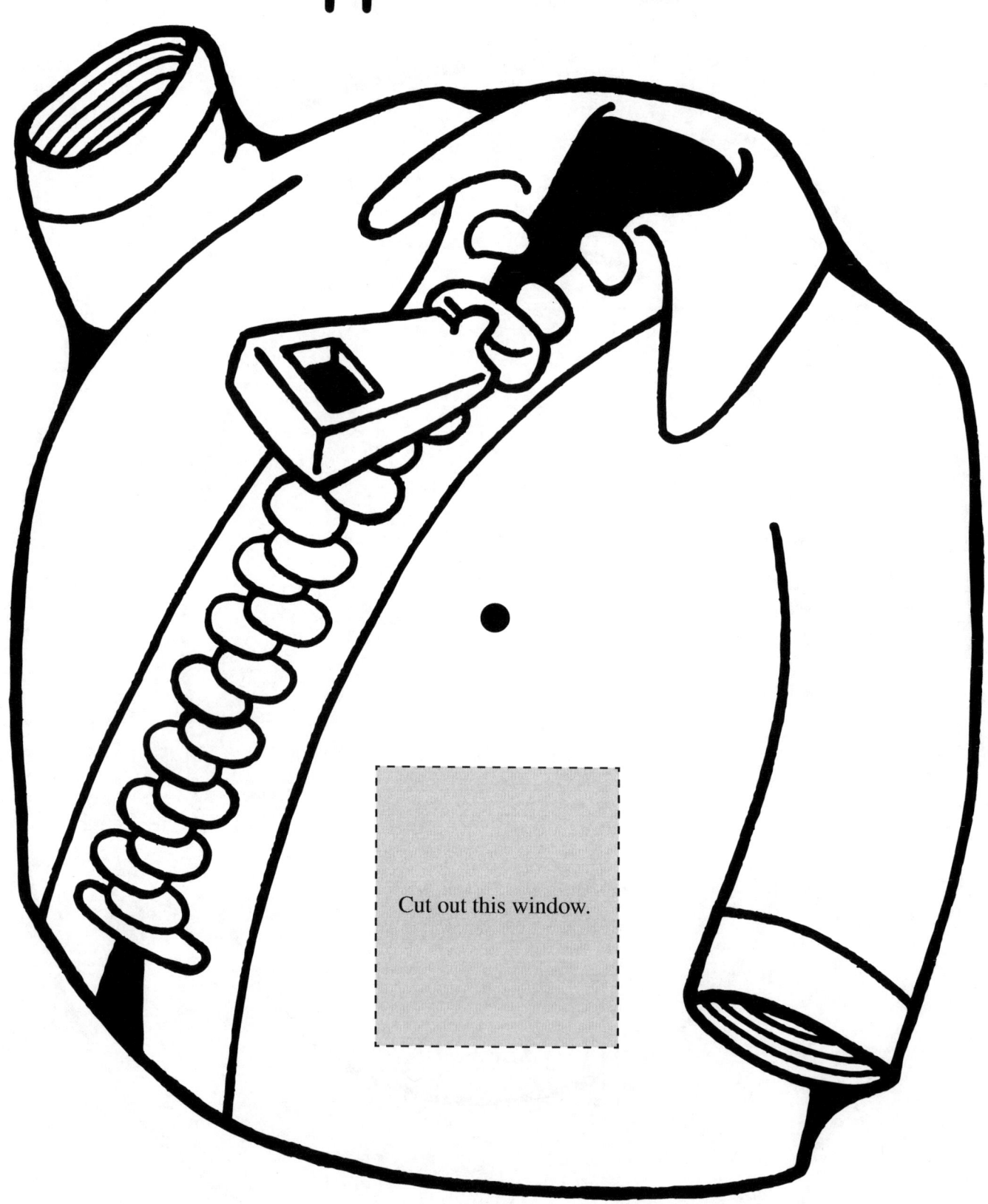

Cut out this window.

Letter Zz

Zz Picture Wheel

zipper

zero

zebra

Zz

©Teacher Created Resources, Inc. #2340 Alphabet Treasury

Letter Zz

#2340 Alphabet Treasury

Zz is for a zebra, running through the grasslands.

Zz is for a zipper, going up and down.

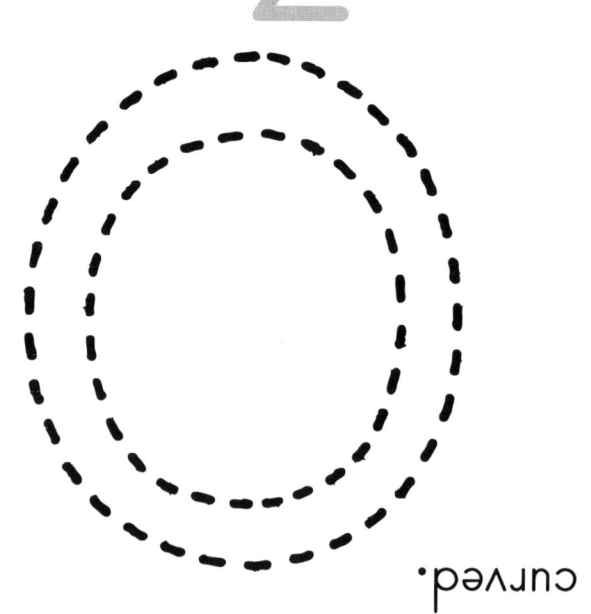

Zz is for a zero, big and curved.

_____'s

Zz

Minibook

©Teacher Created Resources, Inc.